ENCOUNTERS WITH ARCHITECTURE

INSIGHTS FROM A HUNDRED PLACES

I0881551

HOWARD DAVIS is Professor Emeritus of Architecture at the University of Oregon, where his specialty is issues of culture and place in buildings and cities. He is the author of *The Culture of Building*, *Living Over the Store*, and *Working Cities*, and the co-author, with Christopher Alexander and others, of *The Production of Houses*. Davis is a Distinguished Professor of the Association of Collegiate Schools of Architecture and winner of the Herman Award at the University of Oregon. His travels in over fifty countries are the basis for the writing and photography in this book.

The hundred places of this book were visited over several decades, and played an important role in Davis's career. Insights come from everyday places and famous landmarks: some beautiful, some the product of fine craftsmanship, some active places of gathering or commerce, some quiet places of contemplation. All stayed in the author's memory, helping build the framework of his understandings of what is important to people in architecture and cities.

Organized chronologically, the book begins with the author's encounters with buildings and places as a child in New York, and leads to his most recent architectural experiences as a seasoned professor, scholar and traveler. Each encounter is explained on two or three pages, that bring out the reasons for its significance and the lessons learned from it. Readers are encouraged to look for themselves and see how the places they encounter in their everyday lives and travels can enrich their own understandings about the built world that surrounds them.

Illustrated with beautiful photographs, drawings and diagrams, the book will interest people outside architecture who are fascinated by buildings and cities, as well as teachers, practitioners and students of architecture and cities.

Jaisalmer, Rajasthan, India.

ENCOUNTERS WITH ARCHITECTURE

INSIGHTS FROM A HUNDRED PLACES

Howard Davis

Routledge
Taylor & Francis Group
NEW YORK AND LONDON

First published 2026
by Routledge
4 Park Square, Milton Park, Abingdon, Oxon OX14 4RN

and by Routledge
605 Third Avenue, New York, NY 10158

Routledge is an imprint of the Taylor & Francis Group, an informa business

© 2026 Howard Davis

The right of Howard Davis to be identified as author of this work has been asserted in accordance with sections 77 and 78 of the Copyright, Designs and Patents Act 1988.

All rights reserved. No part of this book may be reprinted or reproduced or utilised in any form or by any electronic, mechanical, or other means, now known or hereafter invented, including photocopying and recording, or in any information storage or retrieval system, without permission in writing from the publishers.

Trademark notice: Product or corporate names may be trademarks or registered trademarks, and are used only for identification and explanation without intent to infringe.

British Library Cataloguing-in-Publication Data
A catalogue record for this book is available from the British Library

ISBN: 9781032976341 (hbk)
ISBN: 9781032976334 (pbk)
ISBN: 9781003594598 (ebk)

DOI: 10.4324/9781003594598

Designed and typeset by Alex Lazarou in Adobe Garamond Pro and Avenir

Publisher's Note
This book has been prepared from camera-ready copy provided by the author.

Cover
Design and layout by Alex Lazarou
Photos by Howard Davis

Front cover: Parisian *passages* and boulevard

Back cover:
Top row: Shahjahanabad, Old Delhi, India; Town hall, Hilversum, Denmark
Middle row: SM in Trastevere, Rome; Place du Tertre, Paris
Bottom row: Bethnal Green, London; Piazza dei Signori, Vicenza

For Product Safety Concerns and Information please contact our EU representative GPSR@taylorandfrancis.com Taylor & Francis Verlag GmbH, Kaufingerstraße 24, 80331 München, Germany.
Batch No. NP105990

CONTENTS

INTRODUCTION: LOOKING AND SEEING

I am always wandering here and there from my rooms in Covent-garden, London—now about the city streets, now, about the country by-roads—seeing many little things, and some great things, which, because they interest me, I think may interest others.[1]

CHARLES DICKENS
The Uncommercial Traveller

We all experience architecture before we have even heard the word. The roots of architectural understanding lie in our architectural experience.[2]

PETER ZUMTHOR
Thinking Architecture

THIS BOOK describes encounters with a hundred places influential in my architectural life, beginning about fifteen years before I decided to study architecture, and continuing to the present. Some of these encounters were with ordinary places, some well-known works of architecture, some buildings, some rooms or corridors, some busy urban streets, some peaceful landscapes. They are all places that moved me. I saw them as beautiful, or full of life, or elevating my spirit, or shaking me into a greater awareness of what was around me. In this book I've recalled those encounters in a hundred reflections, and have endeavored to understand and explain the reasons for my reactions.

These reflections, or short essays, include places that affected me deeply, like the view from the outer gate of the Inner Shrine at Ise in Japan or the relationship between the Sarabhai house and its garden, in India. Most of them are of more ordinary places that caused a positive reaction that was strong enough to

1 Charles Dickens, *The Uncommercial Traveller*, p. 1.

2 Peter Zumthor, *Thinking Architecture*, p. 65.

remember—the façade of the Little Singer Building in New York, a 19th-century house-barn in Missouri, the terrace outside an apartment in Athens, the cultural diversity at Gillett Square in London. In all cases, they are buildings and places that stirred me, for a memorable encounter that I remembered decades later.

As a professor of architecture, writer and researcher, I have particular interests: cities and urban buildings, vernacular architecture, how understandings of history can be useful in the present, how buildings and cities can support people and their livelihoods, how cultures make and remake the places that house them. I have traveled to over fifty countries on six continents where I have looked at architecture and places, again and again; and have worked professionally and done research in Latin America, Europe, and Asia, in addition to the USA. Over this time I have developed my own ways of seeing buildings and places, that have served me well in my teaching and writing.

As I began to develop this book, I realized that my own story may contain lessons for others as well. Everyone in architecture has their own ways of looking, their own ways of seeing and interpreting the built world, their own understandings of what's important. And those ways affect how one practices architecture, and how one teaches. Mine are unique to me—my emphasis on the small, on the "connective," on the contrasting, on the human scale—but may also be useful to others. In what ways? Not to copy my own reasons but to bring to the surface the idea that if one is explicit about how one is looking and seeing, and explicit about the ideas that guide one's architectural thinking, that self-awareness might help one look further and understand the sources of ones' successes and mistakes.

So the personal reflections, supported by more objective explanations, have a wider audience than my students and friends alone. They may also be of interest to architects, architecture students, teachers and writers on architecture—and to others who have an interest in buildings and places. And since the book brings together my own feelings and opinions with sharable observations and facts about buildings and places, there are common threads of reference and understanding.

EXPERIENCES AND MEMORIES

How did my observations of the built world begin? I often spent my days off from school with my father, as he went around New York to supervise the ongoing jobs of his electrical contracting business. I loved having a glimpse of parts of the city I wouldn't otherwise see—restaurant kitchens, the basements of apartment buildings, the apartments of wealthy people living upstairs in those buildings, the back-of-house sales counters in electrical-supply houses, the diners where workingmen ate lunch. As I looked, I began to wonder about the city. One of these wonderings was while riding along the Brooklyn-Queens Expressway, looking down from the elevated roadway onto the hundreds of blocks of small factories and four- and six- and twenty-family apartment houses, and asking myself "Who built this?, How could it all have been built?"—one of the first times I looked at the built environment and asked real questions about it. This way of looking at the city played a big role in my eventual decision to study architecture and, as I realize now, to take the particular approach to it that I have. And this looking, looking, ultimately took form in my habits as an observer, spending a lot of time wandering, turning down a street because of the tiniest hint of something interesting, balancing a purposeful visit to some important building or church or museum with a riskier, time-intensive urban exploration.

In thinking about my architectural past, I sometimes wonder why I remember certain things at all. I am able to draw, from memory, a detailed floor plan of the apartment in Brooklyn that I lived in from the age of three to thirteen. This plan, accurate to within a few inches, includes the location of furniture, of kitchen cabinets, of lamps and light fixtures. I remember that the windows were double-hung with counterweights on pulleys built into the jambs, that there was a fringe at the bottom of the (deep, forest

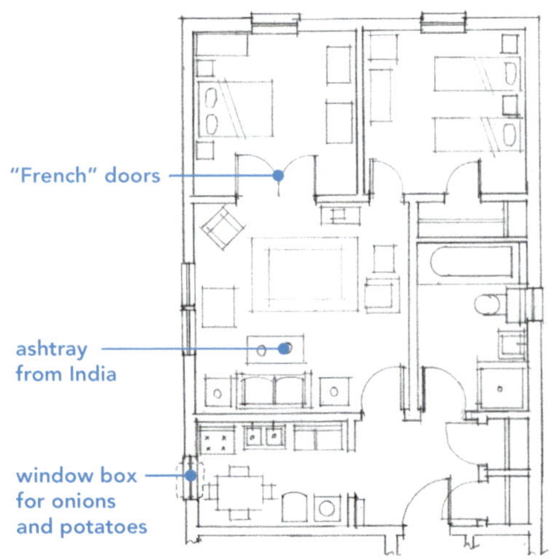

Plan of Brooklyn apartment.
Drawing: Howard Davis

green) sofa in the living room, that on the coffee table (that had a carved, raised rim around the perimeter of the top) there was an embossed brass ashtray (with a screw-on lid) that my uncle brought back from India after the war, that there was a cold-storage box under the kitchen window where we kept onions and potatoes, that there were two "French doors" with glass panes leading from the living room to one of the two bedrooms.[3]

Like many people in and out of architecture, I grew up with a strong awareness of the details of place, and that awareness translated into strong memories. What did I notice? What do I remember? And how did the memory of those observations change over time, perhaps providing evidence for an increasing understanding of architecture and the built world? This chronology helps document the progress of that architectural education—in which what I learned as an architecture student at Berkeley, and subsequently as a faculty member at the University of Oregon, was given form by my lived experience.

The chronological arrangement puts my architectural experiences into their actual temporal sequence. As my world expanded, more and more buildings were included in its orbit, as I began to take multiple trips to different places in the same year, and the variety of buildings and places I looked at increased. This naturally put different ideas and different kinds of ideas together.

[3] I suspect, without evidence, that when that apartment was first rented in about 1930, it was advertised as a one-bedroom apartment, with what we used as the living room advertised as a dining room, and the bedroom with the French doors advertised as a parlor. The kitchen had minimal room for a table, suggesting a separate dining room; and the bedroom with the French doors did not have a built-in closet, suggesting that it might not have been originally advertised as a bedroom, but perhaps a parlor instead.

Three-floor, six-family apartment building in East Flatbush, Brooklyn; one of six identical buildings along the street. Our apartment was on the ground floor, in the rear of the building on the left.

One short sequence, for example, includes a vernacular farmhouse in Denmark, Washington Mews in New York, a walk through a poor neighborhood of Cairo, and Schindler's Kings Road House in California. These are different in scale, type, time of construction, and not least, place. It was this variety, the bringing-together of buildings and places that were outwardly different, that helped catalyze ideas and understandings that did not depend on usual categorizations. The chronological organization shows the possibility of seeing very different places within a single, overall architectural world view.

Architecture is different from most other pursuits in that one is always with it. For most of our day, unless we are hiking in the wilderness, we are in the presence of buildings and designed places: looking at the built world from a car or bus, walking along the street, inside buildings. Consciously or subliminally, buildings are always part of our experience. And I have also been fortunate to travel, with the itinerary often based on particular buildings or kinds of buildings or cities. I have created new opportunities for myself: extending trips to include new purposes, creating fieldwork studies in different places, taking useful detours. And these opportunities have led to many special things, as well as the notable everyday. It has been my luck and privilege to experience the world of architecture in these ways.

THE MONUMENTAL AND THE ORDINARY

It was often the small and particular, in addition to the big or famous, that caught my eye. These encounters include a door lintel in a simple farmhouse in Tunisia, the iron-and-stone detail of a train station in Vienna, the corridor of a town hall in the Netherlands, the door handle in a library in Oregon. Smaller encounters often result from the simple act of walking past the houses and shops of an ordinary street, people cooking food, washing clothes, buying bread. This daily life, and the physical environment that makes it possible, is itself the armature to which more prominent works of architecture are anchored.

On my first trip to Istanbul, I saw the important landmarks—the Hagia Sophia, the Sulemaniye, the Blue Mosque—as impressive and beautiful. But the things that also grabbed my heart include a smaller mosque built on top of shops; an outdoor book market; nineteenth-century vernacular wooden houses. Beauty happens at many different scales, materials, and levels of wealth.

And of course, artists have seen everyday life in ordinary places as subjects for their work: Canaletto's "The Stonemason's Yard," many of Vasi's etchings of Rome, Constable's "The Hay Wain," Bonnard's dining room, the New York photographs of Helen Levitt, the Paris photographs of Eugène Atget, the Dutch paintings of Vermeer and Pieter de Hooch of seventeenth-century daily life in interior spaces.[4] All these elevate the ordinary, the kinds of places otherwise often used as "background."

Once during a Berkeley architecture class, a student asked Christopher Alexander what his favorite building is. After thinking for five or ten seconds, he replied, "Well, there's this fruit stand on the road to Modesto…" Many buildings and places do not have an obvious beauty, in the sense of a Rembrandt portrait or a Mozart piano sonata. But they have life, a modesty of physical expression that foregrounds that life, a strong connection to what is around them—the road, the farm, the gravel parking area, the tree that provides shade, the grass that needs mowing. These ordinary places, that we pass dozens of times in a given day, together provide the framework for our world of built-environmental experience. Those moments of life and beauty build up and are remembered. In her book *The Cities We Need: Essential Stories of Everyday Places*, Gabrielle Bendiner-Viani writes about the importance of local grocery stores, laundromats, dry cleaners, in anchoring people to urban neighborhoods and forming the tight weave that holds together the social fabric of those neighborhoods.[5] The ordinary is not necessarily consciously noticed, but it forms the foundation on which everything else rests.

The architectural historian Dell Upton, in an essay "Architecture in Everyday Life" takes issue with the split between "Architecture" and "architecture," pointing out that "everyday theories have yet to reveal to architects a satisfactory way to inhabit the everyday world professionally because architects focus on the dualities in the theory while overlooking the ways the categories blur."[6]

Certainly I appreciate the great works of architecture and of urban design, and some of these buildings and places are discussed in this book. But the importance of many of the other moments of architectural experience described here is different from the singular ideas of the powerful centrality of the Pantheon or the Hindu temples at Madurai, or the careful asymmetries of the plan of the Acropolis, or the spatial progressions at the Piazza San Marco in Venice or the Katsura Villa in Kyoto. Those places are important

4 Three of Atgets' photographs are on page 299, in a reflection about the Place du Tertre in Paris, and two of de Hooch's paintings are on pages 201 and 202, in a reflection about historic Dutch houses.

5 Gabrielle Bendiner-Viani, *The Cities We Need: Essential Stories of Everyday Places.*

6 Dell Upton, "Architecture in Everyday Life." *New Literary History*, 33, 2002, pp. 707–723.

and beautiful, and need to be thought about when designing. But it is also important to legitimize the smaller moments, to show their connection to the larger world of architecture and sometimes their connection to each other. Buildings and places are revealed and ultimately understood at many different scales and with different intensities of observation. I have a long-standing antipathy to Nikolaus Pevsner's famous statement, "A bicycle shed is a building; Lincoln Cathedral is a work of architecture."[7] The attitude that lies behind that statement has supported the fracturing of the building culture into "thinkers" and "doers," often putting two great professions—architectural design and the construction of buildings—at odds with each other, and relegated 98% of the buildings in the world to secondary status.

PRINCIPLES AND REAL PLACES: THE THINGS THEMSELVES

The author Joan Didion wrote about her student years at Berkeley, trying to understand theory:

> My attention veered inexorably back to the specific, to the tangible, to what was generally considered, by everyone I knew then and for that matter have known since, the peripheral. I would try to contemplate the Hegelian dialectic and would find myself concentrating instead on a flowering pear tree outside my window and the particular way the petals fell on my floor. I would try to read linguistic theory and would find myself wondering instead if the lights were on in the bevatron up the hill.[8]
>
> JOAN DIDION
> *"Why I Write"*

Books about architectural ideas are often organized in a different way from this one. They begin with principles—typological elements and rules of typological combination, or patterns and pattern languages, or mathematical proportioning systems, or various schema of categorization—and then use examples to justify the validity of those principles or categories. But although these represent valid means of explanation, they often fall short of complete or satisfying explanations of particular places. A particular diagram or set of proportions is by itself no guarantee that something will be beautiful, and one is often left with a sense of unfinished business:

[7] The statement appears in the Introduction to Pevsner's *An Outline of European Architecture,* p. 15.

[8] Joan Didion, "Why I Write." *The New York Times*, Dec. 5, 1976.

"…ok, those organizing principles are there, that's well and good, but there's more to it than that."[9]

In this book, the essay focuses on the place itself. "Here is this beautiful building or place or street or window or…; why was I affected by it?" This recognizes that buildings are complex and holistic, and tries to sort out their complexity in ways that keep their unity. But this also is not complete, as even the more complex interaction among principles may not be enough to understand the powerful feeling that a place may evoke.

While the qualities of architecture, its beauty or ugliness, the way it supports human life or not, the ways it fosters community or not, cannot always be easily explained, they are not always unexplainable. And an effective explanation of architectural phenomena, or the qualities of particular places, is neither objective nor subjective. It is neither knowable completely through explicit or numerical means nor altogether a matter of opinion, or personal choice. Beauty is and is not in the mind of the beholder.

My examples use different, multiple modes of explanation. In some cases, as with the vernacular end of the Piazza dei Signori in Vicenza, or the façade of the Little Singer Building in New York, there is a formal explanation, specifically describing relationships among particular parts. In others, as with my first reaction at the gate of the Inner Shrine at Ise or the painting restoration at Chartres or the walk in Cairo, there is little formal analysis, but a lot of strongly-felt emotion. And in yet others, as with the earliest reflection that includes the four small stores in the middle of a Brooklyn block, it is a combination of a description of the urban structure of the surrounding blocks with a more personal remembrance of the character of that small part of the neighborhood.

The combination of feeling and objective explanation is essential. In talking about his design for the Los Angeles County Museum of Art, Peter Zumthor said of the museum visitor, "Look at the objects of art first, get moved or touched or interested, and then we ask, What is this? What do we know about this? But first the emotion, and then the scientific, academic explanation."[10]

Goethe, in *Italian Journey*, after visiting landscape paintings in a Rome gallery, wrote that "What one needs to do is to look at them and then immediately look at Nature to learn what they (the artists) saw in her and in one way or another imitated; then the mind is cleared of misconceptions, and in the end one arrives at a true vision of the relation between Nature and Art. I shall never rest until I know that all my ideas are derived, not from

9 For one critical commentary on the use of mathematical proportioning systems in architecture, see Christopher Alexander, "Perception and Modular Coordination," *RIBA Journal*, 66(12) 1959. Republished in Howard Davis (Ed.), *Early and Unpublished Writings of Christopher Alexander*. London: Routledge, 2022.

10 Dana Goodyear, "From the Ground Up," *The New Yorker*, October 12, 2020, pp. 54–55. See also Zumthor's book *Thinking Architecture.*

hearsay or tradition, but from my real living contact with the things themselves."[11]

And Christopher Alexander's remarkable chapter in *The Timeless Way of Building*, "The quality without a name," recognizes both the importance and difficulty of explaining felt experiences in only a scientific way.[12] Chris once showed me a letter he had written in reply to an inquiry about the language he used in that book, moving back and forth between a precise scientific language and a more poetic language. He wrote that since Descartes, the growing split between science and belief, between fact and feeling, had resulted in different ways of using language, and that his intention was to try to suggest the re-uniting of those two worlds by intertwining their different modes of language.[13]

Different modes of explanation may all be valid, but they are also each incomplete. No one mode of explanation can replace the reality of the place itself, Goethe's "real living contact." The quantitative and qualitative are both important. Science and art—including representational art—are different kinds of abstraction, both necessary for explanation. And in many cases, what is explanation, if not a plausible abstraction? My own approach to this book has been to approach both with respect.

Much of my work, particularly expressed in *The Culture of Building* and *Living Over the Store*, has included attempts to break down unhelpful barriers between generally accepted categories. Many of the architectural ideas that are most important to me work in cross-cultural, cross-geographical and ahistorical ways. Over time I have been building up a point of view that incorporates the big and the small, the rich and the poor, the house and the church, the old and the new, into a single world of building. The variety of examples in this book, and the equality of those examples, reflects that point of view.

[11] Johann Wolfgang von Goethe, *Italian Journey*. San Francisco: North Point Press, 1982, p. 343. Thanks to Philip Shelley for pointing me to this quotation.

[12] Christopher Alexander, *The Timeless Way of Building*, "The quality without a name." New York: Oxford University Press, 1979, pp. 19–40.

[13] The letter was to Stephen Grabow, who was writing the book *Christopher Alexander: The Search for a New Paradigm in Architecture*.

HOW TO READ THIS BOOK

The choice of the hundred places was based primarily on what I saw as the strength and importance of my encounters, as my memory revealed them again to me. The places are at all scales, from the city down to the paving stone, and of different origins: vernacular buildings; historic, modern and contemporary buildings designed by well-known architects and landscape architects; buildings and places on five continents from 500 or so BC to the present.

This book can be read chronologically or episodically.

A chronological reading, cover to cover, will offer an understanding of the variety of places that, over time, influenced my ideas about architecture. There is an understandably large emphasis on New York at the beginning, followed by a gradual branching out to other places. This reading, or even a sequential thumbing through to begin with, will give the reader an overview of the entire book. One thing that will be found, for example, is that as time passed, modern and contemporary buildings became more important. In other cases, places that were initially visited earlier on, were seen as important to me only on later visits—and the dates of those later visits determined their positions in the book.

An episodic reading allows the reader to thumb through the pictures and stop when inspired to delve deeper. Because the one hundred reflections are independent, reflections may be read separately, one at a time or several in any order of interest. It is possible to open the book to a random reflection, read it, close the book, and later do the same thing again.

Whichever way the book is read, it is in the end the hundred places themselves that I hope will pique the interest of the reader to learn more about architecture and the built world, in ways that respect both the special and the ordinary.

CREDITS FOR ILLUSTRATIONS

Photographs by Howard Davis unless otherwise indicated. Drawings and diagrams by Ian Nielsen-Fox unless otherwise indicated.

This page and facing page: All photos of New York

PART ONE
1957–1975

The hundred reflections begin on the next page, with a few encounters from when I was a child, followed by two more from the years I was studying physics. My formal education in architecture began at Berkeley, where my most influential mentors were two brilliant teachers. Alan Forrest was a pioneering architecture teacher, one of the first to develop a graduate program for students who had undergraduate degrees in other fields. He believed in the need for students to take responsibility for their own education, teaching us that the question was as important as the answer, that the architect had a social responsibility to the world, that buildings mattered. Christopher Alexander spent his long career developing new frameworks for understanding the beauty and function of buildings. All this was in the milieu of Vietnam War-era Berkeley, and physical surroundings that included the richness of California architecture. As a break from school I spent six months in a London architecture firm, which for me put the idealisms of my mentors up against the realities of the architectural profession and the building cultures of which it was a part. These were also the years of an innovative housing project in Mexico, working with Alexander, that ultimately revealed the same contradictions.[1]

[1] The project in Mexico is described much later in the book, on p. 303.

FOUR SHOPS, ST. JOHNS PLACE, BROOKLYN

From the viewpoint of a child

Shops on south side of St. Johns Place, between Troy and Schenectady Avenues. Frame from home movie taken in the 1950s.

DURING MY CHILDHOOD in the 1950s my brother and I went with our mother every Saturday to visit my aunt and grandmother, who lived in a third-floor apartment in a tenement building on St. Johns Place, in the Crown Heights neighborhood of Brooklyn. The building was built in 1919 and had 19 apartments: four on the ground floor, and five on each of the upper three floors. St. Johns Place had wide sidewalks providing space for social groups to gather, with an electric bus (powered by overhead wires) running along it, and busy shopping streets nearby. At that time the neighborhood had a mostly Jewish population but also had a small percentage of African Americans, Irish, and Italian families.

Adjacent to the building were two narrower tenement buildings, each with two shops on their ground floor, separated by the residential entrance hall. The four shops included Silverstein's candy store, a small grocery store, a Venetian-blind shop where our uncle—married to my mother's sister and living in the tenement next door—worked for some time, and another store without any signs or markings. Perhaps it served as someone's dwelling.

Part of our Saturday was spent in the apartment, part shopping on nearby streets and walking in the neighborhood, and part outside "hanging out" and playing while the grownups and neighbors talked. Usually visiting were also the children of my mother's brother, who lived in an apartment building on a nearby street, Lincoln Place.

The shops played a big role in our experience of the neighborhood. They were places of congregation, with people going in and out, baby carriages standing outside, people meeting and talking.

The candy store was a place to buy ice cream or a stick of licorice or candy "dots" on a strip of long white paper, a six-cent glass of Coca-Cola, or a fifteen-cent comic book. We might be asked by the grownups to get a newspaper there,[1] or a couple of cigars or pack of cigarettes. The store had a pay telephone in a wooden booth—and although by that time most people had phones in their apartments, some still did not, and so used that pay phone (and learned about incoming calls from a child being paid a few cents to run up to their apartment and get them to come down to the phone). The grocery store had basic needs—milk, packaged bread, butter, tea, canned vegetables. The stores gave variety to a long street of otherwise residential entrances, together forming a small social center, in and amongst the residential buildings and their doorways.

Outside the apartment, this was our world for the day. What we did not know as children is that the four stores were part of the spatial and economic system of the entire neighborhood. Schenectady Avenue, half a block away, was dominated by food stores and stores selling everyday needs; Utica Avenue, another block to the east, by clothing stores and the sale of more "special things" like jewelry and musical instruments; and Troy Avenue had a small supermarket, a dry-goods store, and some other establishments. At the intersection of Eastern Parkway and Utica Avenue, the location of the nearest subway station, was Dubrow's cafeteria, and along Eastern Parkway itself were an elementary school, a branch of the Brooklyn Public Library, churches, and synagogues. And also on St. Johns Place, much closer to Schenectady Avenue, was a small shop on the ground floor of a tenement building, selling only fresh eggs.

What I did not understand explicitly at the time, was what I was experiencing: that this neighborhood had a logic to it: everyday needs could be immediately taken care of by the nearby shops, and more infrequent needs—major grocery shopping, buying clothes—happened farther away. Certainly I did not know anything about

[1] In those years there were seven daily English newspapers in the city, four morning and three evening papers, plus the *Brooklyn Eagle*, the Yiddish newspaper *Forvitz [Forward]*, and others. The newspapers were displayed on a wooden stand just outside the store, and could be paid for through the shop window.

economic geography, but my weekly experience of that place may have been my first lesson in how the physical complexity of the city is related to its economics.[2]

I have thought about this place again and again over the years, coming back to it often in my thoughts about the life of cities. Experienced by me for the last time when I was about 12 years old, these modest buildings in immigrant Brooklyn made a great impression on me—a memory that helped me understand architecture as a means to support everyday life, and that seemingly small and ordinary things can have an outsized importance.[3]

Shops and apartment buildings on south side of St. Johns Place, between Troy and Schenectady Avenues, in the 1940s. Photos: Municipal Archives, City of New York.

[2] Simply put, there will be more local centers selling everyday things, closer to people's homes; fewer larger centers selling things needed less frequently; and fewest largest centers, requiring the most distance of travel, selling things needed least frequently. A long trip is ok for a wedding ring, but not for a quart of milk. The candy store and grocery store were relatively far from the "everyday businesses" of Schenectady Avenue and even farther from the more specialized stores of Utica Avenue. Many blocks had some version of the small stores that were nearby my family's apartment.

[3] I went back to this block in the mid-2000s and found that the shops had been replaced by ground-floor apartments. This happened sometime after the 1950s, perhaps as the ultimate result of the 1916 Zoning Resolution that allowed nonconforming uses to remain until a change of ownership or change of use. The 1961 zoning map showed residential zoning for the property.

EASTERN PARKWAY, BROOKLYN

Connecting the neighborhood to a larger world

EASTERN PARKWAY was just a few minutes' walk from where my aunt's family and grandmother lived, so we often spent time there, just taking a weekend walk from St. Johns Place, or using the great boulevard as a path to some store or Dubrow's cafeteria, or entering the Utica Ave. subway station. We also visited Eastern Parkway every Memorial Day, as it was the location of the Kings County Memorial Day Parade, one of the oldest and most continuous celebrations of that somber holiday in the country.

It was only much later, after we had stopped going to that neighborhood every Saturday, and stopped going to the parade, that I learned the importance of Eastern Parkway as a prime example of the work of Frederick Law Olmsted, the great American landscape architect of the nineteenth century.

Eastern Parkway is one of Olmsted's extensions of Prospect Park, stretching east from the museum and library at Grand Army Plaza into the neighborhoods of immigrants in Crown Heights, East Flatbush, and Brownsville. It had a character of its own, a big contrast from the densely-populated, tenement-lined streets of St. Johns Place and other residential streets, and from the busy commercial streets like Utica and Schenectady avenues. It was first of all very wide, with three roadways and two pedestrian-only walks; it was lined with trees, providing shade in the hot-and-humid summer and crispy leaves underfoot in the fall; the pedestrian walks were paved with hexagonal paving stones and had wood-and-cast-concrete benches along them. The blocks of Eastern Parkway were lined with old mansions and public and religious buildings: schools, a branch of the Brooklyn Public Library, synagogues, and churches. The intersecting streets were commercial streets that themselves intersected more residential streets, parallel to Eastern Parkway, with large houses on President Street (where our doctor had his large house and office) and apartment buildings and tenement houses on other streets like St. Johns Place. In *The Boulevard*

Eastern Parkway in 1939. Credit: New park benches, 1939, gelatin silver print, NEIG_1746; *Brooklyn Daily Eagle* photograph, Brooklyn Public Library, Center for Brooklyn History.

Eastern Parkway in 2024.

Book, Allan Jacobs, Elizabeth MacDonald, and Yodan Rofe write about Eastern Parkway's easygoing, graceful character, the way it absorbs a lot of automobile traffic without being overwhelmed, and the clusters of commercial buildings around subway stops along its length.[1]

Eastern Parkway was a place of social mixing, with people of different economic classes, and many people who were first- or second-generation immigrants. In *A Walker in the City*, Alfred Kazin described Eastern Parkway as the place for middle-class Jews, "... alrightniks, making out 'all right' in the New World, they were still Gentiles to me as they went out into the wide and tree-lined Eastern Parkway."[2] It seemed like a place where people who walked along it were well dressed, as people still are on an evening walk in Italy, Spain, or Greece; a street that helped connect the neighborhood with the larger world outside. This was certainly helped by knowing that the Brooklyn extension of the east- and west-side IRT subway lines were running underneath the street; and that the main branch of the Brooklyn Public Library and the Brooklyn Museum were at the end of it. I felt the street not just as a big street, but as something that helped connect me, albeit perhaps just in my imagination or in thinking about my future, with the larger world.

[1] This paragraph is from *Living Over the Store*.

[2] Alfred Kazin, *A Walker in the City*, p. 9.

MEADOWS, CATSKILL MOUNTAINS, NEW YORK

Remembering the fragrant landscape

WE SPENT SEVERAL SUMMERS in the Catskill Mountains, near the village of South Fallsburgh, renting a "bungalow" for four or five hundred dollars for the summer. This was a simple wooden cottage that consisted of two rooms and a screened porch, in a "bungalow colony" owned by a Jewish family who lived there year-round. Often there had originally been a farm and farmhouse on the land of such resort properties, and the bungalows were built as an additional source of income. The bungalow colony included a swimming pool, a recreation hall for movies or parties, and sometimes a building with rented rooms instead of individual bungalows, and a common kitchen, a "kuch-alein," shared by several families. But we stayed in our own rented bungalow, bringing up

I took no photos of the meadows. This meadow is like the one described. Painting: Sheri Pyron.

boxes of dishes and linens and clothes from our Brooklyn apartment for our two-month stay.

I loved to walk in the gentle hills, on which there were well-worn paths that took me down to the stream; in one place there was a dam that helped form a pond. To get there or up to a place with a longer view I had to walk through two or three meadows and bits of woods; the walk took 15 minutes at most but it always seemed like a venture into the wild. In July those meadows were full of wildflowers—daisies, buttercups, sunflowers—with the fragrance of the soil and grass, and the smell different after the rain. For this child from Brooklyn, where the only "natural" terrain near our small apartment house consisted of a few square feet of "dirt" supporting a privet hedge in the tiny garden in front of the building, these meadows were wondrous places, without a view of buildings or telephone wires, with open skies above and surrounded by deciduous forests that always seemed dark and mysterious.

These Catskills meadows were my introduction to the natural landscape and for some reason I have thought about them often over the years. It is particularly the memory of their fragrance that comes back to me—not the fragrance itself but the memory that it was unique, along with the knowledge that it was characteristic of that place three hours from our apartment in Brooklyn.

And in the words of a poet, albeit with different plants and different places:

> And now the tar weed, sweet vagrant of the valley,
> Useless, unloved, but offering its golden discs by millions
> To waste places, filled the air with its poignant tang,
> Bringing back childhood with a pang of pain–
> Old dreams of childhood lived in this lovely valley.[1]

MARGARET S. COBB,
"Long Valley."

[1] Margaret S. Cobb, "Long Valley," 1919. Thanks to Sheri Pyron for showing me this poem, that was inspiration for her own art in Oregon.

HOUSE, LEVITTOWN, LONG ISLAND

Expanding architectural space

IN THE MID-1950s, our former Brooklyn neighbors—Etta, Eddie, and their two daughters Maxine and Lynne—bought a house in Levittown, Long Island, for $9,000—a price that at the time was above my family's means. The house had four rooms on the ground floor, with a covered carport near the front door, and an unfinished attic.

To me, growing up in Brooklyn, and continually exposed on TV to what I later learned was the "American dream," this was a real house. It had its own piece of land with a lawn in front and a back yard with tomatoes and roses, an upstairs and downstairs, a pitched roof, and a special place for the car. Looking back on it now, it was of course very modest, and different from many of the other places in this book, that are more historical or "architectural" or beautiful. But at the time there were two attributes of the house that stayed with me, and are connected to architectural ideas that are present in many other places.

One of these was the large windows in the living room. They were multi-pane windows in which the sill was just above the floor. This allowed the living room to have a strong connection to the back garden, almost extending the space of the room itself. As a small child, the garden appeared large to me, and the back window made the living room seem bigger because of its strong connection to the garden.

The second, more memorable feature, was the two-sided fireplace, connecting the kitchen with the living room. There were two aspects to this: the fireplace opening itself, which allowed one to see through from room to room, and the fact that the fireplace was in a thick brick wall, a strong architectural feature of both rooms, in a simple wood-frame house. It allowed for entrance to the living room on either side of it, creating a spatial "loop" in the house at the same time as providing a division between the two rooms. What this all did, of course, was set up a linear spatial sequence

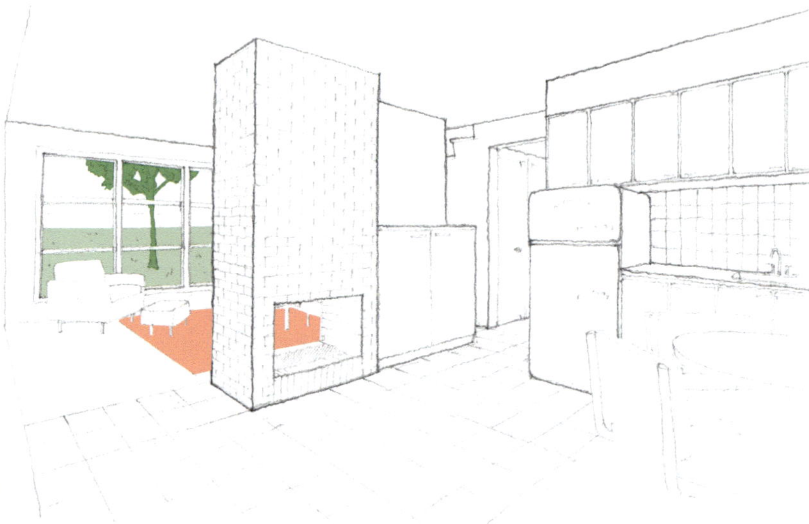

View of interior from front door showing two-sided fireplace and rear window.

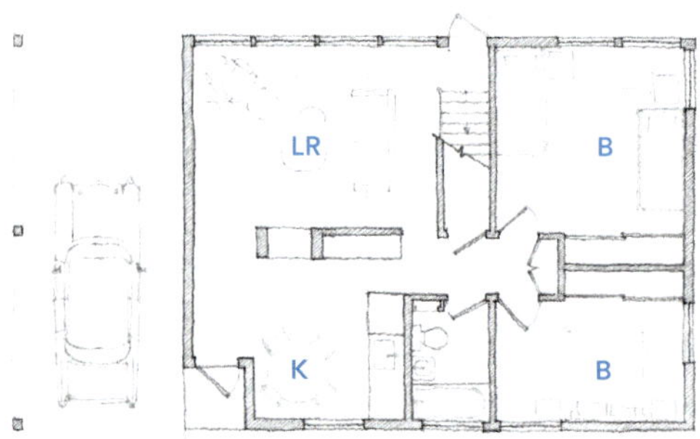

Plan of Levittown house.

from the kitchen to the living room to the garden, using openings between these spaces, in a way not dissimilar from the Dutch room sequences described later in this book (see p. 201).

These features were obviously understood by William Levitt's architects, who were trying to design houses that were, on the one hand, inexpensive and available to modest-income urban dwellers, but on the other seeming as big and comfortable as possible.

Of course, these are simple ideas, repeated in buildings millions of times. I have probably seen dozens, if not hundreds of these examples over the years, many in architecturally more significant buildings. But these two ideas stayed with me, possibly because to a child they were unusual, so at the same time I recognized their value. Our Brooklyn apartment had none of this. Since then I have often thought about these features of simple Levittown houses, and they have helped sustain the idea that architectural quality does not necessarily depend on size or elaborate details or cost, but may be achieved with very simple strategies based on fundamental spatial relationships.

SMALL TOWNS NEAR NEW YORK CITY

A view from the road

WHEN WE GOT our first car (a used 1953 Nash Ambassador) we began to take weekend drives out of Brooklyn: to Long Island, to places north of the city ("upstate," even though we were going only as far as Westchester or Dutchess county), to western Connecticut, and to New Jersey. This was before the days of interstate highways, and even with the suburbs that had grown along the routes of the commuter rail lines, many older, small towns were still vibrant places. They were as yet untouched by (or at least I didn't notice) major changes like the growth of the "exurbs," the transformations of agriculture, or the decline of American industry. So our drives brought us through farm country and towns, and within the towns we drove through the town centers ("Main Street") as well as the neighborhoods of houses that were next to them.

I was fascinated by what I saw through the back, side window of the car, and those views were burned into my memory. The late nineteenth- and early twentieth-century wooden, clapboard houses, set back from the street, with front yards shaded by elms, maples, and sycamores; deep front porches; large houses; plenty of land. Closer to the town center, or on the other side of the town center, houses much closer together[1] or even row houses, were closer to the street, but still places of family life with their own dignity. And the city center itself, with brick buildings among the wooden ones, individual shops often with dwellings on upper floors, and a cluster of highway signs at the main intersection.

I came to realize that there was a whole world out there, places that I could only experience on drives like this.

These trips helped form an understanding of the American built environment outside big cities (although I certainly didn't put it in those terms at the time), and although that understanding was formed also by what I read and what I watched on television, those trips were important. Certainly these places were different from the place in which I was growing up, and although it was only much

[1] Lewis Mumford wrote about how some American cities became denser: "The isolated country house, insulated from its neighbours, perhaps remained the ideal of house-design, even among the classes that were forced to accept mean bungalows or shanties five feet from their neighbours as equivalent…" *The Brown Decades: A Study of the Arts in America*, pp. 174–175.

White Plains, New York in the late 1940s.
Photo: Westchester County Historical Society.

later that I began to understand the relationships between those two kinds of places, I saw these small towns as somehow essential. And I sometimes felt as if the places in which I was growing up were depriving me of that American life.

Thinking back on it now, my eventual decision to study architecture—that came years after the last of these trips—came about for various reasons, and seeing these places was likely one of them.

BROOKLYN TECHNICAL HIGH SCHOOL, BROOKLYN, NEW YORK

Urban and architectural complexity

MY ARCHITECTURAL and urban world expanded when I entered high school, revealing new levels of scale and spatial complexity. I had been admitted to Brooklyn Technical High School, one of New York City's specialized high schools, which had a strong curriculum in science and technical subjects.[1] Located a short walk from the center of downtown Brooklyn, across DeKalb Avenue from Fort Greene Park, attending the school required a round trip by subway and bus, and that twice-a-day commute expanded my growing understanding of the city. I began to experience firsthand the differences among neighborhoods; I met classmates from all over the city, of different backgrounds and ethnicities; I saw stores with neon signs and two floors of apartments above that were built near subway stations; and I began to see how the subway lines and buses linked the different parts of the city together and also helped define the city itself.

There were several different combinations of bus and subway that I could use for the trip, and I tried them all. Done again and again over three years, the trip to and from school helped reinforce my growing understanding of New York. I gained confidence in my ability to move around the city, and that confidence was likely supported by a growing, subliminal understanding of the city's geography.

I was also fascinated by the building that housed Brooklyn Tech, probably one of the largest high school buildings in the country, in which I was one of 6,000 students. It was massive, the largest and most complex building I had ever been in. It was eight or nine stories tall, with a squared "figure 8" plan on each floor, filling most of its long block. It incorporated several multiple-floor spaces including one of the largest auditoriums in the city, a two-story-high metal foundry with wonderful daylight on one of the top floors and a large gymnasium with a running track.

It was impossible to see or experience the whole building, but I was aware of many individual features that made it up: the

1 Besides hands-on classes in woodshop, machine (metal) shop, and metallurgy, perhaps the most memorable and unique class was "Industrial Processes," taken in my first year, which introduced students to such subjects as lumber production, steel production and forming, oil refining, and related processes of industrial production. The textbook, *Materials and Processes*, was written by a teacher at the school specifically for this class.

View of school from Fulton Street in late 1940s. The neighborhood did not change substantially by the 1960s. Photo: Max Hubacher. ©Milstein Division, The New York Public Library.

scissors stairs, "down" nearest the corridor and "up" away from it, both in the same vertical space; the cafeteria filling the seventh floor with several kitchens and connected eating areas; the long hallways.

In addition to the foundry, there were two-story-high workshops with overhead power shafts that used continuous belts to drive machine tools, science laboratories, a radio station, and a library that took the place of the middle corridor on the fifth floor. The library had a fireplace that helped give it a refined and quiet atmosphere, but also bookstacks with their own stairs adding to the building's apparent complexity, in an adjacent volume to the main room.

I was aware of this spatial variety, and also of the fact that all the pieces somehow fit together. It was also mysterious: I knew there were rooms that I never entered and probably never would. This complex building was a real-life civic equivalent of the giant-yet-imaginary New York hotel described in Steven Millhauser's novel, *Martin Dressler: Tale of an American Dreamer.*[2] In this story, the protagonist, who started out working in a cigar shop, became a real estate developer in New York, and his dream building project grew and grew, eventually containing within it vast spaces,

[2] My colleague Glenda Utsey introduced me to this book.

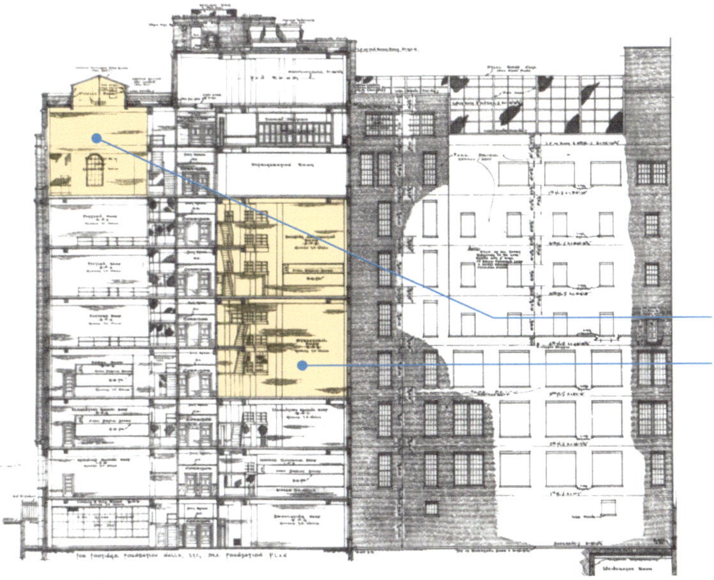

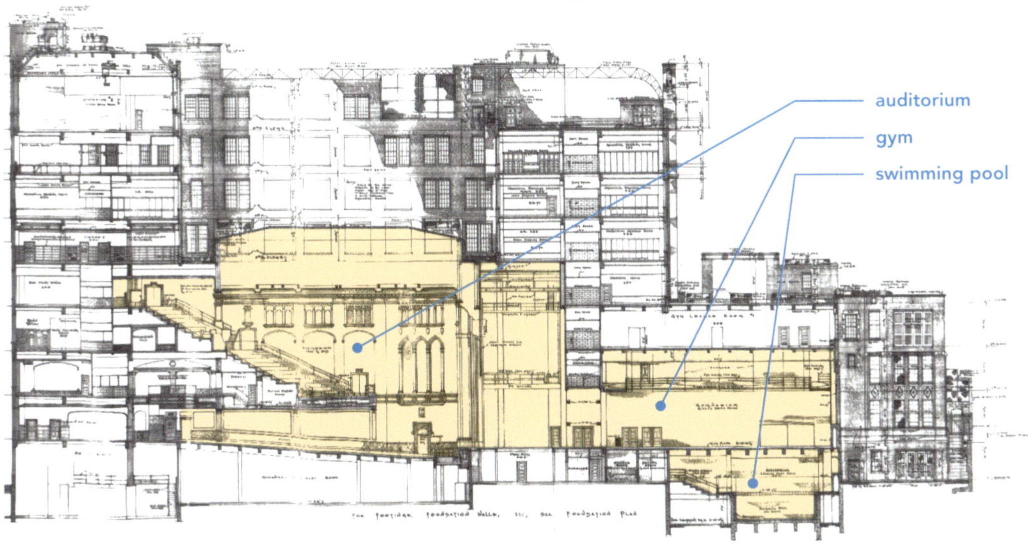

Original section drawings of Brooklyn Tech, recorded on microfiche, showing (top) two-story workshops and (bottom) auditorium, gym and swimming pool. Courtesy Municipal Archives, City of New York.

thousands of rooms, enormous buildings, and parts of cities that never could exist—a New York building itself illustrating one of Italo Calvino's *Invisible Cities*.

As my territory of urban wandering got bigger and bigger, starting with our four-room apartment, so did the extent and complexity of the buildings within that growing territory. The effects of those discoveries were not immediate, and without a clear translation to what I thought about, taught, or wrote about until much later. My attraction to large and complex cities, and to the complex buildings within them, surely comes at least partly from having grown up where I did, and having buildings like Brooklyn Tech as part of my day-to-day experience.

FOUNDATION BUILDING, COOPER UNION, NEW YORK

Functional variety in urban compactness

WHEN I BEGAN my college education at Cooper Union, I was studying in its School of Engineering and Science, and in my second year I began studies in my chosen major, physics.[1] All our classes were in the Engineering Building, an undistinguished building from the early 1960s that housed the departments of its four engineering disciplines (Chemical, Civil, Electrical, and Mechanical), plus physics and mathematics.[2]

But apart from classes, I spent a lot of time across Astor Place, in the Foundation Building, the original building of the college. It housed art and architecture studios and classrooms, plus

1 The Cooper Union for the Advancement of Science and Art was tuition free, made possible partly through its ownership of the land under the Chrysler Building. After passing a rigorous entry exam, I went there because it allowed me to live at home, and study what I then thought would would form the basis of my career.

2 The physics major lasted at Cooper Union for less than two decades. It was instituted by Cooper Union's then-president, Richard F. Humphreys, a physicist.

Cooper Union Foundation Building in 2024.

various facilities used by all students: the cafeteria, bookstore, Great Hall, administrative offices, and general library. We used the Great Hall for our theater group (the "Great Hall Players") and for the public-speaking part of one of our humanities courses, in which we each spoke from the same podium that Abraham Lincoln used in the speech that is considered to have been instrumental in his attaining the presidency. ("Let us have faith that right makes might, and in that faith, let us, to the end, dare to do our duty as we understand it.")[3] It also housed the "Museum for the Arts of Decoration" (now the Cooper-Hewitt Museum relocated to the old Carnegie mansion on the Upper East Side), and the art-and-architecture library on the fifth floor, near the architecture studios, where I first found books on Frank Lloyd Wright and other architects.[4]

So I had ample reasons to be in the Foundation Building, and it was perhaps my walk up to the fifth floor to visit the architecture library that gave me the time and varied environments to begin to appreciate the building. But it is only decades later that I can conjecture how my experience in that building, partly influenced by its history, might have shaped my architectural worldview. Although I was a physics student, and was to remain a physics student three years after my graduation from Cooper Union, many of my sensibilities were toward architecture.

The building has long been known in the architectural world principally for three features. It is the first major building in the country built with rolled iron beams. It has a round elevator shaft; the story told is that Peter Cooper thought that when the elevator would be invented, it would be round. And it has a unique system of ventilating the Great Hall, in the basement, that features air monitors under the seats.

But these features did not strongly enter into my experience of the building. Although I wasn't yet in a position to understand the building from an architect's point of view (and I never even saw all the drawings until I recently found them in the online HABS/HAER archive), I can look back now at what I remember of my experience of the building, and correlate that with how the building is represented in the drawings.

Words that come to mind when I try to describe the building through my experience: foursquare, solid, and permanent; spatially generous; spatially and functionally varied and complex; daylight; darkness; wide, light stairwell. These are all attributes I was aware of at the time, and that I felt and appreciated. Individually:

3 See for example Harold Holzer, *Lincoln at Cooper Union: The Speech That Made Abraham Lincoln President.*

4 The school had a third building, the Hewitt Building, that housed a lecture hall, darkrooms, and graphics studios. This building was replaced in 2009 by the Thom Mayne-designed building that also incorporated functions of the old Engineering Building, that was demolished.

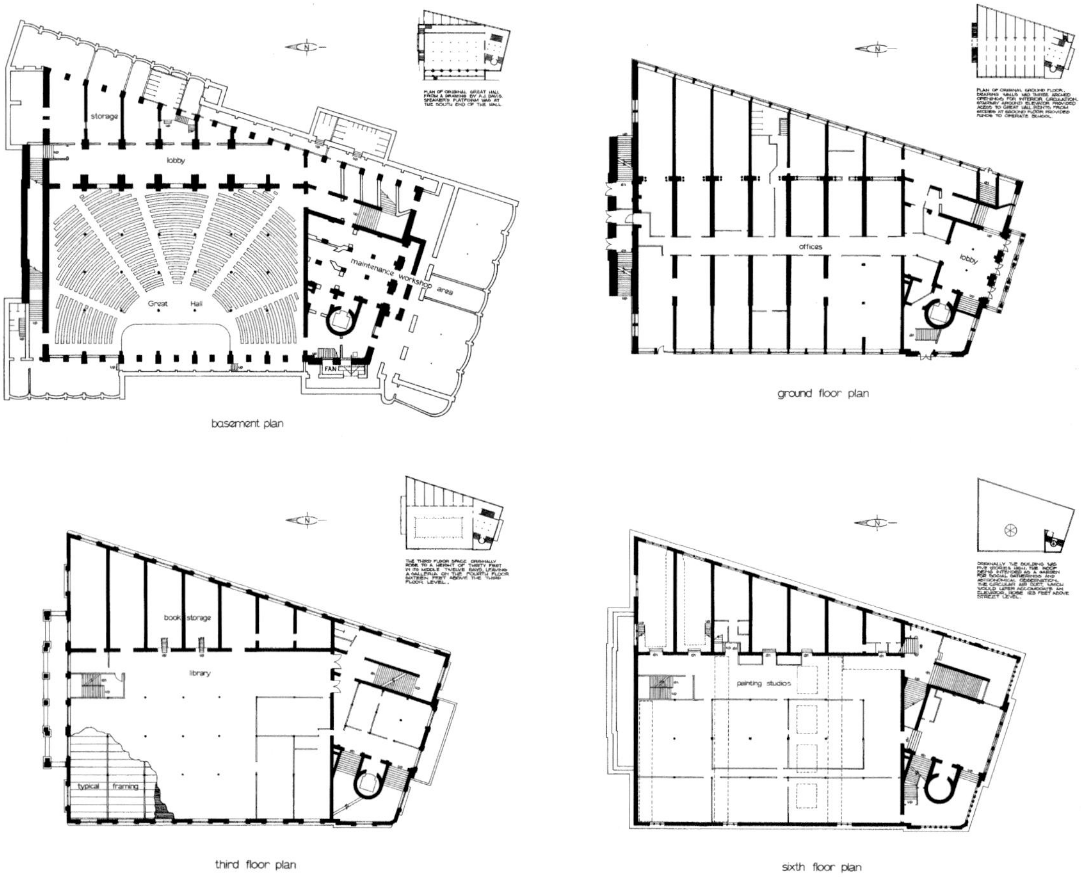

Foundation Building. Plans of basement (Great Hall), ground, third and sixth floors. Historic American Engineering Record, Library of Congress.

- *Foursquare, solid, and permanent.* The building fills an entire block—the Bowery to Third Avenue, East Seventh Street to Astor Place. It is a small block for New York, but my perception of the massing/volume of the building was that it is full of space and activities, functionally efficient.
- *Spatially generous.* At the same time, the individual spaces felt generous: high ceilings, broad corridors (particularly on the second floor where the administrative offices were located), a feeling of height and spatial expanse in the third-floor library. As I now realize, the floor-to-floor height in the Great Hall was about 20 feet; that in the two floors above about 16 feet—all helping to give these spaces the sense of spatial generosity that they had.
- *Spatially varied and complex.* The building had a wide variety of kinds of spaces, seemingly packed together in a very neat

array. When I used the building, it included the following: a 1600-seat auditorium, art and architecture studios, a general library, a specialized library for art and architecture, offices and meeting rooms, classrooms, a bookstore, a museum, a store for books and supplies, and a cafeteria—at least. There was a richness to this mix and I never got to all the spaces—partly because my classes weren't held in the building.

These uses had changed over the century since the building was finished. The main library was originally on the fifth floor, not the third; the museum was not yet in place; and the sixth and seventh floors were not yet built. One of the most striking things about the original building was the fact that it included rental spaces that helped support the institution financially: shops at the ground floor, offices at the second floor, and studios for rental to artists on one of the upper floors.

- *Wide, light stairwell.* Specifically, one of the most significant spaces was the stairwell on the east side of the south, East 7th Street entrance. This was a very light space, with a wide

Great Hall. Photo: Historic American Engineering Record, Library of Congress.

Engraving room. Drawing: Historic American Buildings Survey, Library of Congress.

stair and generous windows all the way up. At the time I certainly wasn't thinking about the inefficiency of this part of the building's "circulation system," but was simply enjoying the experience of going up and down that stair, being inside the building and connected to the city outside as well. That stairwell was important in itself, and not only as a means to get somewhere else.

- *Daylight and darkness.* The spatial generosity of the rooms and the large windows on the exterior (that all overlooked relatively wide streets rather than narrow alleys or yards) helped make rooms—particularly the main library on the third floor and the studios—have daylight that was almost palpable. At the same time, the fourth-floor museum felt dark, looking in from its entrance on its south side.

I experienced this building at a time when I was developing an explicit and broad view of the world; a new connection to politics and my own possible futures, and becoming aware of that new, personal connection. My beginning understanding of the architectural uniqueness of the building emerged along with my use of it, and what it had to offer—not the least of which were my connections and friendships with students studying architecture and art.

LIBRARY, MOUNT ANGEL ABBEY, OREGON

A door handle designed for comfort

MY FIRST VISIT to the library at Mount Angel Abbey was in the summer of 1972, after my first year in architecture school at Berkeley, and fourteen years before I moved to Oregon. I have been there many times since, including visits with students, with architects and friends visiting Oregon, and in connection with a planning project that I participated in at the Abbey. But that first summer, I spent several weeks in New York, and drove back to Berkeley via Oregon, largely so I could see the library as well as Lawrence Halprins' fountains in Portland.

Alvar Aalto was one of the architects who was much admired by our teachers at Berkeley, particularly by Richard Peters, whose architectural specialty was light in buildings. The library, a new building, was one of Aalto's last designs. It had only been finished three years before my visit and as one of Aalto's only two complete buildings in the U.S. (the other was Baker House, a dormitory at M.I.T.), it was much celebrated and I was excited to see it first-hand. I saw Baker House a few years after that, but it was not until 2015 that I had the chance to see Aalto's work in Finland.

I remember it being a gray and wet day. After driving up the approach road through the forest, passing the 14 Stations of the Cross, I came onto the flat top of the butte and left my Renault in the parking area in front of the library—essentially the main "green" of the Abbey—and went into the building. I came through the lobby and entered the main part of the library, and was immediately struck by the warm light of that space, in contrast to the grayness outside. I then began to look at how the building section, with the skylights, was allowing daylight to flood into the space, guaranteeing that the building would have its luminosity even during an Oregon winter of clouds and rain.

It was for me a transcendent architectural experience: a feeling of being in the presence of something that was not only beautiful, but in which there was a perfect convergence of architectural

Main floor of library.

Door handle on men's room in building lobby.

form and human experience. My colleague Virginia Cartwright, in a wonderful lecture about Aalto's several libraries, talked about how the Mount Angel building represented the culmination of a gradually strengthening synthesis of several architectural strategies of plan, section and daylight. Although I didn't know that much about Aalto when I first saw the building, I certainly experienced the result of that evolution.

After I looked at the main part of the library, I came back out to the lobby and found the men's room behind a wooden screen. I put my hand on the door handle to open the door, and immediately came in touch with one of the other things that I had been taught about Aalto: his attention to the smallest details of human experience. The handle welcomed my hand around it. It was not only "comfortable" but brought my hand and the handle together in an intimate way. Its section was not circular but oblong without an edge.

I did not like everything about the building. I felt that the front façade was too austere (and only much later I learned that a covered walkway with a small clock tower had been proposed but never built). In subsequent visits I realized that the basement level did not have the elegance of plan of the main level; the office wing did not have the same resolution as the main spaces. But I did see it as an extraordinary building: both because of the daylight in the main space and the details like the door handle that connected so strongly with the human hand. Like much of Aalto's work, this building supports human experience. It does it through light and touch, at scales ranging from the overall, principal space, down to the door handles of rest rooms.

ORCHARD LANE, BERKELEY, CALIFORNIA

Walking up to California's past

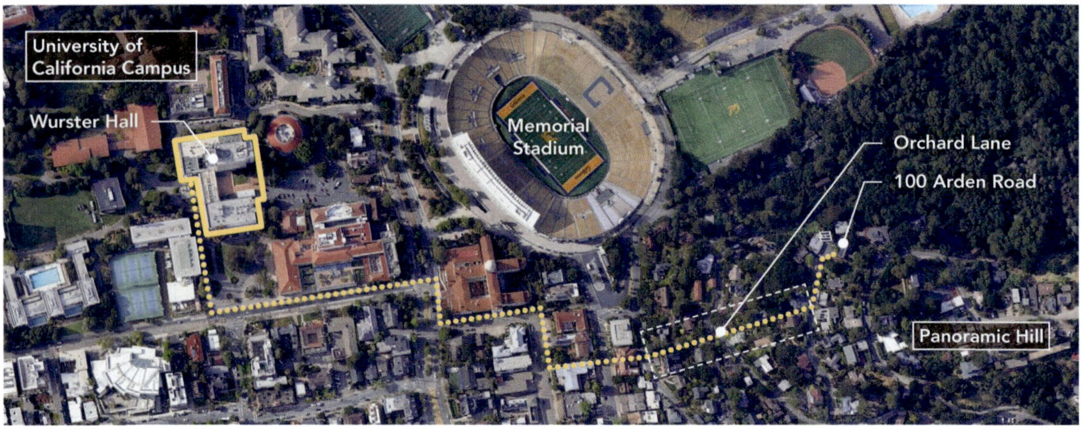

The path from architecture school to house. Google Maps.

ONE OF THE MOST formative aspects of my Berkeley architectural education happened as a result of living for two years in a house on Arden Road, on Panoramic Hill, just east of the campus and close enough to walk to from the architecture department in Wurster Hall. This house, built in about 1912, was the first house built that high on the hill. It was built of redwood, inside and out, and had views out to San Francisco Bay that incorporated four bridges—the Golden Gate Bridge, the Bay Bridge, and the San Rafael and San Mateo bridges. Our neighbor (who lived in a house designed in 1939 by William Wurster)[1] was Eleanor Gardner, who grew up in Berkeley just after the beginning of the twentieth century and who was old enough to remember driving past orange orchards instead of tract developments and shopping malls to get to San Jose.

That house, along with the 20-minute-or-so walk between the house and the school, helped make real for me the architectural traditions of Berkeley and the Bay Area. The first house on the way up the path, No. 1 Orchard Lane, belonged to architect Walter Steilberg, a draftsman and engineer in Julia Morgan's office[2]—and

[1] This information was found on the website https://usmodernist.org/wurster.htm

[2] The architect Julia Morgan was the first woman to graduate from the École des Beaux Arts.

when we were walking up the hill, white-haired Mr. Steilberg himself was sometimes seen in his garden. On the way up were also houses by Bernard Maybeck, sometimes partly hidden in gardens. The Introduction to Charles Keeler's book *The Simple Home*, quoted the 1906–07 yearbook of the Hillside Club in Berkeley: "hillside architecture is landscape gardening around a few rooms in case of rain."[3] But we learned that it is more, connecting to the natural world: the use of local materials, capturing the precious sunshine, easy connections between inside and outside, roof porches, the fragrance of eucalyptus.

Orchard Lane was one of many public pedestrian paths and staircases in the Berkeley hills, the most famous probably being the Maybeck-designed Rose Walk, in north Berkeley. These public ways provided alternative possibilities for public space—divorced from cars and trucks, integrated with houses and gardens. They also brought one very close to the life of houses and gardens, allowing a view of details and sometimes even a glimpse into the house, with reflected sunlight making the redwood-paneled walls glow. Our direct experience of these buildings helped give a reality to what we were otherwise learning about Maybeck, Julia Morgan, and their contemporaries, and helped set the stage for learning about those who continued their tradition later in the century—William Wurster, Joseph Esherick, and Bill Turnbull.

Even when I first saw these places, I came to realize that the world I was glimpsing was not only an architectural world. That domestic architecture, with its strong connections to its context, was part of a complete cultural world, of Berkeley and the Bay Area: a world of political and cultural

Views of Orchard Lane, Berkeley.

3 Charles Keeler, *The Simple Home*, introduction by Dimitri Shipounoff, p. xi.

Views of Orchard Lane and nearby houses, Berkeley.
Top left: the house high on the hill, where we lived.

alternatives that set the stage for the 1960s. These buildings, and the builders' versions that were copied all over Berkeley, represented a strong architectural idea, with their redwood shingles or pink stucco, painted trim, views of the Bay, and easy connections between gardens and inside rooms. But partly through these buildings, I also saw people for whom progressive politics and ideals were a normal part of daily life.

LONDON

The small and the human

> "I love walking in London," said Mrs. Dalloway.
> "Really, it's better than walking in the country."
>
> VIRGINIA WOOLF

I FIRST LIVED IN LONDON when I took six months off from architecture school to work for an architecture firm in Soho. For the first three months I lived in Kilburn, on West End Lane, and the second three months in Islington, in Lonsdale Square. Arriving in the city for the first time, and looking out from the train as it made its way toward Victoria Station, I saw a lot of worn, gray brick, black pipes, chimney pots, what seemed like disordered back extensions to the old terraced houses, not much greenery. To me London seemed run-down and poor, with an ugly and sooty repetitiveness. And I was ignorant about the urban history and geography of London, about its architecture, about the nineteenth century, about the Blitz. First impressions can be deceiving, and they affected how I interpreted what I saw.

Near the Euston Road.

I began to explore the city. After work I joined my office colleagues at our local pub, the John Snow. It was named for the nineteenth-century physician who first found that cholera spread by water, after discovering that a nearby pump was the center of a local concentration of the disease. On weekends I took long walks that often began with a particular focus—a park, a museum, a neighborhood that I particularly wanted to see—but then evolved into a more relaxed urban wandering.

Dalston.

I walked along large and small streets, through mews and parks, passing houses of different styles and sizes and levels of prosperity. I began to notice the stone-slab pavement, the spare Georgian façades, the street signs mounted directly to buildings, everywhere the low scale of buildings along with a real calmness in many of the residential streets. Once I started seeing these things again and again, I began to think about the city in different ways.

Tate Modern, formerly power station.

A back street.

Any foreign place causes people to notice ordinary things more than they do at home, and here the ordinary things seemed to add up to something.

What was that something? The other reflections in this book focus on one or two small, definable things. But London is a sprawling city, with up to a million buildings, over 60,000 streets, and 32 boroughs plus the City of London at the center. How can I say *one thing* about London, in the 700 or so words that I have allotted myself for these short essays, or even in something twice that length?

If there is one such thing for me, it is this. The "one-thing-ness" about London is that its greatness is *not* symbolized in one thing, one center, one set of buildings, one garden, one brick wall. It is not the Haussmanian coherence and beauty of Paris, the unifying power of the *Ringstrasse* of Vienna, the Royal Mile marching up the ridge to Edinburgh Castle, the ancient grids of Xi'an and Beijing, the 1811 gridded plan of New York. These are all wonderful, but for London it is different, almost the opposite. It is the human scale, the attention to and care for the individual, the fact that I never feel small in the city, never overwhelmed by the scale of buildings or grand boulevards intended to impress. London does not completely lack those kinds of things—Whitehall, Buckingham Palace, Trafalgar Square, the Palace of Westminster right on the river, the Wren churches, the great parks, the new buildings in the City, the Thames itself. But when I think about London, I don't think about those monumental things. Instead I think of the small, close, and accessible, and the way in which they seem to be made with attention to the individual.

St James's Square.

What really got to me was the small and human and immediately accessible, the carefully-made places of everyday life. The terraced house giving everyone their own piece of land, including a garden and a front door that opens to the outside rather than an internal corridor; two or three windows wide, two or three or four storys tall, with an "area" surrounded by a black wrought-iron railing, to bring light into the basement; the smallest houses without even the obligation to align the ground-floor openings with those above; the smooth brick wall, laid in English or Flemish bond with grey London brick; the comfortable, shaped feeling of a curved wooden stair rail in an old house; the low scale and ample light of many residential streets; shopkeepers still living over their tiny shop on many commercial streets; the green-ness and care taken with gardens and parks.

Street sign, July 2017.

More than any other great city I know—except perhaps Tokyo—London is a "bottom-up" city. The impossibility of re-planning London after the Great Fire of 1666 contrasted with other cities that followed the grand urban ideas and symmetries of the Baroque. London could not incorporate those grand ideas, while continuing to respect individual property rights. And the term "bottom up" speaks to the devolution of administration and resources to individual boroughs that can be attentive to their own neighborhoods; to the fact that skateboarders could develop enough public support to stop a major development for the arts that would have displaced them, in a highly public place;[1] to the ability to develop a project like Gillett Square (see pp. 237–240), with its respect to local residents, rich and poor, as part of the plan; to the persistence of markets like East Street and Ridley Road, where even poor immigrant vendors from Ghana have a place.

Houses of Huguenot weavers, Spitalfields.

London is not without its problems. Like other major cities, it has what seems to be an insatiable property market, a difficult gap between rich and poor, and major challenges with housing and social services. But even amongst these issues, and what sometimes seems to be an inexorable march of capital[2], the small and local and human continue to pop up.

Stockwell, stacked two-story maisonettes.

My affection for the city has drawn me back dozens of times. In addition to Kilburn and Islington, I have stayed in different neighborhoods on both sides of the river: Peckham, Chelsea, Bethnal Green, Kennington, Stockwell, South Bermondsey, South Kensington, Marylebone, Notting Hill. And when I carried out research, my projects were centered on topics connected to the particularities of the small scale I was appreciating: the ancient lights doctrine; the historic contracts of seventeenth- and eighteenth-century carpenters and bricklayers who built one or two houses at a time; the hundreds of craftsmen, and their small buildings, who made up the furniture-making industry in Shoreditch and Bethnal Green; the weavers' houses of Spitalfields; the geography of small businesses in Dalston and Whitechapel and Upton Park; most recently the ground-floor commercial extensions that appeared beginning in the mid-nineteenth century on thousands of houses in busy streets. My initial perceptions of London came to have researchable histories, giving order and knowledge to my observations—while at the same time my observations and fascination with the city continue.

[1] The renovation of Queen Elizabeth Hall, an important building of the South Bank arts center, was stopped by public support for the skateboarders who used the space underneath that building.

[2] See Anna Minton, *Who Is London For?*

1974

LA TOURETTE MONASTERY, ÉVEUX-SUR-L'ARBRESLE, FRANCE

Small spaces and human use

IN 1974 I VISITED many of the Le Corbusier buildings in France, including several of the houses in and around Paris, the chapel at Ronchamp, the Unité d'Habitation in Marseille, and the monastery of La Tourette at Éveux sur l'Arbresle near Lyon. I spent a night at La Tourette, having dinner with the monks, and sleeping in one of the monks' cells made available to visitors—mostly architects and architecture students.

La Tourette was one of the Le Corbusier buildings that had attracted me the most, through drawings and photographs. I liked its overall form, the contrast with the hill, the strong articulation of its parts, the hierarchies among building volumes of different sizes. When I visited, I was looking at it more through an architectural eye than the eye of a resident. But in addition to the overall form, what struck me the strongest when I first entered the building was the roughness of the construction—particularly the concrete finishes and simple, almost primitive, way in which materials met each other. There was little refinement, but only the most basic joint, forcing the eye and the hand to focus on the material itself —perhaps appropriate for a building the residents of which were expected to live in privation.

My experience of the room was quite different. I was of course aware of its dimensions and proportions—long, narrow, and low. I was able to touch both walls at the same time, and to easily touch the ceiling. But what really surprised me was how the length of the room, and the extreme relationship between its length and width, seemed to divide it into several parts, making what is a small room in area into a room that had clear "activity settings"—an area for entry and dressing, near the door; the place for the bed, in the middle; and a place for working, near the window—plus a small terrace outside for contemplation of the landscape. That terrace and the low concrete wall dividing it from the view helped extend the room and join it with the landscape beyond.

View of monastery. Hemis/Alamy stock photo.

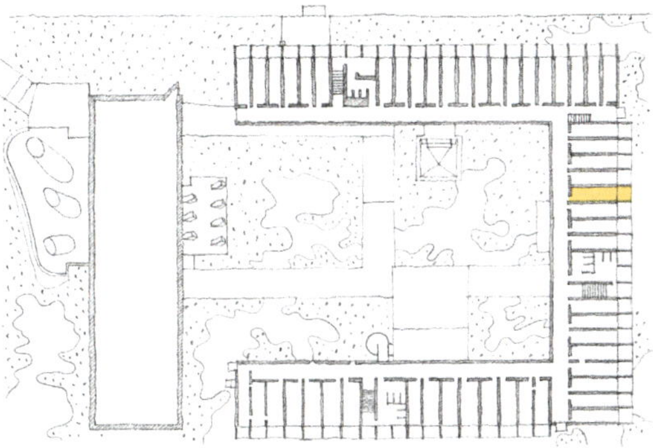

Plan showing individual rooms.

An individual monk's room.
Painting by Sheri Pyron.

I enjoyed this experience, and the question of the relationships between quantity of space and the possible multiple human uses of space stayed with me in my subsequent work and teaching. Almost 20 years later, in India, I had an experience that drew on this idea. We were working with families to design very small houses—they had two rooms and a porch, often in a single line, like a "shotgun house" in the American South. The question arose about where to put the door between the two rooms—in line with the door between the porch and the front room, or on the opposite side. We originally suggested that the door be in line with the entrance door—this would set up a "circulation path" on one side of the house. But the family member responsible for the design said no—if the circulation path cut diagonally across the room instead, it would clearly set up two different activity zones, in opposite corners, thereby making the use of the room more efficient. Although these were small houses, the room dimensions were larger than the width of the La Tourette room, and the houses were used by multiple people, including children, and not only one occupant.

At La Tourette as well as at the small house in south India, the use of the room was not necessarily the same as it might seem from the floor plans alone, where the small size might suggest a singular use. In each case, a small room lent itself to division into even smaller areas of activity that came to be strongly understood as such by their designers, listening to the people who use them.

FARMHOUSE, TUNISIA

Precious wood

MY INTEREST in the traditional vernacular architecture of the Middle East and North Africa took me to Tunisia, where I visited several small towns in the middle of the country: Gafsa, Tozeur, and Nefta. These were oases with large orchards of date palms, and many simple, traditional buildings of mud brick. At the edge of one town, just after sunset, with daylight fading, I saw the buildings blending into the sand of the desert, the landscape and the buildings of the town one and the same.

Traditional doorways of Tunisian houses are often elaborately decorated with ornamented metal fasteners to hold the wood of the door together, within openings in the wall that themselves may have ornamented arches. These doors may be the principal decorative element in a wall that is otherwise largely blank. Privacy is an important characteristic of houses in traditional Islamic culture, and most of the walls that are elaborated and ornamented are often those of the inner courtyard rather than the public façade. Through the street door, the visitor enters the *skifa*, a passage that leads to the courtyard while shielding a view of the courtyard from the street while the door is open.

Typologically, the traditional houses get increasingly elaborate as they get bigger. Much of this transformation concerns the courtyard: increased symmetries, additional side spaces, arcades around the edge, more ornament. But it also may concern the door on the street: larger, more ornament, arched or with a decorated stone lintel. Smaller houses, belonging to the families of less wealth, have more modesty, less ornament, and less complexity.

The Tunisian house that is the subject of this reflection was too small even to have a courtyard at all. Made of mud brick, it had only one or two rooms, a flat roof without even a line to mark where the wall ended and the parapet began, and a façade with a simple door in the center and a window on each side. Instead of an arch there was a wooden lintel over a metal door inside the opening. The house

Tunisian doorways.

Simple farmhouse in Tunisian oasis town. Painting by Zachary Leonard.

measured no more than 15 or 18 feet across the façade: as simple as they come. But the urge for ornament was still expressed. The lintel was carved and painted, with vivid colors forming a strongly-formed marking of the entrance. That single piece of wood, the only thing visible on the house that was painted or carved at all, was precious: the most precious bit of material in that simple building, doing the same thing for the family that lived there as the much more elaborate doorways did for theirs.

In a housing project in the south Indian state of Tamil Nadu, India about 20 years later, we worked with families to design their own small and inexpensive houses, each costing the equivalent of about 500 dollars. Each house had about 300 square feet of roofed space, built with plastered walls of fired brick and mud mortar, and roofs of baked tiles on a wooden frame.

At the end of the finishing work for the concrete floors, the builders inscribed a line in the concrete, a few inches from the wall of each of the two rooms. There was no functional reason for the line. We had not specified it, and it took only a few minutes to do.

I thought it remarkable that the builders of such modest houses saw the importance of making that line, but at the time I did not connect it to the Tunisian door. But this border, on the floor of each room, provided the only bit of ornament built into the house. Like the wooden lintel in Tunisia, the impulse to make ornament was able to be realized even in the most simple and inexpensive dwelling.

ROEHAMPTON HOUSING ESTATE, LONDON

Back to the real world

DURING THE YEARS immediately following architecture school, I visited many of the buildings and places that I had learned about in school—buildings and places that represented all periods of architectural history, including the most recent buildings that followed the Second World War. One of those projects was the large housing developments at Roehampton, in west London, designed under the auspices of the London County Council (L.C.C.), which had been the governing authority for London since 1889.

Roehampton was arguably the L.C.C.'s crowning achievement in public housing (usually known as "council housing" in the UK). It was first of all the largest, and it was for that reason that it could most readily be an exemplar of Le Corbusier's Ville Radieuse, his architectural idea of "towers in a park," including modernist ideas of planning that separated functions from each other. This included the separation of different housing types from each

Apartment blocks at Roehamption, 2024.

Balcony at end of individual dwelling unit at Roehampton.

other (tower blocks, slab blocks, low-rise blocks); functions from each other (dwelling, shopping, schools, recreation); to large extent pedestrians from motor vehicles; and, as I realized on a much later visit, people from each other.

The end of the war through to the 1970s was a golden era for progressive-minded architects in the UK (and Europe). The need for a lot of housing and the need to rebuild following the destruction of the war, the politically-left inclinations that followed the defeat of fascism (including the tendency to see modernist architecture as a rejection of what were seen as symbols of fascism), and a genuine appreciation of modernism's functional clarity, all conspired to produce hundreds of projects incorporating tens of thousands of dwelling units.

Roehampton was among these projects, and as a student at Berkeley I often heard about it, particularly from our teacher Alan Forrest, who had worked in London for one of the leading firms there, Douglas Stephen & Partners.[1]

So I took the bus out to Roehampton, entered the large area of housing and other functions, and spent a couple of hours walking the streets and paths, and looking at the buildings. It's a long time ago, but I remember it being a sunny day, with people outside enjoying the fresh air and sunshine. I walked on the paths alongside as well as away from the vehicular streets; I looked at the

Ground floor of housing block showing pilotis supporting buildings.

[1] Alan was a brilliant Scotsman, from a working-class Edinburgh family, who moved to London after his education at the Edinburgh College of Art, and was recruited by the architecture department at Berkeley after he began teaching at the Bartlett following his professional time with Douglas Stephen.

A street in London.

different building types with dwellings in them; passed by a child-care center; began to understand how the functions were separated from each other; saw a large amount of green space. I was happy to see in the flesh what I had learned about and seen pictures of, and to experience what was regarded as an exemplar of modern British architecture.

Then it came time to leave. I walked out to the main road, found the bus stop toward central London, and began to wait there. And after a couple of minutes waiting for the bus, and on the bus ride itself, I began to realize that I had a completely different feeling from what I experienced inside the development. The feeling was one of having re-entered the real world. I was suddenly in the presence of buses and trucks, noise and traffic lights, trash cans and metal roll-up shutters on shop fronts, narrow stairs leading to flats above the shops, ambulances and newspaper stands, people in all conditions of striving, trouble, and success.

When I thought back on it from the road outside, it seemed like a world apart, an artificial construction, the attempted creation of a utopian world. It was more an idea than a living place.[2]

[2] I returned to Roehampton in 2024, almost 50 years after my first visit. I was more familiar with architecture, architectural history, and with reading buildings than I was on my first visit—and I appreciated the architects' intent to provide dwelling units with good daylight, balconies, and outside views of green space. But while at the estate, I also spent time pondering how influential—and potentially damaging—a single set of architectural ideas could be. And my reaction on the bus back to London was the same—a world apart.

ARCADED STREETS, BOLOGNA, ITALY

Sheltering daily life

ON MY SECOND TRIP to Italy in 1975, I was in Bologna for about three weeks, staying with friends—exploring the city, and using it as a base for shorter excursions to other cities like Florence, Ferrara, and Ravenna. Bologna is different from most cities in Italy. Its architecture, combined with twentieth-century initiatives, brought together aesthetic power and typological order with a set of political intentions based on the idea of community.

For several hundred years, the historic center of Bologna has included arcades in the front of every building. They were there, by law, to give shelter to visitors from outside the city. This straightforward law resulted in a unique aspect of urban form: the continuity of a sheltered public space in front of every building, and providing a path of movement, one step up from the roadway, everywhere in the city—on every street, large and small, in front of mansions for

Arcaded buildings in Bologna.

the wealthy, small buildings with people living over the store, and stately buildings for government and commerce.

In modern times, Bologna's buildings were not seen as historic artifacts to be treated as a tourist attraction, but as living parts of the contemporary city. Since 1960, Bologna had had a leftist city government, regularly re-elected. In the 1960s and 1970s the city underwent a major project of restoration and urban renewal. But differently from the kind of "renewal" that characterized American cities during those decades, in which vast areas of the city were destroyed, and poor people forced to move, Bologna handled it in ways that respected the historic city and all the people who lived in it. The architect in charge of the project, Pier Luigi Cervellati, guided a process in which the buildings remained with their historic typologies respected; the arcades remained and were restored, and people could move back after the construction was complete,

Arcaded buildings in Bologna.

Arcaded buildings in Bologna.

paying the same rent as they did before they temporarily left. What resulted was a city in which all the parts—buildings, streets, pavements within the arcades—had an ordinary, everyday purpose, with little to do with tourism or maintaining the historic city as a public investment that would be repaid by tourists.[1]

I have returned to Bologna only a few times since that first visit. But I have always seen the arcades in an intimate relationship with the daily life of the city. People respect that daily life, protect it, and symbolize its importance. The chance meeting of neighbors, the ways in which shopkeepers can keep their "eyes on the street," in Jane Jacobs' sense, the ways in which the arcades, different as they are from building to building, help give visual unity to the street and the city—all these things help establish and maintain the arcades of Bologna as an architectural phenomenon that is at once physical, social and aesthetic.

1 The variety of arcades in Bologna, and their varied history and social role, is described in the nomination for recognition of the arcades by UNESCO as a World Heritage Site. Samples of relevant text from that nomination follow. The full text is at https://whc.unesco.org/en/list/1650/documents/.

- The portico of the Edificio porticato del MAMbo certainly plays an important and acknowledged social role, which has been maintained to this day. During World War I it was a place of great significance, for it was there that the population would receive their daily ration of bread. It was a sheltered place where Bolognese gathered to buy the barilini, small loaves of bread that were baked inside the building.
- The Portici accademici di via Zamboni have a strong cultural identity related to the presence of the university and the municipal theatre. They represented the place where the great academic conversations took place. Under the institutional porticoes of via Zamboni, young people from different nationalities currently meet, study, have a conversation, enjoy a meal.
- Devotional, commercial and political functions blend together in the Piazza Porticata di Santo Stefano, a place that accommodates the market, the senatorial residences and the Complesso delle Sette Chiese.
- The portico del Baraccano is the one that best represents the charitable function, as it was originally a pilgrim shelter of which we have record since 1416. It was managed by the Compagnia del Baraccano, whose charitable work was addressed to the elderly, wayfarers and orphans.
- The Portico della Certosa has a funerary function. Small shops connected to the cemetery, such as florists, marble workshops and funeral services, prove a social aspect that is still relevant in our time.
- The portici of the Piazza Cavour and the via Farini represent a social ambivalence. If, on the one hand, they are the ideal place for the promenade, combining elegance with architectural refinement, on the other hand they represent a shelter for the homeless. This particular aspect is celebrated in a very popular song entitled "Piazza Grande," by a famous Bolognese singer, Lucio Dalla. The homeless use the porticoes as a place to exchange experiences or to rest, in a city which can offer numerous city-run homeless shelters.

Copenhagen

Island of Thasos, northern Greece

Left to right:
Istanbul
Barcelona
London

PART TWO

1980–1985

In these years I was mostly based in Berkeley. I began to teach under Ray Lifchez, a much loved, dedicated teacher who had a unique, successful way of teaching introductory design. It started with written scenarios about human activity, and then their development into buildings through a succession of specific techniques: collages based on the text, then simple, rough models that made the collages three-dimensional, and only then the typical architectural drawings of plan, section, and elevation. Ray's insistence on teaching students to support human needs in buildings was emphasized through his connections with the community of people with disabilities in Berkeley, and their regular inclusion as guests and informants in the studios.

I also had a one-term teaching appointment in Edinburgh, one of the most beautiful cities in Europe. A year after I returned to California, I moved to Texas, where I spent two years on the architecture faculty at the University of Texas at Austin. I began to travel more extensively, including a trip to Turkey and Greece, and another to Egypt, Italy, and the UK, where I stayed outside Oxford and travelled several days a week to London to carry out research on the ancient lights doctrine. (The law prevented the construction of a new building that would block the light to a window in an existing building, if that window had been in place for a certain amount of time.) That research was ultimately published and was the beginning of several related projects in London.

Left to right:
Edinburgh
Istanbul
Venice

HOUSE IN THE SIERRA NEVADA, CALIFORNIA

Easy comfort or conscious experience

A NUMBER OF YEARS AGO I spent a weekend in California at the Japanese-style house of a carpenter, Len Brackett. He had lived for several years in Kyoto, learning traditional Japanese carpentry through working as a carpenter's apprentice. The house was located on a sloped site in the Sierra Nevada foothills. The house was exquisitely detailed and meticulously crafted with several varieties of wood: planed, jointed, and fitted by hand, with surfaces that were smooth as silk. The house compound consisted of several

Looking across courtyard of Brackett house. Photo: Aya Brackett.

buildings—the main house, the small building containing the *furo*, or bath, a little up the hill, and, since the permanent toilet had not yet been built, a temporary outhouse about 50 or 60 feet down a gentle slope from the main house. There was also a large workshop in which timber was cut and shaped—this place was the location of the workshop for the business as well as the house.

My guest bedroom was a traditional Japanese room, measured in the number of *tatami* mats on its floor—this was probably a four-and-a-half- or six-mat room. The room had sliding *shoji* screens, covered with white rice paper, along one side, separating it from a passage. I slept on a thin futon mattress placed directly on the *tatami* floor, which was a short step above the passage.

In the middle of the night I needed to visit the outhouse. I got up from my futon, stepping onto the raised *tatami* floor, put on my robe, opened the *shoji* screen, put on my slippers, walked down the passage to the kitchen, crossed the kitchen to the outside door, changed my slippers to outdoor shoes, opened an umbrella, stepped into the gentle rain, walked to the outhouse, changed my shoes to ones I found at the outhouse door, and then reversed my steps in the rainy walk back to the house and my bed, closing the umbrella, walking back through the kitchen, up onto the passage, and back through the *shoji* screen to my futon.

This could have been an annoying and laborious experience. If I were in a hotel I would have been a few steps from the bathroom. But instead of being annoyed, I found myself more aware of the sensations of each moment: my feet on the silken floor and then crossing the tile floor of the kitchen, the cool air on my face when I stepped outside, the patter of rain on my umbrella, feeling the few drops that the umbrella did not deflect, walking down and up the slope, lying down again on the futon. The experience was moment-to-moment, each moment felt directly and fully, with changes of touch and temperature and wetness along the way. And much of it was unexpected, relative to my usual experience—not comfortable in the ordinary sense of ease, forcing a different kind of awareness of things outside myself.

The memory of that night has prompted me to remember similar experiences that also raised my awareness of the world around me: the wooden *shoji* screens in a different building, clattering against the creaking house frame during a stormy night in Kyoto; stepping barefoot down the wet stairs at Peter Zumthor's baths at Vals to find a glimpse of the valley through several layers of concrete and stone (see pp. 241–244); walking on top of the

Brackett house in forest. Photo: Aya Brackett.

Side passage in Brackett house. Photo: Aya Brackett.

vaults at Lincoln Cathedral, between the stone ribs and the wooden roof, on floorboards supported on wooden bridges with the curved vaults below; stepping gingerly on the slats of a rope bridge, while crossing a stream in Nepal.

Of course, one of the basic functions of architecture is to help arrange the environment so people are comfortable, "at home" in their place in the world. But comfort is not the same as a retreat from sensation, and an inability to act on one's own behalf. My walk down the hill in the rain represented a heightened sense of awareness: the walk brought me *outside* what is usually regarded as one's "comfort zone." It helped me feel the cool air, the rain, my own body as I walked down and up the slope.[1]

In these few minutes, I was in touch with the world—a larger and more varied world more connected to nature, to materials, to the weather, to the slope of the hill. The world is too big and varied to be known only as one knows his air-conditioned room. It demands attention, and makes us more human when we accept the challenge it requests. And it may be the role of the architect not to close the door on the potential of that challenge.[2]

1 The connection to health that could be supported by such a variety of sensations is described in the book by Christie Johnson Coffin and Jenny Young, *Making Places for People: 12 Questions Every Designer Should Ask*, pp. 140–142.

2 This text is a modification of a short essay I wrote for a student publication at the University of Oregon School of Architecture and Allied Arts: "Foreword: Unsettling the Architecture of Anaesthesia." *Ktisma*; volume 6, 2016. Thanks to Luke Janzen and Daniel Matallana for inviting me to write the essay.

CHRISTIAN SCIENCE CHURCH, BERKELEY, CALIFORNIA

Modern materials, lovely wall

BERNARD MAYBECK designed a variety of public buildings in the Bay Area in addition to many houses, but the Palace of Fine Arts at the edge of the Presidio in San Francisco, near the Golden Gate Bridge, and the Christian Science church near the University of California's Berkeley campus, were arguably his two most well-known buildings. Although the church was only open to the public during Sunday services, its proximity to the campus, along well-traveled streets, meant that as students, we could easily appreciate it from the outside, and begin to understand Maybeck's synthesis of the modern with the historic and vernacular.

The exterior wall of the church is sometimes described as having a variety of stylistic influences: Romanesque, Japanese, California, modern. Esther McCoy, in *Five California Architects*, wrote that Maybeck "was certain of one thing: the man of the Middle Ages could use the most modern materials he could lay his hands on, and would combine them in such a way as to express the spirit of his faith."[1] There is evidence of Romanesque capitals, of Japanese windows in the repetitive shapes of the industrial sash windows, of the use of trellises to support flowering plants, of the use of concrete, of asbestos panels, of the industrial sash itself. Maybeck was a modernist while also drawing on the vernacular, and on the need for buildings to respect the landscape, climate, and social habits of a place. At this church, and particularly on the exterior wall, he used them in a way that helped make the wall itself into a well-designed and well-crafted object.

The variety and contrast of materials (including the solid, fluted square columns; the diamond-shaped tiles on the solid wall; and the industrial sash windows divided into very small panes) all individually helped make the wall visually approachable and touchable. But there were also strategies used, that brought the individual parts together, to unify the entire composition within the larger building. The red diamond-shaped wall tiles visually connect

[1] This quotation is included in the nomination of the building for the National Register of Historic Places, submitted in July 1977.

Entrance to Christian Science church, Berkeley.

Wall of Christian Science church, Berkeley, showing variety of materials.

with the red roof tiles. The roof tiles have similar dimensions as the wall tiles and window panes. The distance between the flutes on the square columns visually connect with the glass panes. The square columns themselves connect with the right angles of the wall tiles and of the industrial-sash windows. The columns are not only objects in themselves but also help form three-dimensional spaces in front of the wall. All of these relationships help unify the entire composition.

The wall, then, is not simply an armature for windows or shading devices or trellises, not just a barrier against rain or cold or wind. Its parts work together to make something that itself has substance and architectural meaning, something which is as pleasurable as a courtyard or view or family kitchen—any of which we experience fully, in itself.

NEW YORK PUBLIC LIBRARY

Symbol and function

I OFTEN DESCRIBE the New York Public Library's Main Reading Room as the most beautiful room in New York.[1] The room is on the third floor of the main library building at Fifth Avenue and 42nd Street; and differently from other major libraries built around the same time, such as the Boston Public Library (finished in 1895), the windows of the main reading room are not visible on the front, Fifth Avenue façade of the building, but instead on the back of the building, facing Bryant Park.

I first started visiting and working in this room when I was a college student at Cooper Union. This was before the room had been restored, including the removal of the remainder of the black-out paint that had been put on the windows during the Second World War and the installation of a modern infrastructure for wifi and a digital indexing system that replaced the catalog system that had been used for decades. I looked forward to the process of searching in the catalog, obtaining and finally reading a particular item from the collections.[2] The building helped me understand that the work I was doing there was important, happening in a beautiful and important place. The room was large and clear in its spatial order; the daylight always seemed to be ample even before the remainder of the windows were made clear again, and there was a sense of purpose among the people working at the large tables.

The room can be understood in two ways. First, in architectural ways: its position in the spatial sequence through the public parts of the building; and second, how it connects, technologically, to the book-ordering and book-delivery system.

The room is reached by a spatial sequence that includes entry up the stairs between the two famous sculpted lions, into the main lobby, up the stairs past the second floor, into a large public vestibule on the third floor, and then through the catalog room into the main, high and light reading room. This sequence was through rooms with a variety of sizes, shapes, and light levels,

1 But certainly the Main Concourse at Grand Central Terminal is at least a serious competitor.

2 The first research project I remember working on in that room was as a student researcher for a proposed little book, involving the design department in the School of Art at Cooper Union, that was ultimately not published. The book was intended to be an artistic and historic account of the first ten positive integers; my role was to carry out historic investigations of the numbers "4" and "10."

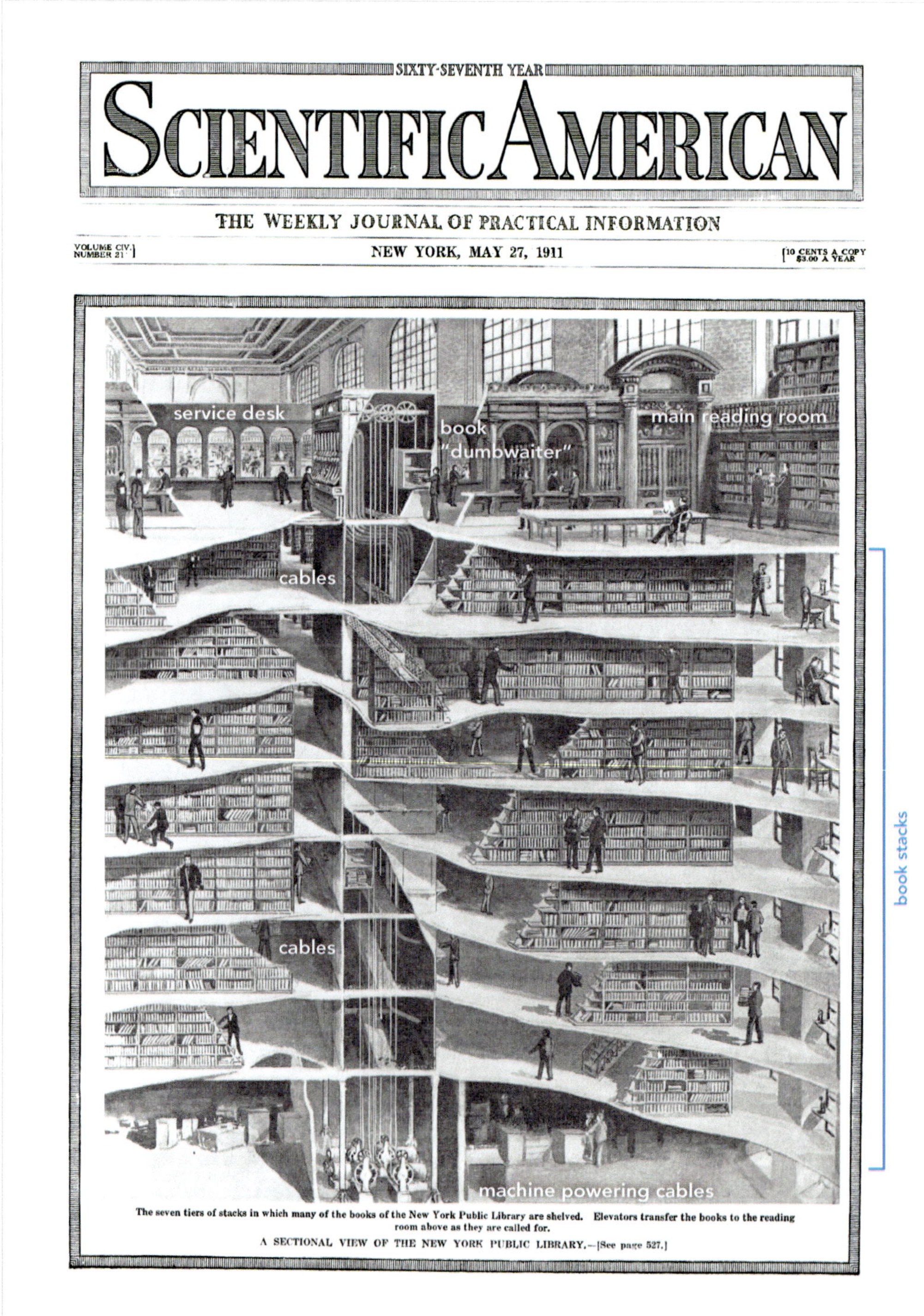
SIXTY-SEVENTH YEAR

SCIENTIFIC AMERICAN

THE WEEKLY JOURNAL OF PRACTICAL INFORMATION

VOLUME CIV. NUMBER 21 | NEW YORK, MAY 27, 1911 | 10 CENTS A COPY $3.00 A YEAR

The seven tiers of stacks in which many of the books of the New York Public Library are shelved. Elevators transfer the books to the reading room above as they are called for.

A SECTIONAL VIEW OF THE NEW YORK PUBLIC LIBRARY.—[See page 527.]

The main reading room at the New York Public Library was the tip of the iceberg of books and the then-modern book delivery system. This issue of *Scientific American* was published when the library opened.

Main reading room, New York Public Library. Library of Congress.

doing everything that architecture could do to make reading and the acquisition of knowledge into an almost sacred act. The reading room is a fine example of neo-classical design, with a well-proportioned system of pilasters, cornices, coffered ceiling, and high, arched windows—all supporting the historic symbolism of the library, including daylight coming from above. This is part of the history that included, for example, Christopher Wren's design for the library at Trinity College, Cambridge, in 1676, and subsequent variations on the same ideas in many different places.

But the room is part of another system as well. It sits atop the stacks, which helped the efficiency of book retrieval by allowing the dumbwaiters that delivered the books to their readers to be efficiently connected to both the center of the main reading room and the book stacks below.[3] Indeed, the two systems come together right in that center, where the books arrive and the researcher enters the main reading room. That overlap is symbolic of the two aspects of the building—a clever technological solution to the problem of book ordering and retrieval, while maintaining traditional ideas of the use of architectural space to act in a symbolic way to maintain the idea of the importance of books and knowledge.

The May 27, 1911 edition of *Scientific American*, a magazine that usually has little to do with architectural aesthetics, devoted its front cover and an article to the new library. After a detailed technical accounting of how the book-ordering and delivery system worked, the authors extended the description to how this system was extended to various rooms dedicated to different subjects—and

[3] Originally, the catalog room contained a vast card catalog, with thousands of drawers, accounting for every item in the library. The researcher filled out a request slip, and gave it to a clerk in the center of the room who sent it down by pneumatic tube to the stacks for retrieval. The researcher was given a slip of paper with a unique number. After retrieval, the item was placed in a tray on a dumbwaiter, and brought up to the central desk of the main reading room. A clerk at the central desk lit the appropriate number on a sign visible to the researcher, who was waiting in the reading room for the item.

concluded with the classification of people. This was perhaps a prescient but unintentional introduction to the twentieth century: "Following the suggestion of the director, the architects, Messrs. Carrère and Hastings, have provided a building which is not only a work of art in itself and a worthy monument to the largest city in the western hemisphere, but which automatically, we may say, divides the thousands of readers who wish to consult the books into the intellectual classes in which they belong."[4]

[4] "The New York Public Library: How the Readers and the Books are Distributed in the New Building." *Scientific American*, May 27, 1911, p. 527.

My experience of this building helped me understand a major lesson of architectural history. On one hand the nineteenth- and early-twentieth centuries were times of technological innovation: railroads and railroad stations, rapid-transit systems, elevators, tall, steel buildings, advanced systems of air handling. But on the other hand, these innovations were often hidden by the historic styles that remained the standard until the flowering of modern architecture two or three decades later. The New York Public Library is a splendid example of this dichotomy.

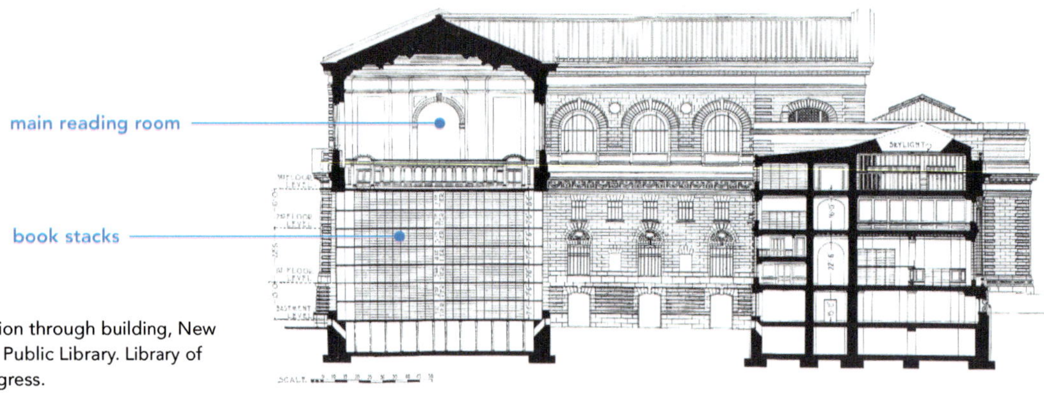

Section through building, New York Public Library. Library of Congress.

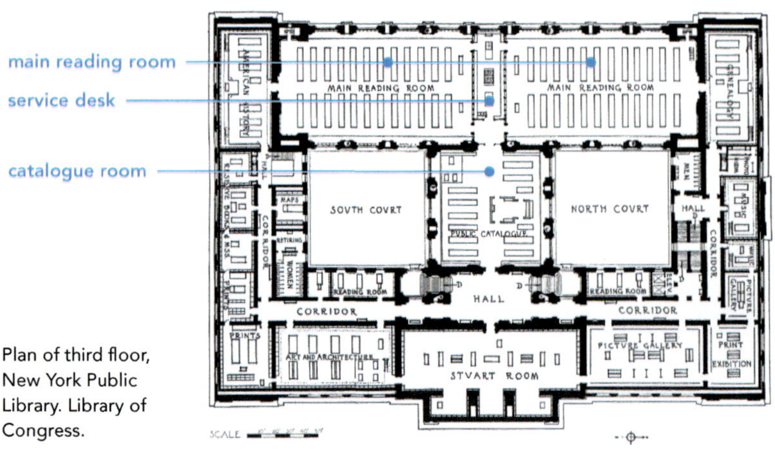

Plan of third floor, New York Public Library. Library of Congress.

WEST 47th STREET, NEW YORK

Wise Men Fish Here

DURING AND FOLLOWING the 1980s, my trips to New York usually included a visit to the Gotham Book Mart, then on the north side of West 47th Street between Fifth Avenue and the Avenue of the Americas. The store was a "real bookstore"—a center of New York's literary community, a place to browse old first editions and current literary magazines, a place with narrow aisles, high shelves, and books everywhere—before the time of bookstore cafés or tote bags. The store's founder and longtime proprietor, Frances Steloff, lived in an apartment above the store.

Entering the store was like entering a different world. But what affected me, beyond the bookstore itself, was the contrast between the bookstore and the local urban world from which I entered it. This block of West 47th Street happened to be the center of New York's diamond-cutting industry, largely dominated by Hasidic Jews. By then many of the five-story townhouses that were along the street in the early part of the century had been replaced

Sign that hung outside the Gotham Book Mart.
Photo: Richard Levine/Alamy.

with six-, eight-, and ten-story loft buildings, with retail space at the street and perhaps the second floor, and workshops in the loft spaces above, where the actual cutting of diamonds took place.

The contrast was extreme. In the middle of an industrial location with hundreds of individual shops, through which passed 95% of the diamonds sold in the United States, items that perhaps had the most value per ounce of anything sold in the country, items that represented the ultimate symbol of wealth, was a bookstore where words and ideas were the primary currency, part of a culture in which very few got rich but in which, for many members of the culture, getting rich was not the idea. These two entities co-existed in the same urban milieu, with the bookstore advertising itself with a metal sign hanging over the sidewalk, "Wise Men Fish Here."

So just in the block on that one side of the street were, at least: one of the most important bookstores in the city, the apartment of its owner and proprietor, retail jewelers, workshops of diamond cutters and craftsmen, a small number of restaurants, and probably other apartments still present in the townhouses that had not yet been turned into loft buildings specifically designed for the diamond-cutting industry. There were also two important businesses for photographers: 47th Street Photo, and Marty Forscher's camera repair shop, located amongst the diamond cutters on an upper floor of one of the loft buildings, known and used by every serious photographer in the city.

This common location of three different types of specialized businesses, along with secondary businesses that served them, helped form my understanding of how cities function. The diamond industry had had at least two centers in the city before it came to West 47th Street. It began at Maiden Lane in the financial district, then moved to the area around the intersection of Canal Street and the Bowery,[1] and finally, in the 1940s and after, relocated itself on 47th Street, where it remains. The economist Alfred Marshall, who carried out his innovative work on "agglomeration" and industrial districts in the late nineteenth- and early-twentieth centuries,[2] might have seen it as a perfect case study. The agglomeration of hundreds of diamond-cutting firms on West 47th Street had the three attributes important to him: a large pool of skilled labor, ready access to customers and suppliers, and knowledge of the trade that could be easily shared.[3] And economists and economic geographers recognize that among this concentration of specialized firms are the firms of secondary industries that serve

1 In one of her first publications, Jane Jacobs wrote about the diamond industry when it was on the Bowery. "Outside [the diamond workshop] on the Bowery, the lusty, tumultuous life of the Lower East Side converges. The 'El' roars, trucks rumble, Chinamen from Mott Street mince by, snatches from foreign tongues are cut and lost in a reek of exotic and forbidding odors. Absorbed in the raucous chaos, the visitor forgets the cool diamonds and the metal until, a few blocks away, he sees the glittering gold-leaf roof of the new building at Foley Square." Jane Jacobs, "Diamonds in the tough," *Vogue*, October 15, 1936, reprinted in Samuel Zipp and Nathan Storring, eds., *Vital Little Plans: The Short Works of Jane Jacobs*, pp. 10–16.

2 Thanks to Francesca Froy for bringing his work to my attention.

3 An anthropologist's account of the strong relationships within the New York diamond industry is in René Rose Shield, *Diamond Stories: Enduring Change on 47th Street.*

Diamond and jewelry businesses on West 47th Street.

them: lawyers, accountants, restaurants, and suppliers of specialized and non-specialized goods.

In a place so heavily populated by a single industry, I saw the Gotham Book Mart as an anomaly: a holdout against the high-dollar businesses all around it. But the character of large cities comes from many such anomalies, the serendipitous mixture of people, the democracy of the street, the gradual change of neighborhoods over time, the union of the ordinary with highly specialized expertise of different kinds. Billions of dollars of diamonds are steps away from Hasselblads and Leicas, and first editions of Virginia Woolf, Jack London and Vladimir Nabokov.

1981

MOSQUE OF RUSTEM PASA, ISTANBUL

The sacred over the profane

ON MY FIRST TRIP to Istanbul in 1981 I concentrated my wanderings in the old city, on the European side of the Bosphorus south of the Golden Horn. With the help of the guidebook *Strolling Through Istanbul* I was able to find many of the mosques and associated buildings designed by the great architect Sinan, who worked following the Ottoman conquest of Constantinople in 1453. He designed scores of buildings, ranging from the famous

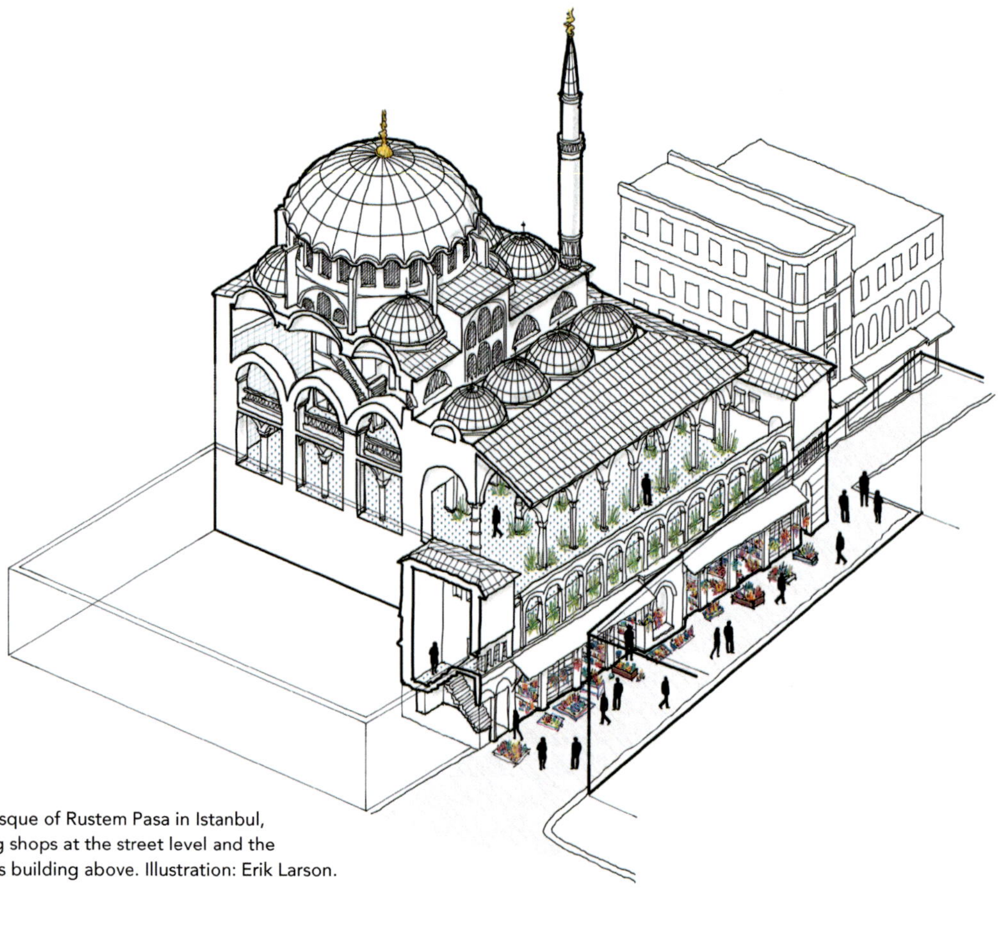

The mosque of Rustem Pasa in Istanbul, showing shops at the street level and the religious building above. Illustration: Erik Larson.

Suleimaniye Cami to much smaller buildings. Like many of Sinan's Ottoman mosques, Rustem Pasa Cami has a large dome marking its center with small domes around it and a courtyard in front; it is known particularly for its brilliantly-colored Iznik tiles.

But what made the mosque unique for me is its position one story up from the street, with a row of shops below. To get to the mosque, a narrow stone stair next to the shops leads the visitor up to the street edge of the courtyard. One side of the courtyard overlooks the street, and the other has the entrance to the mosque's interior. The sequence is powerful. The visitor is hardly aware of the mosque when on the street, amidst the bustle of commercial activity: open shops with goods outside, delivery vehicles, people buying and selling. But then there is the staircase, and the emergence from the staircase onto the quiet courtyard, not completely cut off from the street, but a more peaceful and ordered space. And finally the entrance into the interior, luminous through the dome, and the splendid tile work on the wall.

Mosques and other Muslim religious buildings were often embedded in bazaars and adjacent to commercial buildings, and included such commercial buildings in their initial investment and construction. The rent from these commercial enterprises helped support the mosque's charitable works. In most instances of this, the shops and mosque are on the ground floor, and the mosque is simply surrounded by the shops at the same level. Rustem Pasa is

View of shops below and mosque courtyard above, with minaret.
Photos by Helen Lucas.

Interior of mosque. Photo by Malcolm Fraser.

more unique in the three-dimensional aspect of the phenomenon, but the economic motivation is the same.

Any piece of urban land has a certain economic value, but this value is not evenly distributed throughout the land—either in its plan or in its implied volume. Different uses have different optimal locations within the volume to contribute to the site's financial return—so shops are naturally most lucrative when they are next to pedestrians on the street, and dwellings when they are farther away from the street.[1] This financial idea is not limited to the relationship of dwellings to other uses. In the case of mosques, the sacred space is inside, and its religious nature is emphasized by symmetries. When such an idea is realized on an asymmetrical urban site, the land "left over" at the edge has value associated with the commercial nature of the bounding street, and may take on a commercial use.

In the case of the Rustem Pasa mosque, that happens vertically instead of horizontally. And what is so remarkable about it is the extreme contrast between the boisterous activity of the street and the peaceful beauty of the courtyard and mosque just upstairs.

[1] For a discussion of the economic factors in buildings that combine dwellings and other uses, see Howard Davis, *Living Over the Store: Architecture and Local Urban Life*, pp. 109–113.

OUTDOOR BOOK MARKET, ISTANBUL

New ideas, fresh air

WHILE IN ISTANBUL, I came across the outdoor book market, that I had not been aware of before, in my wanderings around the Grand Bazaar and the nearby Beyazit mosque. Of course I had seen outdoor book stalls before—in New York at the edge of Central Park and outside the Strand Bookstore, in Paris along the Seine and the streets near the Sorbonne, and in other places—but this one was more permanent than the others, clearly anchored in its place, with a space of its own, not simply portable boxes that would be opened and closed every day, perhaps carried away. But outdoors nevertheless.

Its sense of permanence had apparently come about after a long history. The establishment of a book trade in Istanbul dates back to soon after the Ottoman conquest of Constantinople in 1453. At that time there was a book market roughly where this market is now. Bookshops did not only sell books, but were also bookbinders and traders in paper and ink. The outdoor book market may be a descendant of a bookshop of the fifteenth and sixteenth centuries. There is evidence of the continuation of the book trade in this approximate location until the twentieth century.

Spatially, the book market had an order of its own, of course different from the mosques but not so different from the bazaar, that gave it a unique yet appropriate identity. In my memory it was organized around an outdoor space, with a shaded, paved path around its edge, and low plants in the center. The courtyard side of the path had tables with books on them, but no fixed shelves. The inner side also had tables, in front of the open rooms of shops, with glazed cabinets and bookshelves.

My immediate impression was that I was experiencing a place that combined a quiet calmness with an intense intellectual focus. It was in between the noise and activity of the bazaar and the quiet sacredness of the mosque, but yet connected to both of them with its combination of intensity and peacefulness—particularly

Outdoor book market.
Above, taken in 1981.
The pictures to the right, taken by Helen Lucas in 2024, show the Beyazit mosque in the background.

given to the place by the trees and their shade. The location of the market allowed it to be of two worlds at once—the harsher world of buying and selling, and the quieter world of thought and study. It is a simple place, but thinking about it now, several decades after I first encountered it, it exemplifies the power of an ordinary place, with an ordinary architectural order of its own, to have a character that is strong enough to give it a lasting memory and impact.

MOUNT ATHOS, GREECE

Transcendence in the landscape

MOUNT ATHOS, the easternmost finger of the Halkidiki Peninsula in northern Greece, projecting south into the Aegean Sea, is one of the most sacred places of Eastern Orthodox Christianity. It is the site of 20 monasteries and many smaller residences, individual dwellings for hermit-monks, and other religious buildings. The peninsula is mountainous, without direct road service to the rest of Greece, and is generally accessible only by boat. The monasteries are on sites difficult to access, often atop steep rock outcroppings.

The twenty monasteries and other religious buildings of Mount Athos are located on a peninsula in northeast Greece.

As a side trip from a two-week stay in the northern Greek city of Thessaloniki, I made a trip to Mount Athos. To get there, I had to first gain written permission from the Ministry of Northern Greece (now the Ministry of Macedonia and Thrace) in Thessaloniki, which I was able to do as a professor of architecture interested in the buildings of Mount Athos; I could also have done so if I were of the Orthodox Christian faith, wanting to visit as a pilgrimage. (I could not, however, have gotten permission if I were not male; women are not permitted on the peninsula, and have not been for a thousand years.) Very early in the morning of the day my permit allowed me to enter, I took a bus from Thessaloniki to Ouranopolis, then a boat to the port of Dafni, and finally a short bus ride to the hamlet of Karyes, the de-facto border-control point of Mount Athos, where my permission letter was checked and I was given a pass that allowed me to stay on the peninsula for four days. That bus was the last vehicle; from there it was walking and boat journeys—a boat stopped at the tiny ports belonging to monasteries near the peninsulas' shores once or twice a day.

So I mostly walked up and down the hills from monastery to monastery, along narrow but well-worn paths. In four days and nights, I visited six monasteries and stayed overnight at four of them. A typical day consisted of several hours of walking, arrival at a monastery in the afternoon, and then staying at that monastery for the rest of the afternoon and overnight.

Monastery of Simonas Petras seen from below.

[1] In his book *The Broken Road: From the Iron Gates to Mount Athos*, the English writer Patrick Leigh Fermor mentions these four items of welcome at Mount Athos several times. And in his *Mani: Travels in the Southern Peloponnese* (p. 179), he makes it clear that it is not unique to Mount Athos, but to places on the other side of Greece, and probably further away as well, in slightly different form: "… the formalities of visiting are oriental; at least they are that hybrid achievement which we think of as 'Turkish': and, like many Turkish formalities, full of dignity and grace. … The other details of welcome survive intact: the spoonful of jam made from quince or morello cherries or rose leaves, the thimbleful of ouzo or raki, the little cup, iridescently cupola-ed with bubbles, of oriental coffee (or Spartan broth or a scruple of *nepenthe*?), the great gleaming glass of water, which is appraised and extolled by guest and host alike with the niceness of cork-sniffing claret experts."

On each of these visits, a monk welcomed me, offering a tray with the same few items: a glass of cold water, a small glass of *ouzo*, a cup of Greek coffee, and a piece of *loukoumi*, a soft sugared candy that in the neighboring country would be called "Turkish delight." [1] I was shown to my bed (guests were given the rooms with the best view) and then was on my own for the afternoon to wander around the monastery gardens, visit the church and other buildings and outdoor spaces, and experience what was always a great sense of peacefulness and calm. A quiet meal was taken with the monks in a refectory; the locally-grown food often consisted of fresh tomatoes, feta, baked fish, wine, and bread, with watermelon for dessert.

The buildings varied from monastery to monastery, often according to the architectural styles of the countries represented and different communities of the Orthodox Church: mostly Greek, but also Bulgarian, Serbian and Russian. The buildings were always a variant of the hybrid construction system that I had come to Greece and Turkey to see: although they expressed different architectural styles and details, they were also built with hybrids of local stone, prevalent in lower stories, and timber, more evident above.

When I visited Simonas Petras ("Simon's rock"), my bedroom was on the top floor of a nine-story tower that seemed as if it was a continuation of the rock below it. After I was shown to my room I was asked if I wanted to attend services in the church the following morning. I asked what time they started, was told 2:30, and I said, yes, but I might be a little late. So I went down at 6am, the monks had been praying for three-and-a-half hours, in a dark church, with their singing together with the flickering candlelight giving life to the gold and glass ornament, and lighting the icon paintings on the iconostasis. I stayed until the end of the service at 7:30 when I joined the monks at a Sunday breakfast of fish, potatoes, wine, and watermelon.

Before departing the monastery after breakfast, I stepped out onto the narrow wooden balcony on a side of the building that was not directly facing the sea, and looked at the mountainous landscape from that height, with a sheer drop of what seemed like hundreds of feet below me. I

View from the top balcony of Simonas Petras.

Monastery of Xenophontos seen from water.

Courtyard of Iveron monastery.

saw Mount Athos—the single mountain that gives its name to the entire peninsula—among other mountains nearby. And suddenly, for one of the few times in my life, I felt myself to be in a genuinely sacred place—a place whose sacred feeling came from its physical nature, and not only from the religious life that was carried on there. The other times I have felt this have included being in the center of a large Hindu temple in Madurai, in south India, after having come through layers of rooms and spaces; the *hondo*, or main prayer room in a Buddhist temple in Kyoto, with light reflected off small bits of gold; and the mosque of Kairouan, where the forest of columns extended on and on. (My emotional reaction to the Ise Shrine [see p. 154] was not a sense of being closer to the divine.) But this was different, since it wasn't a matter of symbolism, or music, or incense, or all the things that may be done to create or reinforce the sacred. Any religion I have in me doesn't have to do with a connection to a transcendent God—and in this case I was feeling something that was not that, but perhaps similar to it, even if only for the time I spent experiencing that landscape.

Interior hallway of monastery of Gregoriou.

LITTLE SINGER BUILDING, NEW YORK

The whole and the parts

ON MANY OF MY TRIPS to New York, following breakfast after an overnight flight, I took a walk along Lower Broadway. I knew the Little Singer Building from my time at Cooper Union, just a few blocks away, but I only began to appreciate it, and was able to articulate that appreciation, later when I began to be more directly involved with architecture and teaching.

This façade gave me genuine pleasure, and continues to do so. In his book *New York 1900*, Robert Stern writes briefly about the building, and sees it as derived from the "rationalist" work of Viollet-le-Duc.[1] Another source sees it as a variation of a Beaux-Arts building with classical roots. But I was never very interested in stylistic nomenclature, and I was attracted to the building because of its visible compositional order—particularly the scale relationships and three-dimensionality of its Broadway-facing façade.

The design of the façade is based on a careful relationship among its parts, leading to a singularly unique and organized whole. The following five attributes are central to this organization:

- First, the design is composed of a wide variety of parts. This gives the façade interest at these different scales—for example, the whole façade, a window grouping, a single terra-cotta tile. Any one of these is strongly defined, clearly visible and engages my interest.
- Second, the main central bay of the building is emphasized by the narrow bays on its sides—like a picture frame gives emphasis to the picture inside it. This gives the building an overall unity and helps focus the viewer's attention on it.
- Third, most of the façade is made up by a large area of steel and glass. This is balanced by the large, flat terra-cotta tiles. The variety of materials is not randomly

[1] Robert A. M. Stern, *New York 1900*, p. 154.

Little Singer Building, Lower Broadway, Manhattan.

distributed, but in a way that helps give balance to the façade. The areas of terra-cotta strongly define the areas of glass.

- Fourth, the façade is not a two-dimensional, flat surface. It is three dimensional, with depth. For example, the central windows are over a foot back from the horizontal bands of terra-cotta tiles. This makes that whole central bay into a three-dimensional "object" that has interest by itself.

- And fifth, the smallest details, such as the metal columns, the railings, and the elaborate terra-cotta tiles in the smaller side bay were all carefully designed in themselves, giving that smallest scale interest also. So every scale, from the overall façade, to the bays, down to the individual tiles that are bounded by metal has identity and completeness.

Detail of Little Singer Building façade.

Robert A. M. Stern writes that Ernest Flagg, the architect, "set out to express the structure as directly as possible...he abandoned his usual representation of the Classical orders and set the glass back from the façade...The intricate façade seemed as beguilingly transparent as a lace curtain, yet as solid as a thick masonry wall....Henry Desmond said of the designer of this 'rational skyscraper' that 'no other architect has ever so frankly accepted the situation which the skyscraper presents and submitted it to such brainwork...The architect has clearly endeavored to permit the structure to design itself, confining his own role as much as possible to making the structural features as good looking as lay in his power.'"[2]

In other words, the elements are put together with a strong sense of judgment about the two-dimensional relationships and proportions, about the exact size of construction components, about the depth that would produce a particular system of shadows. Although the façade is made up of a clear list of components, they come together as a highly complex, and complete, three-dimensional composition.[3]

2 Stern, *New York 1900*, p. 154.

3 This spatial complexity has affinities with other reflections in this book: the Karlsplatz station in Vienna; Santa Prassede in Rome; and Santa Maria Novella in Florence. In each of these buildings, the clarity of multiple scales of composition help lead to a visually strong result.

1983

VICTORIA AND INDIA STREETS, EDINBURGH, SCOTLAND

Topography and the city

IMMEDIATELY AFTER I arrived for a term teaching at Edinburgh University, I began to experience Edinburgh's highly three-dimensional topography. The medieval Old Town was built on a ridge leading up to Edinburgh Castle, and the linking of the Old Town with new developments around it in the nineteenth century required road builders and engineers to stitch together street systems at different levels. There are few connections between the New Town and the medieval city—a large public garden, that was originally a loch, lies in between them—but some of the connections that exist are distinctive in their three-dimensional geometry.

One of these connections is Victoria Street—that leads down from the George IV Bridge—which helped link the Old Town with newer developments on the south, including the Grassmarket, a low-lying street that was part of the original medieval city. Another is the George IV Bridge itself, that crosses over the Cowgate forming a vivid demonstration of the city's three-dimensionality. A steep public stair led down from Chambers Street to Bannerman's pub in the Cowgate. In one place, shown in a street section drawn by Malcolm Fraser, there are three streets, practically on top of each other, at three different levels. (A legal parcel of land in Edinburgh does not necessarily incorporate everything from the depths of the earth to the sky. In this location, for example, there are at least three separate owners in a single vertical slice.)

Individual houses and rows of terraced houses also respond to the extreme topography. As a result of the sloped streets, areas (the zone of space between the house and the footpath, below the level of the footpath, that bring light into rooms below the ground floor) sometimes allow for more than one "basement" level.

And in one case, a street ends in mid-air. A colleague invited me to dinner at his house, in one of the nineteenth-century extensions to the original, eighteenth-century New Town.[1] The building, at the northern end of India Street, appeared to be a four-story

[1] The original New Town was designed by James Craig in the eighteenth century. The best source is A. J. Youngson, *The Making of Classical Edinburgh*.

India Street, Edinburgh. The photo shows the upper floors only of the farthest house in the foreground on the left; the lower floors of that building are seen in the other photo. The entrance to the house is the second floor (3rd floor U.S.) of the building but at the ground level of India Street on which the photographer is standing.

Looking toward the end of India Street from below. The ground floor was once a post office and is now a pharmacy. The level seen as the ground floor in the other photo is two floors above the street seen in this photo. The pharmacy is on the ground floor of the building, two floors below what appears in the other photo as the ground floor of the house.

terraced house, like many others in the city. As a building at the end of the terrace, it had windows in the end wall.

But looking at the house from Northwest Circus Place reveals a much more complex situation. At their intersection, Northwest Circus Place is about 20 feet lower than India Street, which ends seemingly in midair. The building has two levels below India Street, and the bottom one has a commercial front, with a post office, facing Northwest Circus Place—completely independent of the terraced house above.

From one point of view, the building is similar to shops/houses in which entrances to different uses are located according to the characteristics of particular streets.[2] But in this case, the entrances are at different heights, because the streets are as well, providing a two-floor difference between the two doors. One door is at the dead end of a quiet street, and the other, part of the same building, is along a busy street.

[2] See Howard Davis, *Living Over the Store*, pp. 141–173.

Section drawing including Victoria Street. The different colors show different ownerships in the same vertical "slice" of Edinburgh. Drawing: Malcolm Fraser.

Victoria Terrace, Edinburgh, with Victoria Street below.

Since I first visited Edinburgh, I have remained attracted to its physical beauty. This starts with its geology, but the urban experience of its extreme topography depends on the inventiveness of engineers, architects, and builders—and lawyers—who were not deterred by the city's unique topography, and were able to build densely despite the challenges, and with unusual results. The topography was respected and kept, rather than leveled to make the street pattern "rational" or more useable. These results gave experiential richness to the city, with a three-dimensionality that is perhaps rivaled only by Hong Kong.

BYKER WALL, NEWCASTLE UPON TYNE, ENGLAND

The monumental and the humane

A PRINCIPAL FEATURE of the Byker housing project in Newcastle upon Tyne, designed by architect Ralph Erskine and landscape architect Vernon Gracie, beginning in the late 1960s, is a large, continuous, undulating thick wall, containing 620 dwellings. The enormous wall was placed to help protect the interior of the entire project, with a total of about 2,000 dwellings, from the noise of a proposed motorway just outside the project site, and to help shelter the estate from the north winds. The wall is two rooms deep, the depth of a dwelling unit, with small windows for service rooms (kitchens, bathrooms) facing what was to be the noisy motorway, and larger windows for living rooms and bedrooms facing the quieter project interior. (The motorway was never built.)

The south side, facing the low-rise part of the estate, has access galleries and balconies connected with dwelling units built in wood that contrasted with the brick wall; it has varied colors; and it has a sense of life that continued the closer-to-the-ground low-rise buildings with the south side of the wall.

I had wanted to visit this project since hearing about it from colleagues in Oregon. My first visit was in 1983 with my architecture students from Edinburgh University, on the day of my departure, and the second 21 years later, in 2004 while attending a conference in Newcastle.

The project is known largely for the wall, which drew me to it. But I also appreciated that some existing old buildings, such as a church, were saved and incorporated into the site plan. It is also known for the attention to and investment in landscape design that does a lot to humanize the estate through the provision of places for adults to gather and children to play. Erskine and Gracie maintained their studios on the site, so that they could consult with local residents when the project was under construction.

Erskine and Gracie took great care designing places that people might pass by or linger in, such as in between the private

View of wall with dwelling units.

View of entrance to dwelling unit in low building that is part of project.

space of the dwelling and the public space of the project. The one-bedroom dwelling units in the wall have two outdoor spaces—the public access balcony that has room for plants, toys, etc., near the front door to the dwelling, and a private balcony outside the bedroom. And the landscape budget was high enough that the site could be developed with other places for people—within an understanding that with small dwelling units, outdoor space is important.

The access walkway is wide enough to accommodate plants and furniture, so the façade became a combination of entry gallery, private terraces, and plain wall. This was built with a balanced combination of materials, including stucco and wood slats, horizontal and vertical, all placed to help break down the overall scale of the wall and make visually identifiable pieces of it.

What could have been a large, oppressive building was humane and pleasant. On my first visit in

1983 my experience was a positive one. It was a cold and wet day, so residents were not enjoying the outdoors. But dwellings and gardens seemed well-maintained, and personal items like shoes and children's toys were outside the doors to dwellings; there was an overall sense of respect for the place.

But a more recent article by Anna Minton, written in 2015,[1] is critical of the project. Although some important older buildings were saved from demolition when the project was built, many dwellings—mostly old, two-story Victorian terraced houses—were demolished, driving the original tenants away and destroying their communities. So although I have a positive view of this project's careful design, I also recognize that along with hundreds of other modern projects in the world, it resulted in the destruction of the communities that were once the lifeblood of cities. As I tell my students, very few buildings are "all good" or "all bad." Most buildings are too complex for such blanket statements, and there are things to be learned from all of them.

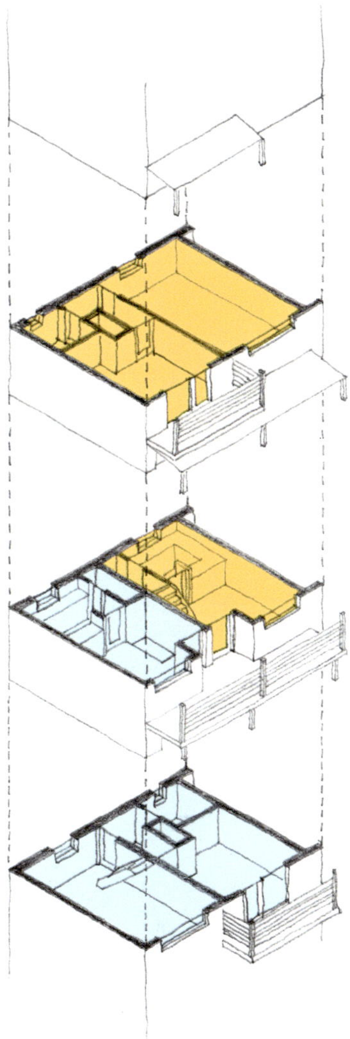

Axonometric drawing showing two-story dwelling units in "wall". Blue and yellow mark separate dwelling units. Most large windows are on the part of the wall facing the balconies, away from the proposed motorway.

Common table for neighbors.

Common area at end of an upper gallery.

[1] https://www.theguardian.com/cities/2015/may/21/byker-wall-newcastles-noble-failure-of-an-estate-a-history-of-cities-in-50-buildings-day-41. Anna Minton is also the author of *Big Capital: Who is London For?*

HOUSE, OPEN-AIR MUSEUM, COPENHAGEN

Simplicity of form, complexity of function

AFTER FINISHING teaching for a term in Edinburgh, I went to Norway and Denmark to look at the vernacular architecture of Scandinavia. I visited wooden buildings still in use in villages and towns, as well as several open-air museums with buildings that had been moved to the museum from different regions of their respective countries. The tradition of these museums began in 1891 with "Skansen" in Stockholm—which gave its name to that type of museum—and came to include similar museums in Europe and many parts of the world. They are often the locus of scholarship into vernacular architecture, and have research departments with historians and archaeologists who, behind the scenes, carry out serious research based on careful and sometimes groundbreaking fieldwork.

For a long time I was attracted to these buildings, and to vernacular buildings in general, for various reasons. They represent a direct response to contexts of place and culture; they are built with materials that are sourced locally, particularly from the local agricultural economy; they are formally and spatially simple. And they are often beautiful. While scholarship over the last several decades has gone beyond simplistic interpretations of the "genius" of "primitive" people,[1] they nonetheless appeal to me despite what I also know about the ways in which peoples native to a place have been marginalized, or worse.

A building that did this very strongly is a house at the Frilandsmuseet, an open-air museum just outside Copenhagen. The building is a "farmstead from Eiderstedt, southwest Schleswig," a place now in northern Germany, south of the Danish border. Many traditional farms are made up of separate buildings, often organized around courtyards, or with buildings organized under two or more roofs. One reason for the separate buildings is to prevent the spread of fire; another is that farms may grow in a piecemeal way and it may be easier to build a new building than to add on to an existing one (particularly with log construction).

1 Many books about vernacular architecture up until about the 1960s took this stance. See for example Bernard Rudofsky, *Architecture Without Architects* and Sibyl Moholy-Nagy, *Native Genius in Anonymous Architecture*.

Farmstead from Eiderstedt, Denmark, in Frilandsmuseet (Copenhagen open-air museum).

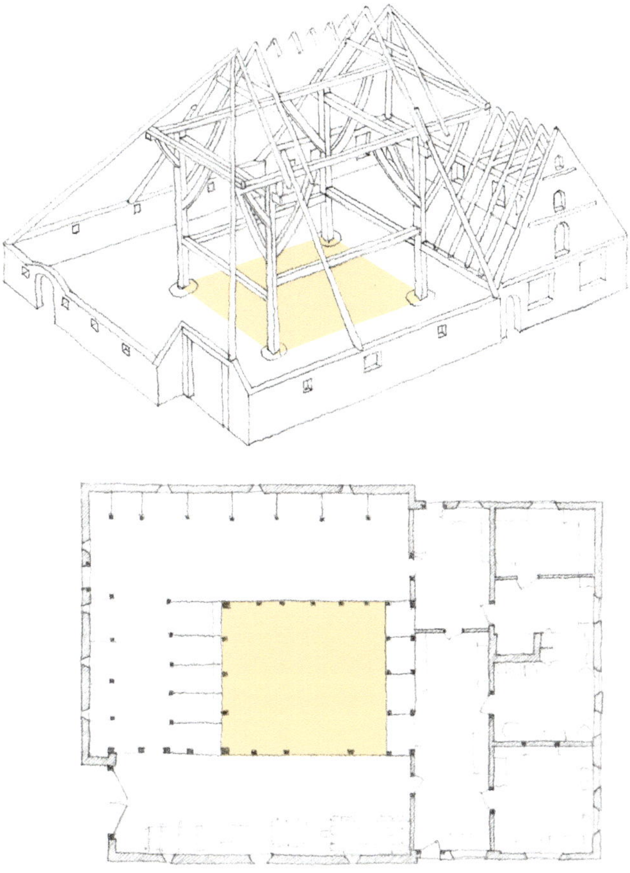

Structural axonometric and plan drawings of farmstead.

When I first saw this building, I was immediately drawn to its extraordinary roof—a single, steep roof that covers the entire building, including the barn in the center, and different functions of the farm, like the dwelling, around the perimeter. The main frame of the building defines the barn itself. According to Kai Uldall, "This concentrated form of construction began in North Holland and East Friesland about 1600, partly because rising corn prices and increasing corn exports necessitated larger barns."[2]

The timber frame that defines the barn-as-center is of course not visible from the outside. But the powerful roof suggests an important space below it, and the frame and history both confirm that.

The courtyard is sometimes not associated with northern climates as vernacular types often emerge as a result of their climatic properties. But in addition to providing shade,[3] courtyards also provide psychological protection from what may be perceived as the wildness of the landscape: they have a symbolic as well as functional role in the house. That symbolism is usually understood inside the house itself—but in the case of the farmstead from Eiderstedt, the great roof marks both the house and the important space that is at the center of it.

[2] Kai Uldall, *Frilandsmuseet: English Guide*, n.p.

[3] In China, for example, courtyards are smaller in the hotter south so that a larger percentage of the courtyard can be shaded, than they are in the colder north.

WASHINGTON MEWS, NEW YORK

Privacy and quiet near an active urban square

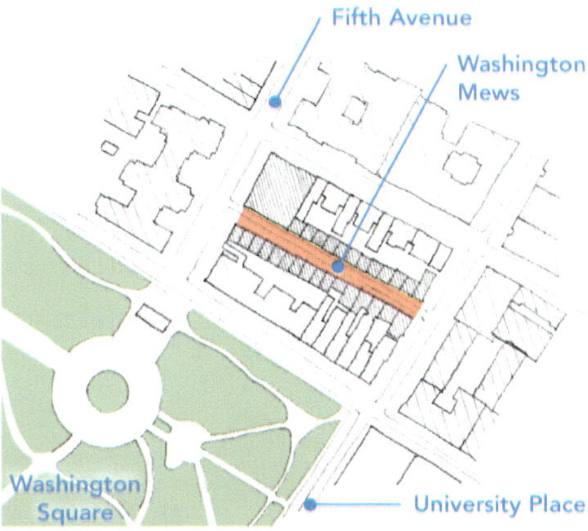

Map showing Washington Mews and Washington Square.

DURING THE YEARS I studied at Cooper Union, I had ample opportunity to visit Washington Square, the social heart of Greenwich Village. It is a place full of life, populated, in good weather, by probably a couple of thousand people talking, skating, reading, playing music, walking dogs, playing chess, splashing in the fountain at its center. It is an everyday place, but also a place for political events, and geographically important, marking the southern end of Fifth Avenue as well as the "center" of the Village. It is one of the pulsing hearts of Manhattan that also include City

Washington Mews looking toward Fifth Avenue.

Washington Square, showing Washington Arch at the southern end of Fifth Avenue.

Washington Square.

Hall Park, Union Square, Times Square, Rockefeller Center, and several others. Its life is continuous, all day and into a good part of the night.

But a mere one- or two-minute walk from the activity of Washington Square is one of the most peaceful streets in the city: Washington Mews, just north of the square and half a block away. At first sight Washington Mews is simply a small, quiet street, and I was always drawn to it. It is only one block long, east-to-west from University Place to Fifth Avenue, and has small, two-story party-wall houses on both sides of it. I liked its scale, its sense of separateness from the city around it, the apparent comfort of many of its houses, all adding up to the idea that it might be possible to live so peacefully in the middle of a great but noisy city like New York.

Why do the street and its small houses exist? Along the north side of Washington Square, and the south side of East Eighth Street, were two rows of nineteenth-century townhouses, originally occupied by wealthy families; behind them are the carriage houses and stables for both rows of houses, accessed through an alley that is now Washington Mews. It is a one-block-long street, connecting University Place with Fifth Avenue, with little reason for anyone to drive or even walk on the street unless going to a house along it. The fact that it is not a through-route of any kind gives it its quiet and privacy.

By itself, New York's rectangular grid offers little opportunity for such extremes of busy-ness and privacy. The grid, like most urban grids, is simple, with only two levels in its spatial hierarchy—the very busy north–south avenues, and the less busy east–west streets. Most of the city does not have alleys like this.

In residential neighborhoods of Manhattan, the east–west streets tend to be residential, often with townhouses and relatively low (for New York) apartment houses, and buildings on the north–south avenues have commercial space at their ground floor and apartments above, often with higher buildings than those on the east–west streets. This affords some measure of quiet to the more residential east–west streets, but the difference is sometimes elusive. After all, the streets are continuous as part of a uniform grid,[1] and vehicles can easily use them—and they do so.

The rarity of streets like Washington Mews makes the houses there very expensive, out of reach for most people. It is an urban anomaly: for people who want to live in places like that, it is almost an impossible dream.

But other models of urban design allow for more explicit hierarchies, clearly allowing the quiet and private to be more prevalent. One of the most spectacular in this regard is the Edinburgh New Town, designed in the eighteenth century by James Craig.[2] In this design, there are three levels to the street hierarchy, allowing the narrowest and least possible as a "through route" to also be the most prevalent. London also has many mews with converted houses. These are the result not only of the provision of places for carriage houses, but also of a history of land development that subdivided long lots, often within England's real-estate framework of nested property leases.[3]

The criticism of Washington Mews, that it is overly exclusive, is valid. But its exclusivity is not inevitable. And after I first experienced Washington Mews I came to notice, in other places, the possibility of urban design with more and different possibilities for giving peace and quiet to residential streets.

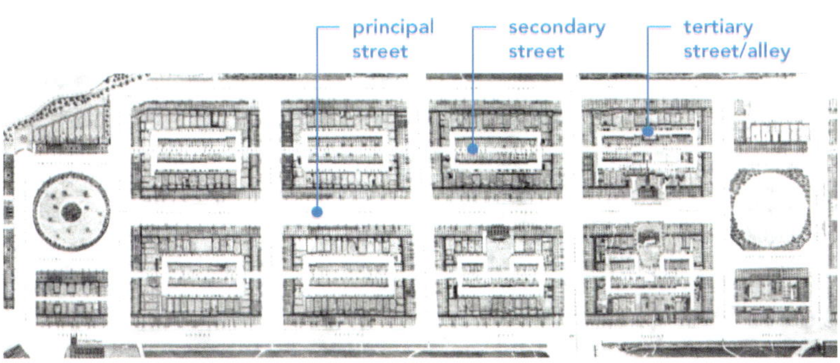

Plan of Edinburgh New Town, designed by James Craig in 1766.

[1] Most of the street grid of Manhattan above 14th Street was mandated in 1811, with the so-called "Commissioners' Plan". Although there were later modifications, including reserving land for Central Park, the 1811 plan was fundamental to the order and character of Manhattan that is experienced today. See the book by Hilary Ballon, *The Greatest Grid*, for a good account of the New York grid.

[2] James Craig was a 25-year-old architect when he designed the plan of the Edinburgh New Town.

[3] One of the best books on the nineteenth-century development of London is Linda Clarke, *Building Capitalism*.

1985

A NEIGHBORHOOD IN CAIRO

A walk in a city

IN 1985 I MADE my first trip to Cairo. I stayed in what was then the Nile Hilton, on the east bank of the river, near the Egyptian Museum and Tahrir Square—a place made famous in 2011 as the center of the revolution that resulted in Hosni Mubarak's removal as president of Egypt. It was late afternoon on a hot day, at the end of a visit to some of the mosques and other religious buildings in the medieval city. I decided to walk back to the hotel. Sunset was still an hour or two away, the weather had gotten a little cooler, and walking seemed better than taking a taxi.

So I set off, without a definite route in mind, only a general direction west, toward the river. I was not in a hurry, and I knew that as long as I got to the river, I could find the hotel. Pretty soon I was no longer in the medieval city, but in a more modern area, with a mixture of historic and modern buildings. Some were apartment buildings, many with shops, occupied by what seemed to be lower-middle-class people. But mainly, the streets were full of life—children playing, men working on their cars and motorcycles, neighbors talking, music coming from radios, dogs barking, street vendors selling their wares and food.

But I wasn't studying the streets and buildings, or even paying much attention to their details or to what people were doing. What I became acutely aware of was not the particulars of what was around me, but my own *intoxication by the city.* I was in a different mental place, with no apprehension or fear about being there, little sense of time passing, absorbed by the city, loving the city, at one with the city. I've had these kinds of feelings in New York and London, but this was at a more pronounced and extreme level than those other cities that are more a part of me. Somehow I felt as if I was being carried along by the city itself.

Part of my reaction came from a strong affinity with the people there, a realization that although we lived on opposite sides of the world, they were the same as people in New York and other

Cairo neighborhoods with ordinary daily activity.

more familiar places, and a further realization of the common humanity of people all over the world—a "Family of Man" moment.[1] But that is not all of it. The other part of it had to do with the city itself in its totality as a living, breathing, pulsing thing, and a sense that I was in it and very much a part of it. And knowing, even then, that this feeling had to do not only with Cairo, but with all great cities.

1 "The Family of Man" was an important photography exhibition at the Museum of Modern Art in New York, in 1955, curated by Edward Steichen, that included over 500 photographs, out of several million submitted by photographers and lay people all over the world. Illustrating the basics of human life in different places on the planet, the photographs were published in a catalog that has sold over four million copies and is still in print. Edward Steichen, ed., *The Family of Man.*

KINGS ROAD HOUSE, WEST HOLLYWOOD, CALIFORNIA

California and Japan

I VISITED the Kings Road House in West Hollywood in 1985, ten years before I first went to Japan. The house was desiged by Rudolf Schindler. I had read about the house and its social ideas—a dwelling for two families with a close relationship to each other, with some shared rooms and other rooms for each family alone; the "sleeping baskets"—redwood-and-canvas canopies on the roof. Having seen drawings and pictures of the building, its indoor/outdoor relationships, experienced mostly through the connection between the living rooms and the gardens, formed a major part of what I saw on my visit.

Kings Road House, R.M.S. studio. Photo: Timothy Sakamoto.

In the house, the wall between the living room and the garden is built with a redwood post-and-beam structure, allowing for a wide, uninterrupted opening. The strength of this connection was reinforced by the use of materials—with poured concrete on interior walls strongly contrasting with the open post-and-beam system—and resulting in strong contrasts between dark and light, and between a sense of enclosure and a sense of openness between garden and room.

The ability to have such a relationship is of course made easier by the fact that the house is in Southern California. Its climate allowed for a major feature of its version of twentieth-century architecture to be the breaking down of the boundary between inside and outside. At the time, I saw this as a strong expression of what I understood as "California architecture." I had already begun to understand this in the Bay Area, but the warmer climate in southern California lends itself more to this spatial continuity.

It was not until ten years later that I was directly introduced to traditional Japanese architecture. On my first trip to Japan, I stayed in a guest house in the area of Ohara, in the northwest

Kings Road House, west elevation. Photo: Timothy Sakamoto.

Kings Road House, Schindler entrance. Photo: Timothy Sakamoto.

part of Kyoto. The guest house was not a traditional building, but a simple modern building in which we sat on a tatami-mat floor for breakfast and supper. The room was connected to a garden, through a large sliding-glass door; indeed, the garden and the room seemed almost as one space. That experience was of course enhanced and multiplied as I subsequently visited many traditional buildings in Japan over the course of several trips.

Twentieth-century architects saw in traditional Japanese buildings a number of qualities they were themselves using: simplicity, spatial and structural clarity, spatial flexibility, the breakdown of hard spatial boundaries including boundaries between inside and outside.

Kings Road House, R.M.S. studio, looking west. Photo: Timothy Sakamoto.

[1] See Robert Sweeney and Judith Sheine, *Schindler, Kings Road, and Southern California Modernism*, p. 76. Judith Sheine writes that "The influence of Japanese designs that Schindler had seen in prints at Taliesin and Wright's Oak Park studio could be seen in the house's lightweight translucent sliding doors and geometric discipline, which, however, emphasized the connections to the outside spaces more than those between interior rooms." Sheine also writes that Schindler worked with three Japanese architects when he was working in Frank Lloyd Wright's Oak Park studio.

Schindler did not spend time in Japan as did, for example, other modernists such as Frank Lloyd Wright and Bruno Taut, but he worked at Wright's studio in Oak Park along with Japanese architects while Wright was in Japan working on the Imperial Hotel in Tokyo. Schindler likely learned about the features of Japanese architecture such as the wood post-and-beam construction and the permeable and changeable boundaries between inside and outside from the Japanese architects he met. If he did not do so, then the Kings Road House needs to be seen as a remarkable coincidence, an example of how architecture may emerge directly from the realities of its place, rather than a borrowed tradition. Most likely it was both.[1]

Vienna

Left to right:
Vienna
Portland, Oregon
Tanjore, India

PART THREE
1986–1991

In 1986 I left Texas for Oregon, where I have been since. I began to see *The Culture of Building* as a real book—and although it was not published until 1999, its possibilities as a book became evident, and my travels regularly provided opportunities to research buildings and places.

An important trip was to India in 1988. What impressed me most was not the colors or food or cultural differences of India—although those were ample—but the fact that within all that were people making their way in the same world I was, with similar successes and challenges. I returned about a dozen times, several for a housing project that built on the earlier one in Mexicali.

In 1989 I joined the Vernacular Architecture Forum (VAF), the primary scholarly group in North America dealing with vernacular buildings, connecting me to a community interested in similar things as me and helped legitimize my interests.

I taught our summer program in Rome in 1990, based at the Campo dei Fiori in the middle of the historic city. This connected me to a different urban reality from that of London or Delhi, with particularly historical understandings. And finally, a trip to Ukraine with VAF colleagues included a remarkable visit at an old village house that played a strong role in my understanding of how people depend on place for their life and identity.

Left to right:
Portland, Oregon
Rome
Portland, Oregon

MAIN LIBRARY, UNIVERSITY OF OREGON

A façade of humanism and classicism —and the local building culture

WHEN I FIRST came to the University of Oregon in the 1980s, I appreciated the combination of classical order and modesty in the buildings in the old part of the campus. This included the primacy of brick as the main wall material, the selective use of cast stone, and the restrained use of ornamental detail—all within the clear lines of classically-ordered façades. The buildings of the campus, along with the pride in the hundreds of campus trees representing a wide variety of species, helped represent what I understood as the humanism and modest restraint of the University.

In fact, this modesty was part of the intention of the architect whose designs gave the campus its original character. The main library was designed by Ellis Lawrence, a Portland architect who was instrumental in the first years of the School of Architecture and Allied Arts at the University, acting as its dean, and who, in the

Principal façade of main library, designed by Ellis Lawrence, facing main campus quadrangle at the University of Oregon.

1920s and 1930s, designed many of the University's buildings as well as its campus plan, based on the traditional idea of campus quadrangles. Lawrence had a modest approach to design, believing that architecture should be close in spirit to the people for whom it was being designed and built.[1] This was not Charles McKim designing Columbia University or John Galen Howard designing the University of California at Berkeley—both strong examples of neo-classical architecture, certainly developed for their particular locations, but also projecting a good deal of power and authority.

Among Lawrence's campus buildings at Oregon, that include the art museum and various other academic buildings, I was particularly drawn to the library. It has a symmetrical façade but without a single entrance in the center; it is brick, with cast stone only used as ornament in particular places; it is centered by the original two major rooms of the building. The building itself is facing north, toward the Willamette Valley that stretches toward Portland, at the end of a major axis of the campus. Its position and symmetry give it importance and centrality; the brick and selective use of cast stone give it modesty. The façade is beautifully proportioned, with what was originally the main reading room (and now the reading room for special collections) forming the *piano nobile* over the ground-floor windows of the Browsing Room. The details add much to the composition, including the projecting "balconies" at the three center windows, the inscriptions over the tall windows of the *piano nobile* (second) floor, and the details of the two entrances, not emphasized in the overall façade but quite visible when one is adjacent to them. Lawrence himself said of the library (at its dedication) that "It is the architect's hope that it is honest, not mere scenery; that it is modest, as the University is modest—not monumental or institutional, but homelike, inviting, quiet. These qualities are what the architects sought for."[2]

The library was finished in 1937, a difficult year of the Great Depression—but this date helps bring to light another aspect of the library that supports its humanistic nature. The library has multiple details—sculpture, friezes, woodwork, paintings—that were crafted by Oregon artists who were paid with Federal money through New Deal programs. Other Oregon buildings from the same era—the most well-known is Timberline Lodge on the slopes of Mount Hood—also had the benefit of such artists. But the Ellis Lawrence library brought together a major institution of the State of Oregon with a group of relatively unknown individuals who left their lasting artworks on the building. They included:

1 Thanks to Judith Kenny, who has done extensive research on Lawrence, for this insight.

2 Michael Shellenbarger, *Harmony in Diversity*, p. 54.

[3] https://researchguides.uoregon.edu/historic-knight/creators. The research guides for the historic University of Oregon buildings were developed by Edward H. Teague, former librarian of the Architecture and Allied Arts Library at the University of Oregon.

> Frederick C. Baker, lighting fixtures; Clarence E. Bates, wood carving; Nellie G. Best, sculpture; Arthur Clough, wood triptychs; Frederick A. Cuthbert, landscape features; O.B. Dawson, memorial gates; Edna Dunberg in collaboration with Louise Utter Pritchard, heads in exterior friezes; Brownell D. Frasier, interior of browsing room; Neal Gardner, sculpture in browsing room; Albert C. Runquist, mural in west stairwell; Arthur Runquist, mural in east stairwell; Phyllis Muirden Ryder, carved panels in Browsing Room; Ernest B. Thomas, cast-stone manufacturer of sculptures in frieze; Nowland B. Zane, murals in east and west stairwells.[3]

And the brick façade is made from the clay soil of the Willamette Valley, which once had dozens of brickworks and kilns, providing another connection to the local place.

In multiple ways, this building fits its time, place, and purposes, and helped me to formulate an understanding of the ethos and character of the University of Oregon. An understanding of the building comes not only from an analysis of its visible architectural order. This understanding also requires placing the building in its particular building culture that includes the sensibilities of its architect, the skills of the craftspeople who made it and provided some of its most visible features, and the local soil that made up its most prominent material.

Detail at library entrance.

RED FORT, DELHI, INDIA

Fire and water

Building at Red Fort, Delhi.

I VISITED the Red Forts in Delhi and Agra for the first time in 1988. The original visit was part of my first trip to India, lasting only three weeks, but during which I was introduced to the Mughal architecture of north India and Rajasthan, to the modern buildings of Ahmedabad and the imperial architecture of Lutyens' New Delhi, to informal settlements, to the khadi shops of Gandhi, to the humanity and beauty of the country that I returned to nine times.

The Mughal forts in Delhi and Agra, and other places in northern and northwestern India, are built largely in red sandstone, which is relatively easy to carve and shape, with finer details in white marble. These building complexes are landscape constructions and not only buildings, and I was also struck by their different ways of working with water: channeling it, making large ponds and putting buildings in the middle of them, making fountains and inclined surfaces with marble, carved into shapes that allow flowing water to ripple, taking advantage of gravity.

Interior of pavilion at Delhi Red Fort.

Edge of floor at Delhi Red Fort showing niches for oil lamps.

Access to water has played a major role in historic landscape construction in India. The country has, across its vast area, varying climates that may be alternately very dry and hot for a few months, and then very wet with monsoon rains for other months. Water is saved and accessed in large "tanks," or constructed ponds, with steps leading down to them for animals and people (different stairs for men and women, and for different kinds of animals); in stepwells, allowing people to go down to water through deep stone stair constructions;[1] in systems that irrigate rice paddies and other agricultural fields; in low-lying backwater canals among the rice paddies in places like the southern state of Kerala.

Each time I visited the forts, the large pools of water and fountains inside and outside the buildings were dry, so I was left to imagine how the buildings and landscapes had been designed to control water in ways that made it not only visible, but the most important feature—as if the design was done specifically to make water visible in different ways, emphasizing its fluidity, its motion, and the ways in which it modifies light.

Looking at a pavilion that once had watercourses carved in marble going through it, I imagined a hot night, with the senses engaged by the results of these strategies of design. I imagined the tinkling of water rippling over a carved marble slab, listening to the

[1] See for example Morna Livingston, *Steps to Water: The Ancient Stepwells of India* for an account of one way water was used in traditional India.

Detail of floor at Red Fort.

music of lutes and tablas and sitars; feeling the smooth coolness while touching the water; the distorted flickering of oil lamps seen through the sheet of falling water coming over the edge of the floor, along with occasional rainbows of color; the fragrance of delicate flowers and burning oil in the lamps. All this on a dark, perhaps moonless night, where the only earthly sources of light were the oil lamps located in small niches ("*chinikhana*") behind the water and hanging from the ceilings in the pavilions—and the tiny reflections of that light on the tiny jewels and cut glass sewn onto people's garments.[2]

Behind all these sensual phenomena is, of course, craft: the craft of stonemasons and stone carvers, of architects and landscape architects, of hydrologists and water engineers, of gem-cutters and jewelers, of tailors and seamstresses, of musical-instrument makers, of musicians and composers. The peaceful and beautiful evening that this place conjures up goes further, and invites us to see it as part of a sophisticated culture of design, making, and performance.

2 There are of course many buildings and designed landscapes in the world where water is such an integral part of the architectural design: the Alhambra and Generalife Gardens in Granada, the Villa Lante and many other gardens in Italy, some of the temples in Kyoto, Scarpa's Querini Stampalia in Venice, Zumthor's baths at Vals, and Mies van der Rohe's Barcelona Pavilion. In many cases the sensual experience depends not only on the large but on the small detail—hundreds of carved elements at the scale of an inch, for example—that together produce a finely-articulated visual and aural experience.

NEIGHBORHOODS AND HOUSES, JAISALMER, INDIA

Carved stone, community space

MY FIRST VISIT to Jaisalmer, a desert city in Rajasthan about 100 miles from the Pakistani border, began with a journey in 1988 on a steam-hauled train from Jodhpur. The city is visible from miles away, marked by an old fort on a mesa that rises up from the desert, with the same yellow color that covers most of the buildings in the city. The fort is no longer used as a fort, but is a tightly-built area of houses, courtyards and streets.

It was the combination of the solidity of the sandstone, the detail with which it is carved, and the variety of spaces that result that impressed me (and brought me back for another visit 12 years later). The craft of working with and carving sandstone was still alive in the city. Handcarts and donkey-pulled carts were helping

Street in Jaisalmer.

deliver the stone. Stonemasons were building houses and house additions, repairing walls, laying new pavement, and carving the complex *jalis* that provide both light and shade to interior rooms with the blazing sun outside.

The houses are variations on courtyard houses that are common in the desert. Their courtyards are several stories tall, instead of the one or two stories found in village houses. The courtyards bring light down into the middle of the house; they act as chimneys allowing hot air to rise and leave the house (daytime temperatures range from an average low of 48°F (9°C) in January to an average high of 107°F (40.6°C) in May) and, because they are often open to the rooms around them to help air flow, they also help reinforce visual connections between different parts of the house. The ornamental carving of the stone, combined with the complex spatial connections among the rooms, gives the houses a wonderful sense of connected spaces at different scales, resulting in beautiful light reflected off the golden stone.

One everyday detail was the washing stone, a special stone among many, on the top surface of the porch, a raised area outside each front door. The carved stone projected out beyond the top edge of the porch surface with a spout, through which water

Shaded courtyard in Jaisalmer.

Clockwise from top left: Looking down on street in Jaisalmer; Interior of house in Jaisalmer; Children playing on raised porch in Jaisalmer; Clothes-washing stone in Jaisalmer. The spout is over an open drain.

was directed down to an outdoor drain that was below street level, along the front of the property. Clothes could be scrubbed and rinsed on that stone— a beautiful example of the craft and specificity of function with which these houses were built.

The houses and outdoor spaces were experienced at three scales: the interior of the house, the house façade and porch just outside the front door that socially connects the house with the street and surrounding neighborhood, and the vibrant public spaces of the streets and markets. These spaces brought together the ordinary activities of daily life with the solidity and beautiful color of the stone. The combination of the highly-refined craft and detail with the ordinariness of the vegetable market gave dignity to a simple shopping trip to buy onions and okra.

TOMB AND MOSQUE COMPLEX, SARKHEJ, AHMEDABAD, INDIA

Stone softening daylight

IN INDIA IN 1988, I spent several days in Ahmedabad, the capital of the state of Gujarat. Ahmedabad was one of the centers of the Mughal Empire in India, and is also important in the development of Western modernism in India, with buildings by Le Corbusier, Louis Kahn, and Charles Correa.

I went to the mosque/funerary complex at Sarkhej, to the southwest of the city center. The complex consisted of several buildings and courtyards, on the edge of a tank, a large contained pool of water—the kind of building-and-landscape configuration found all over India. Built in the fifteenth century, it is a highly-refined example of the use of stone in the construction of *jalis*.

Main space of building at Sarkhej lined with *jalis* resulting in dappled light.

The *jali* is a perforated screen made of carved stone. It has a similar function to the *mashrabiya* (Arabic) in the Middle East and north Africa, which are typically made of wood. The *jali* and *mashrabiya* can do several things. They can act as a screening device, admitting daylight while blocking intense sunlight. They provide privacy to women inside, allowing them to look outward while preventing them from being seen from the outside. They are often exquisite examples of traditional craft. And they may help create wonderful, luminous rooms.

It is this luminosity that struck me during my visit to Sarkhej. When I walked into the building containing the tomb of an important religious leader, I was immediately awestruck by the luminosity of the room, by the way in which the carved *jalis,* which covered the outer wall, were not only creating patterns of sunlight on the interior surfaces of the building, but at the same time creating a golden light throughout the volume of the entire space. The sunlight, reflecting at hundreds of different angles off the small-scale elements of the *jalis*, was modulated in a way that reduced the intensity and prevented the glare—allowing the color and gentle warmth of the light to be strongly felt.

In India, there is still a tradition of stone-carving, that I first saw in practice in the desert town of Jaisalmer, in the west of Rajasthan, where craftsmen were carving *jalis* to be placed on existing and new *havelis*—urban houses—in the old city. But this tradition incorporates more than dwellings, and also includes public buildings and religious buildings.[1]

The golden light filling the building resulted from the carving of hundreds of identical stone openings. Each was a couple of inches in area, all with the same angles that reflect and soften the sunlight, that together made up screens around the entire perimeter. As with many anonymous craftspeople who made beautiful things, the names of the carvers are forgotten.

[1] The architect Joseph Allen Stein used a modern version of the *jali* in his design for the India International Centre in Delhi. (This is described beginning on p. 183.)

SARABHAI HOUSE, AHMEDABAD, INDIA

Interlocking building and landscape

MY TIME IN the Sarabhai house was very short. In December 1988, on my first trip to India, my friend and I arrived in the early afternoon to see the house, as we thought had been agreed with Mrs. Sarabhai. But she said that our visit had been arranged for the morning instead. Since we were already there, she graciously invited us to look at the house anyway—but quickly, as she had guests coming. So it was a very quick look—just a few minutes, and only the ground floor.[1]

That short visit, however, turned out to be a significant architectural experience. What struck me most about the house was the presence of the garden while inside the house, and the strength of the connection between inside and outside. The lower parts of the ends of the barrel-vaulted spaces were open, and the linear spaces moved the eye from the house to the garden. The materials were varied: brick in the vaults, concrete beams supporting the vault, plaster walls, tiled floors. The combination of these materials related to both the smooth planes of the house and the varied scales of vegetation in the garden. The house felt like a giant porch, with the garden as the central feature and focus.

If an architect can have an ideal physical context for a unique approach to design, Le Corbusier found it in the heat of Ahmedabad. Many of Le Corbusier's buildings are characterized by explicit spatial penetrations and ambiguities. These include the ramps in the Villa Savoye, the Carpenter Center at Harvard, and the Millowners' Association building in Ahmedabad; the *bris-soleils* in many of the buildings; the continuous space at ground level, going under the main volume of the building, formed when buildings are raised on *pilotis*; the way in which the outer walls at Ronchamp curve and fold inward to make portals that bring people into the building; the idea of the roof garden itself, forming a thick boundary between the building and the sky. In a climate such as that of India, with hot sun and monsoon rains, such spaces are

1 The house was designed by Le Corbusier for the Sarabhai family, a wealthy textile-manufacturing family who were influential in various ways in India's progress following Independence.

Photographs showing connection of Sarabhai house interior with garden.
© Fondation Le Corbusier / ADAGP, Paris / Artists Rights Society (ARS), New York 2025.

particularly important. The edge spaces can help provide shade, and the more overtly interpenetrating spaces help reinforce the equivalence between inside and outside. A good part of the Millowners' Association Building is simply a giant parasol, which helps shade both the roofs of enclosed rooms as well as the outdoor spaces between those rooms. The parasol keeps both the sun and the monsoon rains off the roof terrace.

Both the Sarabhai House and the Millowners' Association building bring together some of Le Corbusier's typical design ideas with the climate of Ahmedabad, with strongly-defined architectural strategies that protect against the sun and the rain, resulting in buildings that are strongly anchored in place.[2]

[2] In an article about the Sarabhai House, which she observed and studied over a year living in Ahmedabad, Susan Ubbelohde writes about the strong place-qualities of the house, that include the strong relationship between the house and the garden:

> "The Sarabhai house performs an especially elegant dance with [the] realities of summer living: dawn—awakening to the world; afternoon—a protective refuge from the oppressive heat; dusk—opening to the slow cooling of the garden; night—cool terraces and roofs under the moonlight and stars…Over the course of a summer day, the house reinforces and then transforms our understanding of public and private, inside and out, repose and activity: the cave and the pavilion. Though modern in terms of form, the house recapitulates this daily traditional performance from late March until the rains arrive in June."

Sarabhai House, Ahmedabad, India. Edmund Sumner-VIEW / Alamy Stock Photo.

I took no photographs inside the house: the time allowed was short, and I didn't want to make further requests of Mrs. Sarabhai. But when I began to look for pictures to illustrate the smooth connection between the interior and the garden, I couldn't find the right ones: the contemporary books with color pictures did not illustrate the point nearly well enough. But then I looked at Le Corbusier's *Oeuvre Complet,*[3] and found the right pictures. They were chosen by Le Corbusier himself,[4] and one interpretation of that choice is that he was trying to use those photographs to illustrate what I noticed in the house a few decades later.

3 Le Corbusier, *Oeuvre Complet, 1952–57,* "Home of Mrs. Manorama Sarabhai, Ahmedabad, 1955," pp. 114–131. See particularly the photographs on pp. 123, 126, and 127.

4 Concerning the photographs in the *Oeuvre Complet,* Daniel Naegele wrote that "Though Le Corbusier, himself, did not take the photographs, he did select them, crop them, edit them, and place them on the books' pages together with other photographs, text, titles, page numbers and drawings." Daniel Naegele, "Seeing what is not there yet: Le Corbusier and the architectural space of the photograph."

1989

DOGE'S PALACE, VENICE

The thing itself

IN VENICE, the prominent location of St. Mark's Square, just outside the seaward entrance to the Grand Canal, has meant that the Doge's Palace[1] (Palazzo Ducale) has always been part of my experience of the city, over many visits to the city. I have been inside the building only a few times, so my encounters with it have usually been by looking at its two principal façades: the south façade from the water side and the west façade seen across the Piazzetta from the main part of the square or the Sansovino-designed library. In 1989 I visited Venice in preparation for leading students there the following year, and started looking at the building a different way; I began to focus more on the beauty and power of the façade's unusual composition.

The words that come closest to describing my experience of the façade when I started to look at it closely are, in order: *solid, wall, Gothic, delicate, alive.*

It is perhaps the apparent contradiction between some of those words, and contrasts between attributes of the façade, that help describe its unusual aesthetic composition, and its success as a façade in the most important and visible place in Venice.

[1] The Doge's Palace, first built in the ninth century and expanded and renovated many times since then, was Venice's main governmental building when the city was a great maritime-trading power.

View of Doge's Palace, on right, and Piazza San Marco from water at beginning of Grand Canal.

Our understanding of Gothic architecture, often seen in churches and cathedrals, is usually concerned not with a solid exterior wall, but with the "de-materialization" of the wall seen from the interior. Historically, this represents the transformation of the solid wall of the Romanesque, which preceded the Gothic, into a delicate Gothic lacework of thin columns and ribs, giving primacy to stained-glass windows. The Doge's Palace contains both, with the solid wall sitting on top of the lacework of columns and ribbed, pointed arches.

This powerful contrast is emphasized by the horizontal line at the bottom of the solid part of the façade that effectively cuts the façade in half. Although a strong halving of a major plane or object is often frowned upon in two-dimensional architectural composition, in this case it is not problematic. The open arcades below work well with the solid wall above—partly because the wall itself contains openings, at two different scales, that visually "connect" with the openings formed by the columns in the arcades below. The arcades are understood to hold up the wall above them, thereby helping to visually unite the two very different entities. The beautiful finials at the top visually connect with the lacework of arches below. And the variations in the positions of the large windows, and the irregular placement of the small roundels above those windows, all help to give emphasis to the solidity of the wall.

An even closer look at the façades reveals that the solid walls are made up of a complex pattern of pink and white stones (this is Istrian stone and Veronese marble), fixed over fired brick—materials that are typical for Venice. These stones provide a scale that is similar to that of many of the entities below—column diameters, capitals, roundels in the quatrefoil tracery, the railings at the edge of the arcade at the *piano nobile* level. This similarity of scale of small parts also helps to visually tie the large parts together, contributing to the unity to the façades.

But the experience of the façade goes beyond these explicit understandings. The façade has a life to it. Its irregularities suggest its complex history including a human process of design and building. The building has a beauty that is not fully explainable by my text, or likely by any text. And the strength of the building, emphasized by the solidity of its upper half, seems altogether appropriate to its position at the "entrance" to Venice which was, for several centuries in the life of the building, a major economic and political power in southern Europe.

End of façade of Doge's Palace facing the Piazzetta.

Details of façade of Doge's Palace.

Most descriptions of the Palazzo Ducale rightfully classify it as a "Gothic building," as it is in much of its detail. Indeed, Ruskin saw the arched openings with the quatrefoil roundels as the most developed version of Gothic architecture.[2] But the knowledge of Gothic details on the building, and Ruskin's interpretation of it, do not by themselves add up to make the building beautiful. My experience and feeling about the building were prompted by the building itself, sitting there on its site between the water and the church. The unusual nature of the powerful wall, supported by the open arcade and the delicacy of the arches below, were themselves what prompted my reaction. Certainly the detail was present, and that formed part of my reaction, but it really became important to my understanding of the success of the façades after the initial and surprising encounter with the building, as a whole and living thing. And now, after many visits to the building, with more knowledge about the buildings' details and materials, I still have that reaction first when I see it.

[2] John Ruskin, *The Stones of Venice.*

WILHELM PELSTER HOUSE-BARN, FRANKLIN COUNTY, MISSOURI

Spatial clarity and functional complexity

IN 1989 I attended my first annual meeting of the Vernacular Architecture Forum (VAF), an organization that I remained involved with for the next 25 years or so. The VAF's meetings are unique among scholarly organizations in their balance between visits to buildings that have been investigated by members who are based in the meeting locations, and academic paper sessions. The 1989 meeting was based in St. Louis and the field visits included buildings and archaeological remains in the surrounding landscape. These included German and French settlements, as well as Cahokia, an important Native American site.

Our visit to the Pelster house-barn was a welcome surprise and I realize now that it helped crystallize an emerging interest of mine in the hybrid building that was to manifest itself 23 years later with the publication of *Living Over the Store.*[1]

The house-barn was the second dwelling built by Friederich Wilhelm Pelster, who immigrated to Missouri from Germany in

[1] Howard Davis, *Living Over the Store: Architecture and Local Urban Life.*

Pelster housebarn, Franklin County, Missouri.

Pelster housebarn. Historic American Buildings Survey/Library of Congress.

1842 with his wife and two sons. His first dwelling was a simple log house that was accompanied by a barn. This second house, a house-barn, combined family dwelling, and livestock and farm activities in a single building. Similar buildings can still be seen in Europe—in the summer of 1990 I saw several of them in the Austrian town of Langschlag, near the Czech border.

Built on a sloped site, the Pelster house-barn has four stories, and the rooms and spaces are all contained within a simple overall volume. It was that combination of simple overall form and complex functional organization that attracted me to the building. This combination of density and complexity also attracted me to many other buildings where the use of the site is maximized and an economy of construction thereby attained. In this case, the minimum building envelope, enclosing a highly complex array of functions and spaces, likely came early in the planning and construction, albeit with an early understanding of what the internal organization would be.

Stairway and threshing floor. Historic American Buildings Survey/Library of Congress.

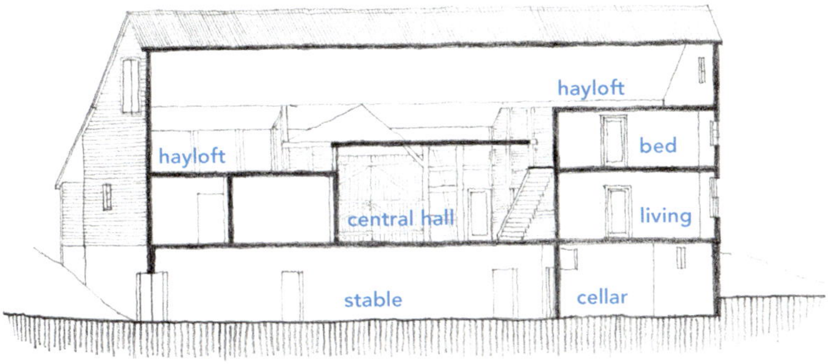

Section drawing of Pelster housebarn showing interior organization of rooms.

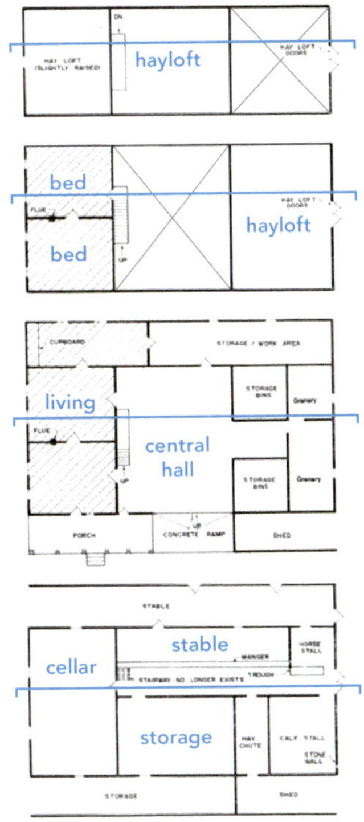

Plans of Pelster housebarn. Top to bottom: Level 4, Level 3, Level 2, and Level 1. Blue lines indicate position of section cut.

The plans clearly show the spatial complexity. The main room, entered on the second floor, is named differently in different documents about the building: "central hall," "threshing floor," "*diele*". Although this variety of names is based on recent investigations and understandings of the building, it does suggest a space in which there may be ambiguity between domestic and agricultural functions. For example, in the north German city of Lübeck, the *diele* is a multi-use room on the main floor that included such activities as eating, children playing, reception of personal and business guests, and delivery and export of goods; the room included a lift that took goods up and town to storage floors above. In the Pelster building, that room is central, with purely domestic rooms on one side, storage rooms on the other, and open above to bedrooms on one side and a hay loft on the other.

Other features of the plan also suggest a functional mix: the door between the "cupboard" and a "storage-work area"; the internal stair itself in the central hall that connects the different parts of the domestic end together; the door from the porch into the central hall (in addition to a door directly into the domestic rooms).

The compactness and simplicity of the overall form of the house likely came about as a matter of economy of construction: the amount of exterior wall and corners are minimized. Within this simple form, Mr. Pelster decided on the specific functional relationships of the farmhouse, bringing together functions of dwelling and working farm building. The simplicity of the overall form, along with the apparent pragmatic and functional approach to the spatial organization, help describe the essence of this vernacular building that was apparently rare in America, but is still an actively used building type in Europe.

PUBLIC HOUSING, NEW YORK AND VIENNA

Urban indignity and urban dignity

GROWING UP in New York I was used to public housing that was deliberately separate from the ordinary buildings in their neighborhoods. They were "the projects," connoting different economic and social worlds, six or twelve or twenty stories tall, with identical apartments stacked on top of each other, with plain brick walls and standard metal windows plugged into them, devoid of ornament or of detail that would give the buildings any visual appeal. However, this is not how they began, in 1935. The original buildings of the New York City Housing Authority (NYCHA) blended in with other buildings in their neighborhoods, helping maintain the street frontage, and incorporating shops at their

Public housing in New York, near the Williamsburgh Bridge.

ground floor. These are the First Houses, on the Lower East Side, and still exist. But that approach changed, so that by the 1950s the NYCHA buildings all fit within standard models, as buildings segregated from their neighborhoods often helped to emphasize the racial and economic divides that characterized American cities. The word "project" immediately connoted a world that was socially and economically apart—even as it did, indeed, provide the benefits of low-rent housing for people with low incomes.

On my first trip to Vienna in 1990, I was taken by an architect friend to visit the Karl Marx Hof, the best known of the public housing projects built by the city of Vienna following the First World War. One of the war's outcomes was the need for thousands of new dwelling units in the city. The Karl Marx Hof is a massive project, over a kilometer long, that symbolizes for many people the social progressivism of Vienna. It included over 1,300 apartments, and common facilities such as laundries, a library, kindergartens, medical offices, and business offices—together serving some of people's basic needs of daily life, beyond the apartments themselves.

I appreciated the social goals of the Karl Marx Hof, but the building itself seemed separated from the city around it. It was a massive intervention that called a lot of attention to itself. But

First Houses in 1936 and sculpture in its playground, done as part of Depression-era federal work program for artists. NYCHA Archive.

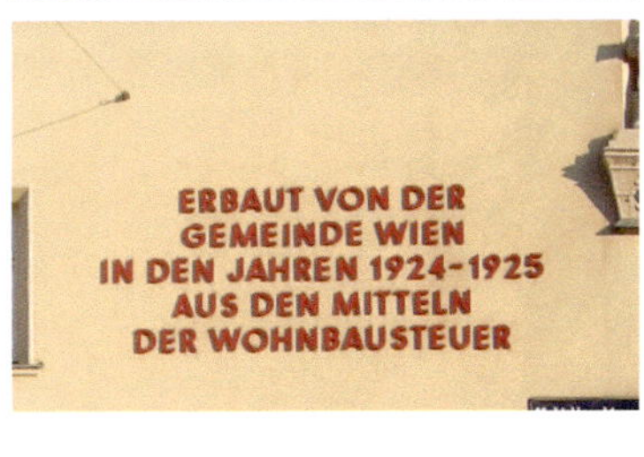

Public housing in Vienna, showing buildings' relationships to streets and other buildings. Sign at right: "Built by the Municipality of Vienna in 1924–1925 using housing tax funds." A sign like this appears on every public housing project in Vienna.

in Vienna I also began to come across other, smaller apartment houses, also public housing built by the city as part of the same program, but more woven into the urban fabric. They were fitted into sites on existing urban blocks, similar in height to neighboring buildings; they had façades that complemented nearby buildings to make the street wall—often with a similar scale, distribution of windows, and similarity of materials. Many of them also had public facilities: kindergartens, dairies, bakeries, laundries—functions that served ordinary, daily life.[1]

Over several trips to Vienna since that first one, I have come to appreciate two major characteristics of the city. One is its formal grandeur and beauty—the parks and boulevards, the Ringstrasse of the nineteenth century, even the buildings built for the royalty of the Austro-Hungarian Empire. The other is what seems to be its livability of its public spaces and the ways in which they are shared, the ease of getting around the city, the ways in which many residential neighborhoods away from the city center have developed strong community networks that have made local improvements and enhanced locally-owned businesses.

This strong sense of local community is exemplified by Vienna's public housing, in which about 60% of the city's population live, with no stigma involved in doing so. In the city, there are about 400 housing blocks built from 1923 to 1934, with a total of 64,000 apartments. The rents increase only with inflation, and then only when inflation exceeds 5% in a year. People spend only a small percentage of their income on rent. The public housing program of Vienna has once again become a model, as other countries in the West are struggling to build enough housing to satisfy the need of people who cannot afford to rent or who own dwellings in building cultures dominated by private profit.[2] The way that the buildings physically blend into the city around them is a metaphor for their social inclusion.

[1] For the best account of the history of public housing in Vienna, see Eve Blau, *Red Vienna.*

[2] Francesca Mari, "Imagine a Renter's Utopia. It Might Look Like Vienna."

KARLSPLATZ STATION, VIENNA

A path not taken

WHEN I FIRST SAW it on a visit to Vienna in 1990 (to participate in a meeting on low-cost housing in India), the Karlsplatz station, designed by the Austrian architect Otto Wagner and opened in 1899, impressed me because of how the iron, stone, and marble were individually articulated and fit together. The stone and marble were the main cladding materials, but were not load-bearing. Instead, a metal frame was loadbearing, and the masonry materials fit inside the frame. This represented a reversal of a classicist attitude toward these two materials, in which the masonry might be loadbearing and the metal acting as smaller detail—for example a window sash in a masonry wall.

Karlsplatz station.

Detail of wall at Karlplatz station.

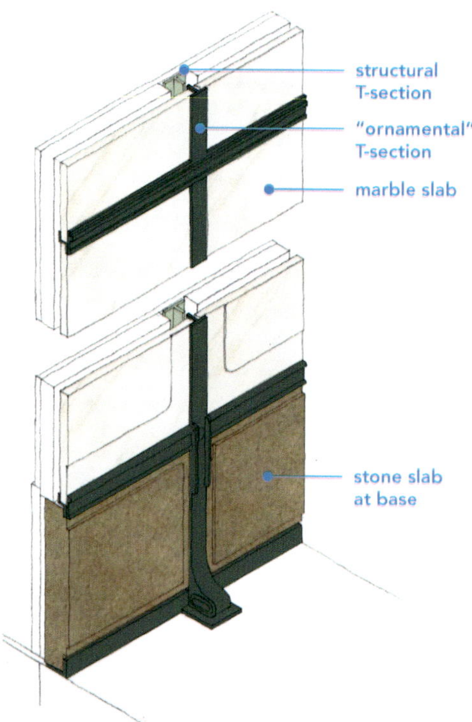

Drawing showing assembly of materials in Karlsplatz station wall.

The characterization of the Otto Wagner Karlsplatz station as an Art Nouveau building was never as important to me as was the station as an example of Wagner's straddling of historicism and modernity in his buildings. Wagner's buildings had plans characterized by classical symmetries and proportions but at the same time modern iron and steel columns, and colonnades helping to reinforce spatial ambiguities and connections. In many of his buildings (the station and the Post Office Savings Bank were prime examples), the overall plan was classical, but his use of materials allowed him to make the elements, such as walls and ceiling vaults, into modern constructions.

Wagner wrote about the relationships between construction and the aesthetics of a building, and recognized that modern construction techniques, which allowed for less time in building and therefore labor costs to be decreased, still needed to be balanced by the building's aesthetic content. But Wagner did not use these modern techniques to develop an altogether new, twentieth-century aesthetic. He was trying to utilize and make sense of the new building technologies that were available and that he saw as inevitable, within what persisted as a classical sensibility to architectural order.[1]

He saw this combination of sensibilities as having a unique potential. His idea of exterior cladding applies directly to the Karlsplatz station: "For the exterior cladding of a building ... a panel system will be used for the planar surfaces. Since these panels can be assumed to have significantly less cubic volume [than loadbearing masonry], they can be designed for a nobler material (for example, Laase marble)."[2] He could still achieve the aesthetic effect of masonry at a lower cost.

The materials are shaped and placed in beautiful scale relationships. The large stone panels at the base are shaped to form a reveal that results in a shadow between the stone and the metal; the sections of the metal bars are shaped so that the lines they form have scale and shadows; each material has its own surface texture. But the visible metal is not load-bearing—it is ornament on the face of the building, in front of the metal T-bars that actually are load-bearing. So Wagner wanted to express the structure, but protected the actual load-bearing structure within the wall with a kind of veneer incorporating both metal and stone or marble.

The ordering system is "classical," but achieved with a building system that is modern in its use of contemporary materials and method of assembly. It is in the scale relationship that the building straddles, and unites, different eras and styles. The large-scale, expressed through the overall composition, is classical—or more precisely, classical rendered through the specific, twentieth-century "Art Nouveau" style. The smaller scale, expressed through the details and construction, is modern. And the modern itself is achieved by combining the use of old materials—iron, stone, and marble—and their shaping and assembly in modern ways.

The combination of materials, and the high level of their spatial articulation, formed my strong, positive experience of this building. Many vernacular traditions, such as Japanese wooden architecture, as well as modern architects such as Louis Kahn, do something similar.

This building and similar buildings of Wagner reveal a fork in the road of modern architecture. One path was represented by this building. It showed the possibility of moving forward with modern materials and techniques—and for architecture to be a strong representation of modern industry—but at the same time not giving up an architecture that could incorporate coherent, positive architectural and urban space. Dutch architects such as Berlage, Dudok, and deClerk, for example, were also connected to this idea. The other path was represented by Le Corbusier, by the International Style, and largely by the dissolution of coherent public space. That is the "path taken," leaving the "bridging" architecture of Otto Wagner and some of his contemporaries behind.

1 A detailed description of the construction system of the Karlsplatz station, and its relationship to then-contemporary architectural ideas is in Edward Ford, *The Details of Modern Architecture*, pp. 213–217.

2 Otto Wagner, *Modern Architecture*, p. 96.

1990

CHURCH AND ORPHANAGE, FLORENCE, ITALY

Faith and humanism

I HAVE BEEN to Florence several times, appreciating the lightness, harmony, and human scale of its Renaissance buildings. As I first realized in 1989 and 1990, Florence is full of small buildings and spaces that are humane, approachable, and often delightful. I have been attracted to many buildings and gardens in the city: the Pazzi Chapel at the church of Santa Croce, the Laurentian Library, the church of Santo Spirito, ordinary neighborhoods with party-wall houses built around the time of the Renaissance or a century or two after it ended, the Boboli gardens. But there are two Florentine buildings the façades of which have always stood out for me: the church of Santa Maria Novella, with its façade designed by Alberti, and the Foundling Hospital, designed by Brunelleschi with its sweet terra-cotta roundels made by Andrea della Robbia.

The power of Santa Maria Novella's façade comes from the singularity of its composition. The architectural historian Rudolf Wittkower wrote extensively about its relationship to the church's original Gothic façade. Its parts work together geometrically to keep the main door, leading to the aisle and ultimately the altar, as the focus of the entire, complex organization, giving the façade a remarkable unity. Wittkower analyzes the façade in terms of the squares that make it up, or the curved scrolls that connect the second story with the first. He writes that "It is clear then that Alberti's theoretical precept that the same proportion be kept throughout the building has been fulfilled. It is the strict application of an unbroken series of ratios that marks the unmedieval character of this pseudo-Proto-Renaissance façade..."[1]

My own observation adds to this. The circular window, not included in Wittkower's diagrams, plays a strong role in the façade's unity. It is at the bottom—rather than in the center—of the central bay of the pedimented upper story, visually pulling what is around the window down toward the door. The secondary doorways on the sides of the main portal do the same thing in their relationship to

1 Rudolf Wittkower, *Architectural Principles in the Age of Humanism*, p. 47.

Façade of Santa Maria Novella.

Diagram of façade of Santa Maria Novella, suggesting the importance of the circular window and doors on either side of main door in giving emphasis to the main door.

the three openings that are around each one of them—they are in the second bay, on either side of the main door. These two moves make the main portal the strong focus of the façade. These decisions about the façade's two-dimensional geometry make it come to life, and evoke in me a clear feeling of unity and powerful connection to the center. When I look at the façade, in person or even as a picture, I see its life coming from real things, and not only the proportioning system that helps guide its composition.

Façade of Foundling Hospital.

Detail of Foundling Hospital façade, emphasizing sculptures by Andrea della Robbia.

The Foundling Hospital (*Ospedale degli Innocenti*) is powerful in a different way. Its façade does not have the singularity of focus of Santa Maria Novella. It does have a delicacy and lightness that come from its thin columns and low scale. Indeed, the windows on its façade are much more at the scale of a parapet than a full floor, and the *della Robbia* terra-cotta figures in the roundels, the *bambini di terra*, are the punctuation marks of sweetness on the façade. That façade, more than anything else in Florence, projected to me the humanism of the Renaissance. The program of that building—taking care of abandoned children—seems to merge perfectly with the delicacy and innocence of the façade itself. And the loggia was typical on such buildings: in his book on Brunelleschis' buildings, Howard Saalman writes that "some of the important [hospitals], built in the fourteenth and fifteenth centuries, had an arcaded loggia, facing the public street or piazza before them. As a public space between hospice or hospital and street, the loggias were the meeting-place of inmates and visitors, as well as a secluded spot for convalescent or elderly patients sitting and watching the outer world go by."[2]

These two buildings are very different, but together they rrepresent the combination of the faith and humanism of the Renaissance. Each takes on its role fully and purely, which seemed apparent at my first encounters with them.

[2] Howard Saalman, *Filippo Brunelleschi: The Buildings*, p. 33.

CHURCH OF SANTA PRASSEDE, ROME

Complex relationships of scale

IN ROME, I first visited the church of Santa Prassede, a basilican church just to the south of Santa Maria Maggiore, in the summer of 1990, when I was teaching the University of Oregon's Rome architecture studio. I was surprised and pleased when I first walked into the nave, finding that the repetitive order of spatial bays that one would expect in a basilican church was more complex than usual, resulting in nested spaces at two different scales along the nave, that reinforced rather than destroyed the nave's overall space.

View of nave toward altar.

Santa Prassede was originally built in the ninth century with Roman *spolia* used as columns that help form the nave. In the thirteenth century the church was renovated, to improve its structural performance, with the insertion of three large arches resting on pilasters, each pilaster in the place of one of the columns, for a total of six pilasters. The role of the arches was apparently to help support the weight of the roof, and to stiffen the structure against lateral forces that were perpendicular to the long axis of the nave.

The pilasters project from the plane of the two nave walls. The church has a flat, coffered ceiling that is divided by the arches; the ceiling rests on the side walls and the top of the arches.

Together with the altar wall and the wall separating the narthex and the nave, the three arches form four large transverse bays, and with the pilasters, the two columns between the pilasters holding up each nave wall form three small bays.

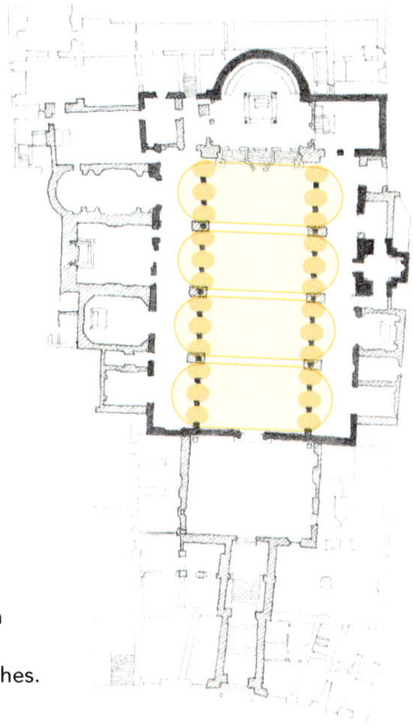

Diagram superimposed on plan showing different scales of space in the church of S Prassede following construction of large pillars and arches.

This is a highly unexpected way of building the nave of a church because it provides an additional scale to the overall space. The nested rhythms, indicated in the plan above, provide for a high level of spatial order inside the nave. There are clearly evident levels of scale, and alternating repetition involving the pilasters and the remaining pairs of columns between them.[1]

In 2023 I described this church to a colleague in Rome, when we were having dinner at a restaurant in the Testaccio neighborhood, and he talked about similar structures in music, in which a sequence of slow bass notes "frames" a faster series of notes two or three octaves higher. This similar complexity gave the building a stronger spatial "weight" and presence, while maintaining, even reinforcing, its spatial unity. In the church, this was the aesthetic result of a structural upgrading of the building, done simply to prevent its collapse. Or was that the only reason—were the arches and pilasters also understood to be the bass notes of the church?

[1] "Alternating repetition" is a term used by Christopher Alexander to describe repetitive spatial sequences. See Christopher Alexander, *The Nature of Order, volume 1, The Phenomenon of Life*, pp. 165–172.

View of ceiling showing arches.

View of nave from side aisles.

COSMATI PAVEMENTS, ROMAN CHURCHES, ITALY

Tile floors 900 years old

IN ABOUT 1989, I began visiting Rome on a more regular basis, thanks partly to the student program that our department offers there every summer. I began to appreciate the churches—Santa Maria in Trastevere with its exquisite mosaics, San Luigi dei Francesi with the remarkable Caravaggio paintings, and the smaller churches which draw one in closely to the smaller details, like those of the floor.

In Roman churches ones' eyes are not only drawn upward to the vaults and ribs, to the flat coffered ceilings, to the high windows that are the principal sources of daylight, to the sunlight on the opposite wall of its source. There are different kinds of wonders looking down. One set of these wonders, in dozens of churches, is formed of millions of tiny tiles, made and placed by generations of the Cosmati family, after the beginning of the last millennium—around 1100–1300.

The tiles are of simple shapes: squares, triangles, rhombuses, hexagons...not many others. They are made of a variety of stones, including marble and onyx. The three variables of material, shape, and size provide the geometric basis for a large variety of spatial patterns—and that opportunity was amply used by the craftsmen who made those floors.

Cosmati-made floors in Roman churches.

The geometry of the laying of tile, and the process of making a floor, are described in detail in the book *Cosmatesque Ornament*, using the floor of the church of San Clemente as a case

Cosmati-made floors in Roman churches.

study. The quincunx—a five-part pattern with its geometry based on four circles forming the corners of a square with a larger circle at its center—is a common geometric basis, with religious connotations, for the layout of Cosmatesque floors. The materials used were based on what was available; in Rome this often was spoglia from earlier buildings. And quoting from a book on the subject, "One can suppose that once the general layout of the pavement was completed, using white marble bands, various artists could work simultaneously on the 'filling operation,' each occupied with a concrete area or a type of geometric pattern whose execution the artist had mastered. In this way, the total time of execution of the pavement was enormously reduced. Therefore the succession of tasks that led to the construction of the pavement of San Clemente followed an order that began by establishing the whole in order to address the parts, going from the general to the particular in a process regulated principally by subdivision."[1]

The individual tiles are at a scale of about a square inch, so a portion of floor that is one square foot has about 150 tiles; 50 square feet, 7500 tiles; an entire church perhaps a few hundred thousand tiles or more—with each of the tiles cut, shaped, and placed by hand. So it is not only the decorative pattern itself that drew my attention, but also the knowledge of human effort that went into the craftsmanship of those surfaces that people have walked on for hundreds of years. There are differences—some subtle, some more apparent—between the areas of tile patterns within a particular church, and these differences provide visual relief and continuing interest to those—including me, many times—who are drawn to look at the floor.

1 Paloma Pajares-Ayuela, *Cosmatesque Ornament*, pp. 265–266.

The fact that there are literally millions of these small tiles on the floors of Roman churches, each individually shaped and placed, is itself staggering. But it becomes even more so when thinking of the craftsmen who made those floors. Dozens or scores of them, spending their work lives in one craft, on their hands and knees all day, making these beautiful patterns a square inch at a time, in a church location opposite to that of height and light and the direction of God. All the while knowing that their work was important and beautiful, but perhaps not thinking that it would still be there in a thousand years, having been walked on by tens of millions of people.

Cosmati floors in Rome. Quincunx at San Prassade at top, floor of Santa Maria in Trastevere below.

1991

THE SIDE OF THE ROAD, INDIA

Life on the verge

OVER ABOUT ten trips to India I have traveled by train, car, auto-rickshaw, and bus, and each mode of travel has had its own idiosyncrasies and pleasures. On my first trip in 1988, I travelled between cities largely by train. With the world's largest railroad system, train travel is one of India's marvels. Arriving at a station is like the curtain going up on a great performance: red and green and violet saris in the bright sunlight; families sitting on the platform with bundles of possessions; vendors hawking fruit, water, cooked food, sweets; all this lasting for the few minutes that the train was stopped, the act repeated at the next station down the line; this happening simultaneously in the 7300+ train stations all over India: altogether a few tens of thousands of times a day.

In the city, auto-rickshaw travel is more unpredictable: a largely open vehicle, weaving in and out among cars and trucks and buses. In Chennai one driver introduced herself with plastic-protected newspaper articles reporting her achievement as the first woman auto-rickshaw driver in Tamil Nadu. In Ahmedabad I stated my destination as "Drive-In Road" and the auto driver asked if I was going to see "Mr. Doshi," which I was. And bus travel is even more exciting—on one terrifying middle-of-the-night trip on a two-lane road in Kerala, sitting in the right hand seat just behind the driver, I had to close my eyes numerous times when the bus passed the one just in front of us, with what seemed to be inches to spare between our bus and the one barreling down the same right-hand lane, toward us.

On several trips we traveled mostly by road—using buses and with Mr. Nelson's old, white Ambassador.[1] And at least as much as others, this mode of travel brought me close to people and their daily lives. An important feature of the road is the verge—the area between the active roadway and the front of buildings that face directly onto it. In towns the verge may be fairly narrow with very little space other than a small raised porch and perhaps a little bit

[1] Mr. Nelson was the head of the Centre for Development Madras, our client for a low-cost housing project.

of land to park a car or motorcycle. But in smaller villages, and near rural building clusters, the verge may be much wider—30 or 40 feet, or even more—and when these places are active and occupied, a wide variety of everyday functions and activities may happen there, often in the shade of tall, broad trees. These include chai stalls, selling the sweet, milky tea for a few rupees; auto and bicycle repair; sales of coconuts from the nearby grove, with a man using a sharp knife to cut the fruit and make a hole in which to insert a straw to drink its milk; people sleeping on charpoys (woven cots) in the shade; tiny shops selling beedis (hand-rolled cigarettes) for smoking and paan (betel leaf) for chewing; people simply passing the time of day. I felt a real peacefulness in these places, resulting from the loveliness of the trees combined with the human life in the shade they provided. And they are indeed *places*; providing space for the road to connect with all the human life alongside it.

Daily life at the side of the road in India.

The verge in the town was similar, but denser and shallower. People sitting just outside their houses or shops; open shops and tea stalls on the road edge of houses; more people and more activity, but the same sense of connection between the movement along the road and the established houses and businesses next to it.

India continues to modernize, and on my most recent trip in 2017, to visit the workshops of the handloom silk industry in Kanchipuram, we were on a newly-built road in Tamil Nadu. It was the local version of a freeway, with two lanes in each direction. It was a faster road, perhaps intended to approach the functionality of something like an American freeway or a German *autobahn*. So I was surprised to find that even here, the "occupied verge" was present and in use, and that drivers could enter and leave the roadway pretty much anywhere, but on these faster roads with the use of an "unoccupied verge," closer to the roadway lane, that was used to bring the vehicle up to speed before it entered the driving lane itself. But on the outside, on the occupied verge, was the same variety of people and tiny shops, there to take advantage of the possible business from people on the faster road.

The American freeway, or "limited-access" highway, has had the consequence of severing land and communities. It is only now that bridges are beginning to be built to repair wildlife corridors, and beginning efforts to repair the cities and neighborhoods that have been cut in half by freeways. I can't speak to the safety issues that may be connected to this Indian hybrid between a limited access highway and an active, populated street, but it does seem that the "life in the verge," instead of being a severing of local life, is instead an intensification of it, taking advantage of local economic opportunity to make places that connect people and foster community. In these cases, that simply continue the idea of the occupied verge, the road remains a social asset rather than a divider.

VILLAGE HOUSE, NEAR LVIV, UKRAINE

The power of place

BUILDINGS, and particularly houses, are central to the establishment and maintenance of cultural identity and daily life; this may be particularly true for simple farmhouses that anchor people to the land.

In the summer of 1991, I visited Ukraine as part of a group of ten colleagues, led by a Ukrainian-American scholar of vernacular architecture. Traveling by train and minibus, we stayed for a week each in Lviv and Kyiv, and visited those cities and various places around them. We were hosted in different places by architectural historians, archaeologists, and specialists in the traditional, vernacular houses of different regions of the country.

That summer was the last in which Ukraine remained under Soviet rule. Signs of the impending change were everywhere. People knew what was about to happen, and acted as if the country was already independent. On a train journey from Lviv to Kyiv, we sat up all night with bottles of vodka brought by several Ukrainian scholars who described how they had been the guinea pigs for a "70-year-long failed experiment." Churches were being restored—we came upon the reconsecration ceremony for a church in one village where hundreds of people were walking through the fields

People walking over fields to attend re-consecration of church, 1991, just before Ukraine gained independence from the Soviet Union.

Reconsecration of church.

and over the hills to the church. At another church, a priest showed us a collection of gravestones that had been brought to the churchyard after having been submerged in a river for several decades. The yellow-and-blue Ukrainian flag was flying everywhere. A well-known poet welcomed us into his studio, and showed us his collection of audio tapes with recordings of traditional Ukrainian music.

Archaeologists were working to find and document the existence of material evidence of Ukrainian culture before Russian rule. This included house foundations at one site, and a wooden fort spanning a narrow pass between two mountains, at another. The evidence for the fort consisted only of the holes in the stone that would have supported the beams, and this evidence was the basis for a detailed wooden model that conjectured the design of the fort itself. Such a mixture of scholarship and politics was present in the work of many people we met; they saw the importance of their work in establishing the justification for a free Ukraine.

Farmhouse near Lviv, Ukraine, similar to the one described.

But the most poignant expression of the relationships between politics, society, and buildings did not come from scholars, but with our visit to a simple village farmhouse. It had a typical linear plan, including two rooms separated by an entrance hall, each room with a stove at the end near the hall, topped by a flue that met the other, leading to a single chimney. (In the Austro-Hungarian Empire that once encompassed this farm, house taxes were based partly on the number of chimneys the house had.)

An elderly couple was living there, and they invited us in. We sat on wooden chairs and stools in their simple kitchen. They told us their story over warm glasses of milk, just taken from their cow. The farm originally belonged to the man's father, who refused to sell it to the local collective. That refusal prompted his exile to a labor camp in Siberia where he spent several years; he died after his return. The couple were poor—the family's failure to submit to the Soviet system had left them alone, with next to nothing. But that "next to nothing" included their house and their small farm, that had stayed in the family through all those decades; it was the center of their existence, allowing them to maintain their dignity, their livelihood, and their place in the world. The wife told us, with tears, that we were the first people to whom they had been able to tell their story, and by the end of our visit they were not the only people in the room who were crying. That "vernacular" house, anchored in the landscape of their village, was like their beating heart—without it they would have ceased to exist in the world.

After our two weeks in Ukraine, several of us flew from Kyiv to Prague for a few days, and then home. Three weeks later the Soviet Union collapsed.

Paris

Left to right:
Kyoto, Japan
Paris
Paris

PART FOUR
1992–1999

In these years I developed and began to teach courses at Oregon that were strongly based on my own interests. These included a lecture course on issues of culture and place in architecture that I co-taught with two colleagues, and an advanced design studio. This studio was usually based on a complex urban building, often to be located in New York, that brought together different uses and social/economic opportunities. I was also carrying out research for *The Culture of Building*, including work in various archives in London and New York, as well as continuing the housing project in south India—and always seeing the opportunity for more exploratory travel.

In 1995 I visited Japan for the first time, and that turned out to be the first of several trips, focused in Kyoto. Traditional Japan was a revelation. The care and precision with which things are shaped and finished—ranging from a sliding wooden screen, to a public bus, to the reversible seats on an express train, to a wooden toothpick—puts the building-and-craft culture of the country onto a different level, worthy of its own investigation.

Left to right:
Kyoto, Japan
Kyoto, Japan
Ine-cho, Japan

PASSAGE DES PANORAMAS, PARIS

Webs of public space

ON A VISIT to Paris in 1992 I had recently learned about the *passages* (arcades), so I visited several that still existed on the Right Bank. I had probably visited one or two before, but this was the first time I started to think about these covered pedestrian ways as a distinct urban phenomenon. I realized their uniqueness, with tiny shops, daylight from above, and a clean and quiet way to walk through parts of the city. They were mostly built in the nineteenth century (the first in 1799) as a means of accommodating the growing interest in shopping and buying as the Industrial Revolution proceeded. They were the precursors of department stores—but where each shop had its own proprietor.

Walter Benjamin, the twentieth-century philosopher, wrote extensively about the *passages* in Paris as a means to describe and analyze the complexity and depth of the city itself. He listed, for example, shops in the Passage des Panoramas: Restaurant Véron, reading room, music shop, Marquis, wine merchants, hosiery, haberdashers, tailors, bootmakers, hosiery, bookshops, caricaturist, Théatre des Variétés. He compared the arcades to each other: "the Passage Vivienne was the 'solid' arcade. There, one found no luxury shops."[1]

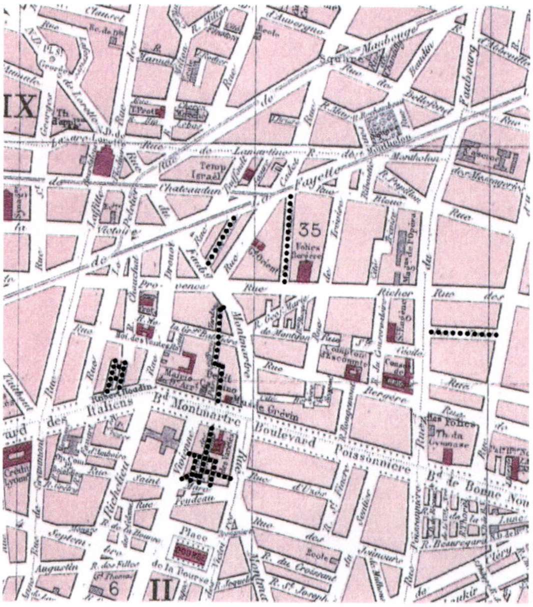

Map showing Parisian passages as lines of dots.
Map: A. Vuillemin, 1893. Public domain.

My own reaction to the arcades supported an increasing awareness of the complexity of the city, including different types of public ways. These ranged from the great boulevards to the older streets that were left in between them after their construction, to the arcades at the smallest, pedestrian scale. This was all connected to a growing understanding of the role of the

Paris *passages* and how they meet the streets.

streets and public places of Paris as the places where the urbanity of Paris thrives. They are the places of planned and unplanned meetings, places for individuals to watch the city, places of commerce and of movement.

Some of the arcades built in the first part of the nineteenth century were destroyed by the Haussmann clearances,[2] but not all, and there are still places where the arcades form a system of routes through the city that is parallel to the streets and boulevards. This system is shifted from the larger streets, like in a Tartan grid. One walks through the arcade from one end to the other, comes out onto a boulevard, with blue sky and trees above, crosses the street, and then re-enters an arcade on the other side of the street. The

1 Walter Benjamin, *The Arcades Project*, p. 37.

2 Baron Haussmann directed the demolition of large areas of the city and the construction of many of the boulevards.

narrowness and maximum two-story height of the arcade, the small size and careful architectural detailing of the shops, the continuity of the arcade from street to street, all together provide another scale of urban experience, tighter and more particular than the streets, but part of the same complex network of public space.

My experience of Paris has largely to do with its networks of streets and public spaces. Of course, the great buildings are important—Notre Dame, Sainte-Chapelle, the Musée d'Orsay, the Bibliothèque Saint-Geneviève—but I see those buildings not as individual places, but extensions of the complex public space network of the city. And the *passages* are only one element in the complex network. It also includes boulevards (many of which are nineteenth-century constructions); streets (many established in medieval times); public gardens and parks; paths along the Seine; public squares; cafés (functionally public although privately owned); churches, synagogues and mosques; the Bibliothèque Nationale; and the Hôtel de Ville. Even the back stairs of many older apartment buildings, used by service people, are sometimes seen as an extension of the public space of the street.[3]

This elaborate and robust network, extending its roots and branches everywhere, makes for the spatial unity of the city that supports its human variety and history in different ways at very different scales, including that of the *passages*. For me, this is not only an academic issue. It is one way I have come to experience the order and reality of cities, including Paris. I don't only see the immediate building or tree or street that is in front of me, but I am always aware of the urban structure of which that building or tree is a part. It is that awareness that has attracted me to the *passages*. I see them as not only charming in themselves, but also as parts of a highly ordered and almost living urban organism.

3 For helpful discussions of how public space and the perception of public space in Paris changed during the nineteenth century, with focus on the apartment buildings built after Haussmann's transformations of the city, see Sharon Marcus, *Apartment Stories: City and Home in Nineteenth-Century Paris and London*. In the Introduction to that book, Marcus writes that her account "shows discourses promoting urban mobility and legibility at work in Paris from 1820 to 1828, extending the visibility and fluidity of all urban space even to the homes and women who, in an ideology of separate spheres, would have been associated with sequestered private space. Those architectural and urban discourses made the apartment house and the female porter who managed it emblems of the continuity between the street and the home" (p. 5).

A SLUM, MADRAS (NOW CHENNAI), INDIA

The value of paper

WHILE WORKING on a housing project in Vellore, in the Indian state of Tamil Nadu, our client was Mr. Nelson, the head of the Centre for Development Madras (CEDMA), an NGO that worked with poor people in Madras (now Chennai) and Vellore.[1] He had made contact with people in Madras who heard about our work in Vellore, and were interested in making improvements to a particular slum settlement in Madras. The settlement was on a long strip of land adjacent to an area of publicly-built housing. It was organized around a makeshift, unpaved street, with very small houses every 20 feet or so, on each side. The houses were so low that one had to kneel to get into them; it seemed as if they would have been used only for sleeping or staying out of the rain. They were made of scavenged materials—bits of sheet metal, wood, cardboard, with the doorway as the only opening. They could not have been more than 60 or 70 square feet in area. Some of the people

1 This project is described in two articles: Howard Davis and David Week, "The Village Meets the City" and Howard Davis, "Learning from Vellore."

Small houses in Madras (now Chennai) slum, showing piles of trash and bags used to collect and store trash.

who lived there, identified to us as "gypsies," were sitting on the ground outside the houses. And near them, outside each house, was a small pile of trash—paper, cardboard, bits of packaging of different kinds. These were very poor people, whose lives were vulnerable in all kinds of ways.

While walking through the settlement we asked a man we met if he lived there. He said that he did not, so we asked him why he was there, and he told us that he was there to buy the piles of trash. It turned out that the settlement was made up of a group of scavengers who went out every night or day with cloth sacks to pick up discarded things and bring them home, keeping them for sale until a buyer came to purchase them.

And in that moment my understanding of "the people with the trash" suddenly changed. Those piles of used paper and cardboard represented their total assets, and the people and these assets were part of a regular economic cycle. When I first started learning about India I was told that "everything is used, everything is recycled"—and this seemed to be a strong demonstration of that. These people, living in their makeshift houses, were people with economic lives, trying to get by, perhaps with dreams for their children's futures, like billions of people on the planet. They were part of the complex economy of India and the world, in this case contributing to a circular economy of reuse and upcycling. And this observation has helped form my understanding of "housing," emphasizing the house not just as a building, but as an important part of a shared human system of exchange and community.

1992

TEMPLE OF ATHENA NIKE, ACROPOLIS, ATHENS

Keynote of the Acropolis

The temple of Athena Nike on the Acropolis, to the right, seen from the bottom of the Propylaea.

I HAVE MADE eight trips to Greece, the last in 2022 when I visited the north, near the Balkans and Turkey, where I was struck by the difference between that lush farmland, and the drier landscapes of the south and many of the Aegean islands. My previous trip, in 2016, included a visit to the new Acropolis Museum,[1] designed with a place for the Parthenon marbles, in their proper orientation. And up on the Acropolis itself, I again marveled at the little architectural gem (Vincent Scully called it the "keynote of the Acropolis") that is the Temple of Athena Nike.[2]

Athena Nike is tiny compared to the other major Acropolis buildings—the Parthenon, the Erechtheion, and the Propylaea—but this small temple plays an important, outsized role with respect to those other buildings and the Acropolis itself.

Indeed, the building has sculptures that mark the Athenian victories. But the temple is also a strong part of a larger spatial system of the entire Acropolis. My principal connection with the

1 The museum was designed by Bernard Tschumi Architects.

2 Vincent Scully, *The Earth, The Temple and the Gods: Greek Sacred Architecture*, p. 178.

temple has been from below or when walking up the steps of the Propylaea. I see it in its relationship to other buildings and to the hill of the Acropolis. The smallest parts of it that I can discern are the column capitals, and certainly not the detail of the sculptures—I am seeing it to large extent as a part of something much bigger that depends on the relationships between the temple, other buildings, and the landscape. This is confirmed by a leading historian of the Acropolis, who wrote about a web of meaning on the Acropolis, and how the temple is an important part of that web.[3]

Within that view, the temple is like an ornament relative to the Acropolis. With its two solid side walls (which in a larger temple would consist of columns) and two tetrastyle[4] ends, the building is about as small as a temple can get. That simplicity, almost purity, is striking. Like a diamond in a simple gold necklace, the building acts to provide an exclamation mark in a very strategic place. That place, the southwest "corner" of the Acropolis, near the top of the Propylaea, calls for such an object, like putting a tree or a statue in just the place in a garden that is needed to re-orient you or bring you to a peaceful place or a particularly beautiful view. The top of the stairs is now marked by a small, solid object that helps unify the larger spaces and buildings around it.

These observations are reinforced by the commentary of architectural historian Robin Francis Rhodes, who writes that

> The Nike temple is not usually seriously considered in analysis of the Periclean building program ... After all, it is so small and so Ionic, barely more than a treasury; yet it is hard to deny the significance of the Propylaia or the unique insight into the meaning of the Acropolis it provides, and Nike's bastion and terrace are visually one with it. Even her temple is conceived in a piece with the gateway...
>
> The Panathenaic procession,[5] embraced by the Propylaia, was greeted first by little Athena Nike. From every angle her Ionic temple stands out, isolated atop the ancient defensive bastion of the Acropolis—a beacon of divine sanction and protection. In spite of her scale, in many ways Nike is the most immediately noticeable, the most striking element of the great entranceway to the Acropolis.[6]

And Athena Nike is an Ionic temple, whereas the Parthenon and Propylaea are both Doric. It was built between 426 BC and 421 BC, begun only six years after the completion of the

[3] Jeffrey Hurwit, *The Acropolis in the Age of* Pericles, p. 239.

[4] A tetrastyle is a building end with four columns.

[5] The Panathenaic procession, honoring the goddess Athena, took place every four years.

[6] Robin Francis Rhodes, *Architecture and Meaning on the Athenian Acropolis*, pp. 113–115.

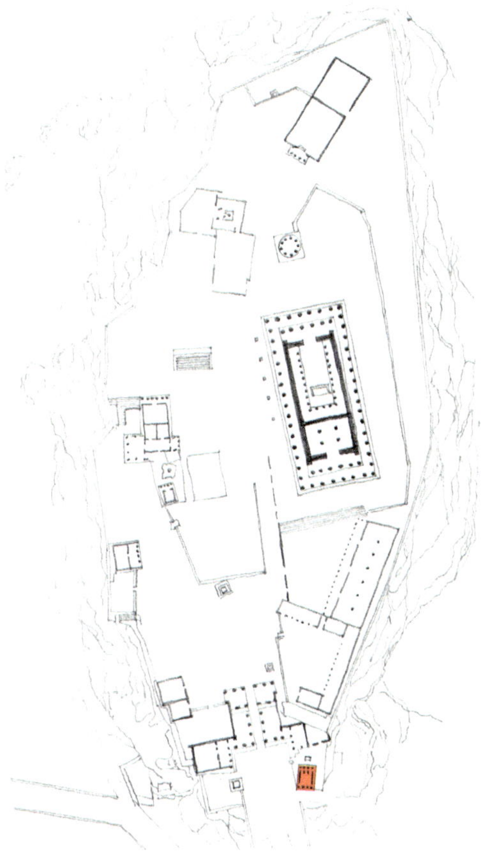

Map of the Acropolis showing the temple of Athena Nike next to the Propylaea.

Two close views of the Temple of Athena Nike.

Parthenon—the two buildings were almost contemporaneous. Why Ionic? Rhodes writes that its architect "...designed a building whose decorative precision and elaboration, like fine jewelry, elevated it beyond the realm of treasuries and fountain houses into close and fitting harmony with the temple façade of the most monumental gateway every constructed. This would have been impossible in the Doric style."[7] The style of the building is seen in connection with other buildings of a different style, reinforcing the idea of a coherent, overall system of the Acropolis, of which Athena Nike is a critical part.

7 Rhodes, *Architecture and Meaning on the Athenian Acropolis*, p. 118.

APARTMENT TERRACE, ATHENS

Outdoor life at high density

Apartment terrace in Athans.
Photo: Artemis Anninou.

WHEN I STAYED with a friend in Athens in 1993, I became aware of an ordinary feature of modern apartment buildings in the city that helps give them a unique, local, and pleasant character. My friend's dwelling, on the upper floor of her apartment building, had a deep shaded balcony, with awnings to control the sun and space sufficient not only for a dining table and chairs for eight or ten people, but also for individual chairs, small tables, and plants—all making the space into a room for multiple modes of living outdoors. The balcony was attached to the main living room of the apartment and acted as an extension of it. This was not unusual in Athens: most dwelling units in modern, multi-story apartment buildings had this.

This is not a feature of ordinary American apartments where most apartment balconies are just a few feet wide, with enough room for a single chair or a few chairs facing outward, and perhaps a small table. The balconies on ordinary apartments are not "rooms," with multiple activity areas and where daily life ordinarily takes place. They are narrow and do not form strong centers of activity, as do the Athens balconies.

Apartment terraces in Athens. (The Parthenon is in the distance.)

Because of their climate, the countries of southern Europe—Spain, Italy, Greece, the Balkans—are of course places where ordinary daily life takes place outdoors during most of the year.[1] The deep Athens balconies are simply the translation of the patios and terraces which are an ordinary part of Greek houses that are on the ground, into denser urban situations.

The development process of these Athens apartment buildings, built beginning in the 1950s, is connected to the ubiquity of these terraces, and affects their social success. The buildings were often built on lots that originally had a one-story detached house on them, the owner of which undertook the development. The owner, retaining the land that had increased in value, and the builder,

1 The importance of a connection to the outdoors, and the nature of the outdoor space, can play a large role in the design of housing. In London and other places in the UK for example, two-story "maisonettes" were part of multi-story apartment blocks built as part of social housing schemes. The front doors of the maisonettes open to an outdoor access balcony, and on the other end of the dwelling, there may be private outdoor terraces. Although the climate is not Mediterranean, this simulates older, on-the-ground terraced houses that are ubiquitous in English cities and towns (and based on much earlier houses in rural settings). The presumption is that people like being able to step directly from their dwelling to the outdoors, even if they are several storys above ground. Both the Greek apartments and London maisonettes are related examples of how architectural features of traditional life may be incorporated into modern design.

investing in the construction, each kept a stake in the property with several apartments each. The buildings often included shops and workshops. And they housed a range of social/economic classes of people, helping to give large sections of Athens social diversity and a rich street life that comes from this diversity.

The deep balconies contribute to this diversity. They allow people to maintain their traditional relationship to the outdoors without making it "precious," and by so doing, help support a social mixing in situations of development that in other countries would result in social segregation—and a difference between buildings that have outdoor terraces as a matter of course, and those that do not.

Residential street in Athens showing apartments with balconies above shops.

ENTSU-JI TEMPLE, KYOTO

Including the borrowed landscape

ENTSU-JI was the first Japanese temple I visited, on my first trip to Japan, joining a student group led by my landscape-architecture colleague Ron Lovinger. I arrived in Kyoto in the morning, after a long flight to Osaka from San Francisco the day before, a night in the airport hotel, a ride on the airport express train to Kyoto, and a taxi ride from Kyoto Station to the hostel where the students were staying. I was thoroughly exhausted from the trip, and Ron and the group were waiting for me to go to Entsu-ji.

We set off by public bus, changing buses once or twice, and finally arrived at the last leg of the journey. In the gray drizzle we walked up a paved road, through the forest to the temple entrance.

Looking toward garden and "borrowed landscape" at Entsu-ji Temple, Kyoto. Mount Hiei is in the distance. Painting: Sheri Pyron.

We left our shoes just inside the entrance, walked in, and proceeded along what I remember as a relatively direct path to the main hall, or *hondo*. Ron explained that the mountain in the distance was Mt. Hiei, a sacred mountain (that now has a Buddhist monastery at its peak). We sat on the *tatami*-mat floor of the *hondo* and looked out across the garden to the landscape in the middle distance, and Mount Hiei far beyond—an example of what Ron called the "borrowed landscape"—the visual incorporation of far-away landscape elements in a nearer view of a garden.

The garden was relatively small, covered with stones and moss, with a low hedge in the back parallel to the open wall and *engawa* (walkway at the edge) of the *hondo*. A line of trees marked the hedge. The trees were outside the garden—except for one of them, that was on the building side of the hedge.

That "inner tree" did everything. It turned an ordinary place into an extraordinary one, by turning the hedge into an object that, instead of dividing space, united the garden with the landscape beyond—and because of its orientation, helped to connect me with the sacred mountain in the far distance. It is a simple gesture, with an enormous impact. There is also something of an intention to it—it is a visual phenomenon but it also deliberately calls the viewer's attention to it, making a strong point of the connection.

The "borrowed landscape" is an important feature of Japanese garden design—the "background" is not just something in the distance, but a carefully ordered part of the composition. This hedge is a beautiful example of what Chris Alexander would call "deep interlock,"[1] reduced to such an elemental level that the idea was brilliantly clear at first sight. Visiting Entsu-ji Temple turned out to be a fitting start to my first trip to Japan—a trip that strongly brought my attention to the precision and deliberateness of everything that was designed.

[1] Christopher Alexander, *The Nature of Order, Volume 1, The Phenomenon of Life*, pp. 195–199.

DAISHEN-IN, MYOSHINJI, KYOTO

A modest example of exquisitely detailed buildings

ON SEVERAL TRIPS to Japan I stayed in a guest house at Daishen-in, a modest temple—one of about 50 in the large temple complex of Myoshin-ji, in the northwest part of Kyoto. I stayed in a four-and-a-half- or eight-mat room,[1] in visits over about 15 years.[2]

Daishen-in is not rich. It shows signs of wear, and lacks the polish and elaborately articulated detail of some of the other Myoshinji subtemples,[3] and certainly of a royal building complex like the Katsura Villa. It is an "ordinary" set of buildings, but yet evokes strong feelings of belonging and beauty.

Most buildings in the complex include an *engawa*, a circulation passage at the edge of the building over which the main roof extends for protection against the sun and the strong monsoon rains. The *engawa* is often open to gardens on one side, and bounded on the other by sliding walls that, when open, reveal

Gate at Katsura Villa.

Ambiguity of inside/outside at Katsura Villa.

1 In traditional Japanese architecture, the size of rooms is often described by the number of tatami mats that they contain, each of which is about 6' × 3' (but historically slightly different from place to place).

2 These stays all took place while helping teach a summer program for architecture and landscape architecture students, organized by a landscape-architect colleague, Ronald Lovinger, my teacher of things Japanese.

3 Ryoan-ji, with its famous rock garden, is one of them.

Daishen-in entrance hall.

Daishen-in view across inner garden from main prayer hall.

tatami rooms inside; in one place there is a roof over a "bridge" that leads to another *engawa* on the other side of the garden—this allows for easy movement during rain.

Traditional Japanese buildings are optimized for summer and not winter. Their broad roofs, that may extend past the edge of the floors, keep out the sun as much as possible. The construction helps control breezes through the house; the wooden floor is raised above the ground to help the breeze move the air below the floor; the moving screens[4] allow control of the breeze through the building with a flexible enclosure. All of it takes full advantage of a post-and-beam system that is structurally essential to the openness of the wall.

The same year that I began to stay at Daishen-in, I also visited, in Kyoto, the Katsura Villa for the first time. This is a complex of buildings and gardens built for royalty, ranging from pavilions to watch the moon or drink tea, to gates and fences—all built with the same attitude that respected the sanctity of the detail and the craft that makes it. And in that first visit, I realized that I was experiencing a similar set of ideas as at Daishen-in: particularly the ambiguity of the boundary between inside and outside.

At some of the Katsura Villa buildings, the outer edge of the roof eave did not correspond with any change of material in the floor below. So not only was the vertical plane minimized, with

[4] These are both kinds of sliding screens at the edge of rooms. Shoji screens are translucent, often covered with translucent rice paper, while fusuma screens are opaque, covered with fabric or opaque paper.

Garden edge.

Engawa at Daishen-in. Photo: Rigel Wakil.

only columns rather than a fully-built wall, but the position of the boundary between inside and outside is ambiguous. That boundary is a zone of three-dimensional space rather than a two-dimensional plane.

The boundary is widened even further by the edge of the garden that the *engawa* is adjacent to. That edge, in the ground, consists of several layers of gravel and worked stone that help drain the rainwater that falls from the eave, providing a wide boundary between the *engawa* and the planted part of the garden.

In a way, the Katsura Villa and Daishen-in are opposites of each other. The Katsura Villa was built for royalty, and Daishen-in is one of the most modest temples in a complex of about 50 of them. But there is a clear similarity between these two building complexes, including the idea of continuous, connected space. So powerfully and elegantly realized at the Katsura Villa, it is present generally in the traditional wooden architecture of Japan. At the modest buildings of Daishen-in it remains part of ordinary daily life, experienced a dozen times a day, moving from room to room and sitting at the wooden edge of a garden.

CHURCH OF ST. JAMES PICCADILLY, LONDON

The sacred and the everyday

PICCADILLY, the broad street that runs west from Piccadilly Circus to Hyde Park Corner, today houses a varied collection of uses, including upscale retail shops in buildings with residential and office uses above, the Royal Academy of Arts, nineteenth-century arcades lined with more upscale shops, the Ritz Hotel, and the church of St. James Piccadilly. The church, along with its churchyard, is a quiet refuge in this busy street. Designed by Christopher Wren, construction of the church began in 1676, a decade after the Great Fire of London of 1666 (although this neighborhood was not burnt in the fire). The area was built, beginning in the seventeenth century, partly because of its proximity to the royal palace.[1]

The nave of St. James Piccadilly.

[1] A good summary of the history of the area is in F. H. W. Sheppard (General Editor), Introduction, *Survey of London, Volume XXIX, The Parish of St. James Westminster, Part One: South of Piccadilly*, pp. 1–20. This work talks about several attributes of the immediate area in its eighteenth-century days: the proliferation of coffee houses, the change of coffee houses to exclusive clubs, and the inward facing nature of St. James's Square and neighboring streets. But the account expressed in this reflection is a contemporary interpretation of the church and its relationship to its surroundings.

One of my favorite Christopher Wren churches, St. James Piccadilly, is one of Wren's most spatially simple. Finished in 1684, its nave is made up of a simple barrel vault supported by smaller barrel vaults that are themselves held up by the columns that define the nave, and the outer wall. The upper gallery is supported by wooden constructions. Wood predominates in places where people are, near the ground level, with painted plaster and glass above. The church's spatial order is straightforward, and that simplicity is reinforced by the clear glass windows in the nave windows. In Wren's design, all the windows were originally clear glass, but were replaced with stained glass during the nineteenth century. After the Blitz in the Second World War that damaged the church, the windows were replaced again with clear glass like the original.

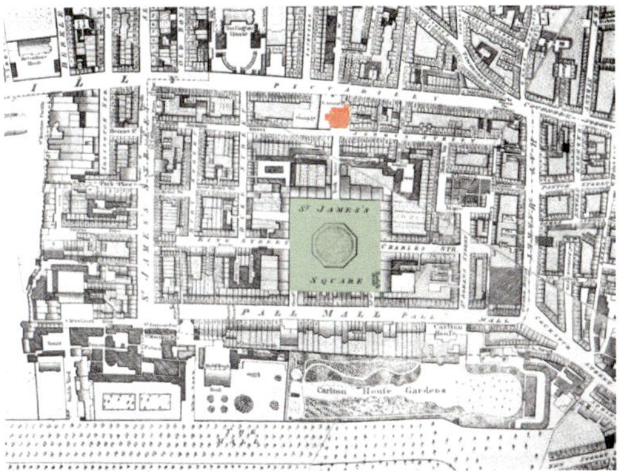

St. James Piccadilly (in orange) and St. James's Square to its south.

Churchyard between Piccadilly (left) and the church.

In addition to its straightforward architectural design, the church appeals to me because of the way it is strongly embedded in the city, at multiple scales and in multiple ways, playing a strong role in connecting parts of the city with each other.

The church building itself is at the northern end of Duke of York Street, which connects it to St. James's Square, helping to tie the active commercial and institutional street of Piccadilly with the residential peacefulness of St. James's Square. One enters the church yard from Piccadilly, and immediately feels a sense of peace and quiet: the church yard, experienced before entering the church, provides a welcome transition from the busy street. If coming from Piccadilly, the church is entered from a north door, under the tower and steeple; the nave is then to the east. But the church can also be entered from the south, opposite the north door, and that is quite a different experience. The south door is at the end of an axis that stretches down the Duke of York Street and ends at the north entrance to St. James's Square.

The church is thereby anchored to two very different urban streets: Piccadilly, with its variety of uses, traffic, and many people on foot; and Duke of York Street, lined with Georgian houses of consistent design and scale, leading to the peaceful

Looking north on Duke of York Street from St. James's Square toward the church of St. James Piccadilly.

Looking out from the church of St. James Piccadilly toward the south, showing building at the corner of Jermyn Street and the Duke of York Street. Photo: Sian Therese.

St. James's Square. So the church is very much tied into the city around it.

The church is also anchored to the city at a smaller, more intimate scale: the clear glass windows allow for views of the neighboring buildings. In the church, when one looks toward the south wall, one gets a view of the buildings across Jermyn Street and down Duke of York Street. So even though a person is in the sacred space of the church, there is still the experience of being in the city as well.

These connections to the city at two different scales are quite different from many other churches, mosques, and other religious buildings in the world. Often, part of the building's role is to remove worshippers from the ordinary and the everyday as much as possible. St. James Piccadilly is different. It has a balance between connection and separation, between the everyday and the sacred, perhaps helping make a deliberate point about the sacredness of everyday life.

APARTMENT HOUSES, NEW YORK

Simple rules leading to complex plans

GROWING UP in New York, large apartment buildings seemed ordinary to me, and although my family and friends tended to live in smaller buildings in Brooklyn, my wanderings in the city put them into my experience. I began to pay more attention to them when I was doing research at the New York Public Library on 42nd Street, where I came across *Apartment Houses of the Metropolis*, a commercial book published in 1906 or 1907, containing the plans and exterior views of hundreds of New York apartment houses. These were mostly on the Upper West Side and in Harlem, but also included buildings in other parts of the city, including Brooklyn and the Bronx. The books were intended for rental and real-estate agents, presumably to show their clients before they visited the apartments themselves.[1]

I began to see the buildings as quite remarkable, fitting into New York's grid and typical modules of land division, and designed to appeal to the growing middle class of the city. Many of the plans

[1] At the library I handled the original volumes, but they are now available online through the New York Public Library website [Digital Collections].

Apartment building on Upper West Side, one of thousands of similar buildings in the city.

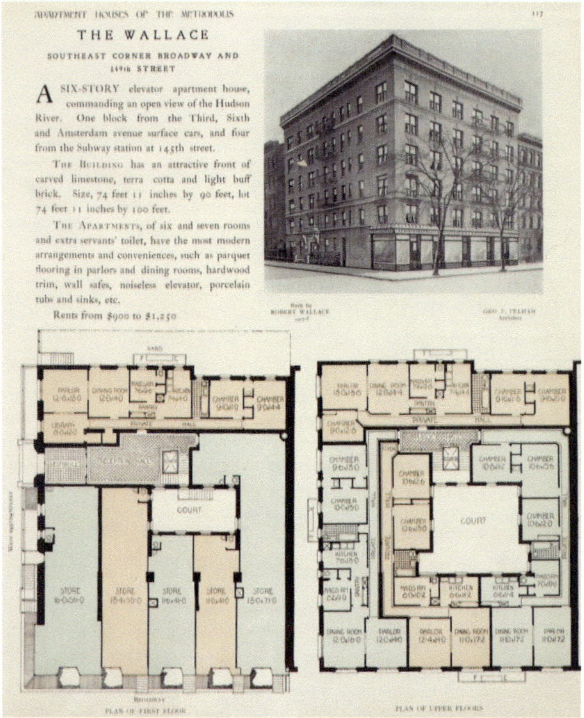

The Wallace, southeast corner Broadway and 149th Street. Plan of first floor, plan of upper floors. The New York Public Library.

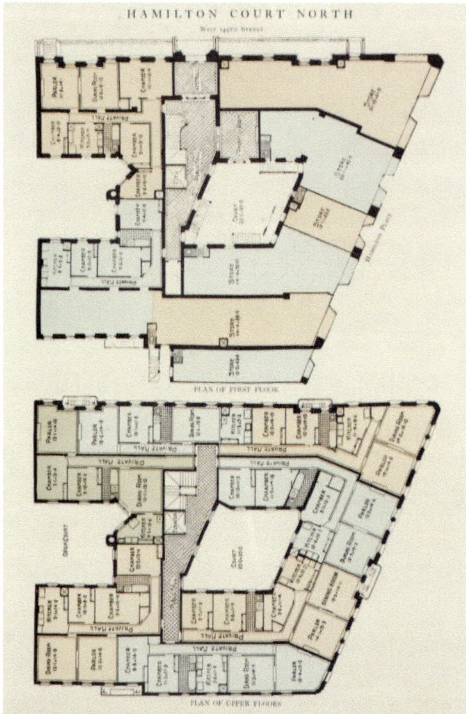

Hamilton Court North. One of the shops on the ground floor is directly connected to an apartment. The New York Public Library.

were for buildings designed for corner sites, sometimes with stores on the ground floor and apartments above. The standard 25-foot basic lot width that applied in much of Manhattan, combined with the 200-foot north/south dimension to the rectangular blocks led to 100'x100" corner sites, or in-block sites that were multiples of 25', or sometimes 75'/2. These standard dimensions guided many of the basic plan types, but within those types there was seemingly infinite variation of detail and exact dimension.

The drawings fascinated me, and since finding them I have spent dozens of hours studying them. They show the ways in which the architects of the buildings maximized economic efficiency while at the same time providing a sense of gentility for the middle-class and upper-middle-class families who would come to occupy them. While the buildings are all different, sometimes only in very subtle ways, they share the same principles of plan layout:

- Public circulation space is minimized even if it means that apartments have very long corridors giving access to all their rooms, even if it means that living and dining rooms are located at the ends of those corridors, and even if it means that two or sometimes even three residential corridors, belonging to different apartments, are adjacent to each other. Minimizing public corridor space while putting more circulation space inside apartments helped to maximize rental income from the apartments. And having apartment doors closer together might have helped increase a sense of community.

- When possible, major rooms—living rooms and dining rooms—are located facing the street rather than internal courts or light wells.
- Internal courts and light wells are reserved for kitchens, maids' rooms, and minor bedrooms.
- Locating the public stairs along the inner court provides daylight to the stair landings while keeping the stairs away from the much more valuable "real estate" of the exterior walls that face the street.

Over time, these buildings, representing one of the important vernacular building types in New York, have together housed millions of the city's people. My discovery of the plan books brought me into the buildings in an almost real way. It allowed me to understand the principles of their design, but I could also imagine myself walking down an apartment corridor with two other people doing the same thing in adjacent corridors, three feet away on each side, each of us in a different apartment.

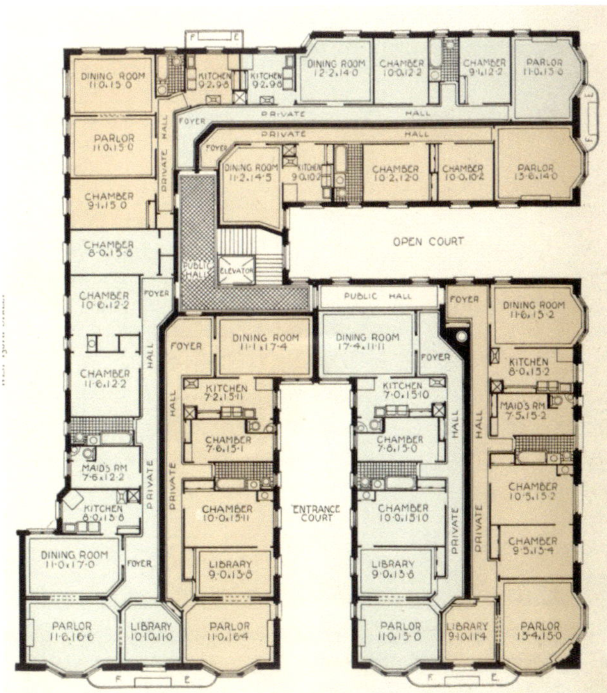

At the upper left of the plan are three adjacent corridors, each part of a different apartment. The New York Public Library.

INNER SHRINE, ISE, MIE PREFECTURE, JAPAN

Tearful beauty at the outer gate

I HAVE VISITED the Ise Shrine three times, each time as a day trip out of Kyoto. Ise consists of a large, forested district, a park, containing dozens of buildings associated with its sacred functions. The Inner Shrine, location of the most sacred building, is approached after a long walk from the entrance through the forest.

The Inner Shrine at Ise is the most important building in the Shinto religion, the indigenous religion of Japan. Its central sanctuary contains one of the religion's most important objects—

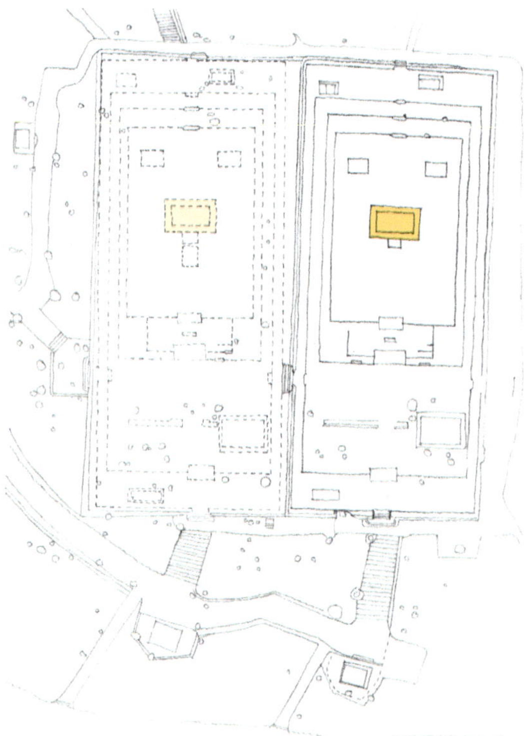

Plan of the two adjacent sites at Ise. The one on the right had the Inner Shrine and assocated structures built in place during all three of HD's visits in 1998, 2003 and 2006.

Steps to outermost gate and enclosure at right-hand site.

the sacred mirror. The only person allowed to enter the building is the Emperor of Japan, and how close others can even get to the building depends on their status, with more important people allowed into more innermost enclosures. I knew that I would be allowed to go no farther than the outermost enclosure.

My first visit was on a drizzly day with a high, overcast sky. I walked through the forest, passing through stands of tall cypress and cedar trees, crossing wooden bridges, passing numerous wooden buildings and shrines, all built with great skill and perfect detail. I finally came to a short path, near the end of which were two staircases leading up to raised areas. The second, farther staircase led up to the site of the Inner Shrine. I walked up that stair, risers made of squared logs with gravel forming the surface of the tread, and passing a tree located right on the edge of the staircase requiring the stairs to be shaped to accommodate it. At the top of the stair, there was a gateway, and through that gateway was a low fence around the enclosure that was only a little smaller than the entire site. The next gate was through that fence, and then two or three more enclosures.

But at that first gateway, I was stopped and could go no farther. I could only see the ridge of the roof of the innermost building, the one that presumably had the sacred mirror. I could see the successive enclosures, and the trees that helped frame the view.

I found myself in a place of sublime beauty. The trees and the wooden enclosures were in perfect balance, making the fences at least as important as the buildings in the experience of the place. The mist and drizzle, by taking away the sharpness and contrast of shadows, helped bring out the smaller details in the view. I stood there for about 40 minutes, so transfixed by the beauty of this one view that I was on the verge of tears running down my face.

The encounter described here was one of the two or three most powerful in this book. In addition to the beauty of the site itself, my reaction was probably due at least partly to several other things: walking up the stair being the culmination of a long walk through the forest after a three-hour train ride, my longtime attraction to the traditional wooden architecture of Japan and my knowledge that this was one of its best examples, and that I was in the presence of one of the most significant buildings of an important world religion. But I also know that that is not all. The place was physically beautiful from the point of view of its materials and details, and of how architectural space was formed by shaped

Building along outermost enclosure.

materials and the living, tended landscape. I would have experienced the beauty of the place even if I didn't know anything about it, and if I had been transported there by helicopter instead of walking to it through a beautiful forest.

But the most remarkable thing about the Ise Shrine is its construction. There are two adjacent sites, alternately rebuilt every 20 years with buildings and fences of exactly the same design. I went up the second stair, having passed the first that led up to an empty site. My three visits took place over a six- or eight-year period beginning in 1998, and all happened during a time when the buildings on the right-hand site, the farther stair, were in place. The dismantling and reconstruction on the adjacent site happened in 2013—so as I begin to write this, in 2020, the right-hand site has been dismantled; the left-hand site is occupied but will be replaced again by buildings on the right-hand site in 2033, made once again with new materials. This cycle of rebuilding every 20 years on alternating sites has happened about 65 times, for over 1,300 years, at least. In this place, architecture and craftsmanship are both kept alive, through a process that is repeated, every century, by five generations of craftspeople.[1]

[1] The dismantled materials are reused for temples in other places. All the wood for the construction of the Ise Shrine is harvested, dried, cut, and shaped anew, every 20 years. See Kenzo Tange and Noboru Kawazoe, with photographs by Yoshio Watanabe, *Ise: Prototype of Japanese Architecture.*

TUNG PATTANA, CHIANG MAI, THAILAND

Ambiguous boundaries and tight community

ON MY FIRST visit to Thailand in 1998, two colleagues and I visited a large number of informal settlements and slums in and around Bangkok and Chiang Mai. One of these, Tung Pattana in Chiang Mai, was a linear settlement located along a klong (canal). It was the site of a project that, in addition to the cleaning of the klong, involved the construction of a wooden footpath along the klong that connected all the houses, allowing people to walk throughout the community, raised up above the mud and water, and giving each house a dry area outside its entrance.

Thailand is hot, rainy, and humid for large parts of the year, and the houses are open to allow any breeze to cool their interiors. But one thing I noticed at Tung Pattana was that this openness was not only a phenomenon of thermal control. It was accompanied by a social openness, or more precisely an ambiguity of the typical boundary between public and private space. I first noticed it while walking along the wooden footpath, and, finding myself amongst some chairs and tables outside a house, and then walking a few feet more, I realized that I had actually entered the house without having noticed it. I was not aware of having crossed anything like a "property line" or entering a door, or passing from "public space" to "private space." I did not enter a space with beds, but I was clearly "inside" the house. In another situation, there was a related phenomenon along a busy public street near the center of Bangkok, where my path along the sidewalk took me in between an open shop at the ground floor of a shophouse, where the goods spilled out onto the sidewalk, and a table set up at the curb, where the family was sitting eating lunch. My path—the public path—took me in between two functions of the house that we would ordinarily consider to be private.

Tom Kerr, who took me to Tung Pattana, writes about the blurring of the inside space and outside space in poor and informal

Public spaces in Bangkok are shared and blur the boundaries between pubic and private. Photos: Thomas A. Kerr.

communities, where people tend to use the whole settlement as an extension of the stage of their family and communal life.

> It is really a wonderful thing...In middle class neighborhoods...up go the compound walls and the high fences and broken-glass-topped walls to destroy whatever smidgens of that blurriness persist. But in poor communities, it's still there.
>
> Another last thought: maybe it's because of the hot weather, or because most of these communities are close to major markets and are full of vendors and people doing home work and working nearby, and because the houses are small, the lanes invariably become much-used space, and sometimes the houses become glorified storage places and bedrooms for sleeping only at night. A lot of the socializing happens out in the lanes, where it's cooler than inside the houses, and where

> many people set up tables or stools to sit and chat and watch and cut up vegetables and do piecework. And there's also that pan-Asian love of sitting and watching the crowd on the lane go by.
>
> All this is part of that flow between the private within and the public without you describe.[1]

[1] Tom Kerr, email, Nov. 10, 2021.

In many places, this phenomenon is not only an architectural one, but a functional sign of the nature of community itself, which shares space among its members—space that reaches into what many people ordinarily see as only private. As in tens of thousands of communities all over the world, from Native Americans to Indigenous Australians to Southeast Asians, and many others, the concept of a strong separation between private and public space is not something based on lived experience, and is in fact strange. Making this distinction is often an artificial construction, consistent with modern legal and economic systems that cannot recognize ambiguity and "hybridity" as legitimate parts of life.

The Peruvian economist Hernando de Soto advocates for the legal definition of property boundaries in informal settlements as a means to unlock the value of land, allowing banks to make loans based on clearly defined collateral. But as was also pointed out to me, many local communities are opposed to this, seeing that it would encourage the land market to run rampant while also destroying community.

WAKALA AL-GHOURI CARAVANSERAI, CAIRO

An apartment house for traders and merchants

IN DECEMBER 1998, while at a conference in Cairo, I visited a building that had fascinated me for a long time, through drawings and photographs: the Wakala al-Ghouri caravanserai. This is a five-story building with a clever organization, combining commercial functions with a compact array of three-story apartments, all arranged around a large courtyard.

View of courtyard. The first two floors are for warehouse space and storage, and the three floors at the top are the apartments.

Apart from some New York apartment buildings that have one- or two-triplex units near their top, this is the only multi-unit apartment house I am aware of that has multiple three-story apartments as its basic dwelling unit. The lower two floors are for warehousing and storage, and the upper three floors have 19 apartments, each with three floors. The building may be entered either directly into the courtyard on the ground floor, or by way of a stair along a side of the building that goes up to the second and third floors. At the second floor (one floor above the ground floor), an arcade around the courtyard gives access to about two dozen commercial spaces, and at the third floor, the corridor's location is shifted to be able to give access to 19 apartments that face either the courtyard or the street. Each apartment has a large two-story reception room—called a "*qa-a*" in

Arabic—and an internal stair that leads up to the private quarters of the dwelling.

Although each dwelling does not have its own courtyard, the typology of the three-story apartment is present in another domestic building in Cairo, the Bayt Suhaymi, originally built in the seventeenth century. As with the apartment in the Wakala Al-Ghouri, the lower floor is where public life meets the house, and includes a multi-story *qa'a*. The building de-emphasizes the path to the more private quarters—adding to the privacy that is typical of many houses built in places with Islamic traditions. The Bayt

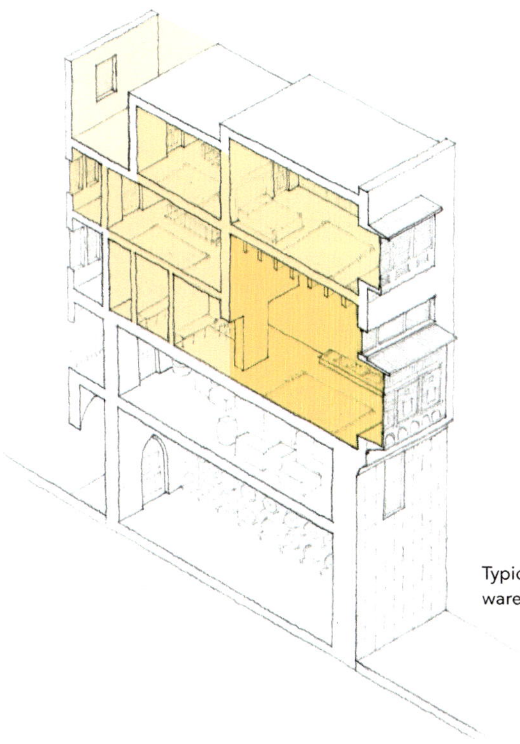

Typical thrree-story apartment on top of warehouse space, showing two-story *qa'a*.

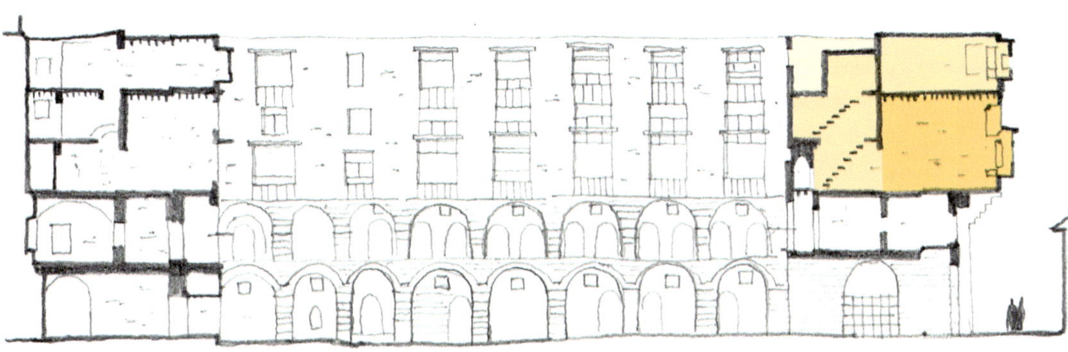

Building section.

Suhaymi has a courtyard and a rear garden, and like many houses built in the Islamic tradition, the courtyard is not visible from the street and accessed only by a shifting entrance hallway called the *skifa.*

This building type has been compressed in the Wakala Al-Ghouri, into a party-wall apartment type that is repeatable in a single building. While the Wakala Al-Ghouri lacks individual courtyards and gardens, the apartments maintain the idea of verticality that supports the privacy of women and daily family life while having a ceremonial room for guests at its lower, entry floor. The three-story apartment maintains the typology of the individual house, while assembling 19 of them in a single, compact building.

Front façade of Wakala al-Ghouri caravanserai. Rooms for goods are on the lower two floors.

GRAND CENTRAL TERMINAL, NEW YORK

The railroad as urban shaper

WHEN I AM in New York, the information booth in the center of the main concourse of Grand Central Terminal, with the four-sided clock above it, is focal. It is often the place where I meet a friend coming in by train from Connecticut to spend a day together, or meet students who are joining me in New York for a few days of architectural and urban exploration.

I sometimes think of that main concourse as the center of the world. Although there are now fewer long-distance trains at

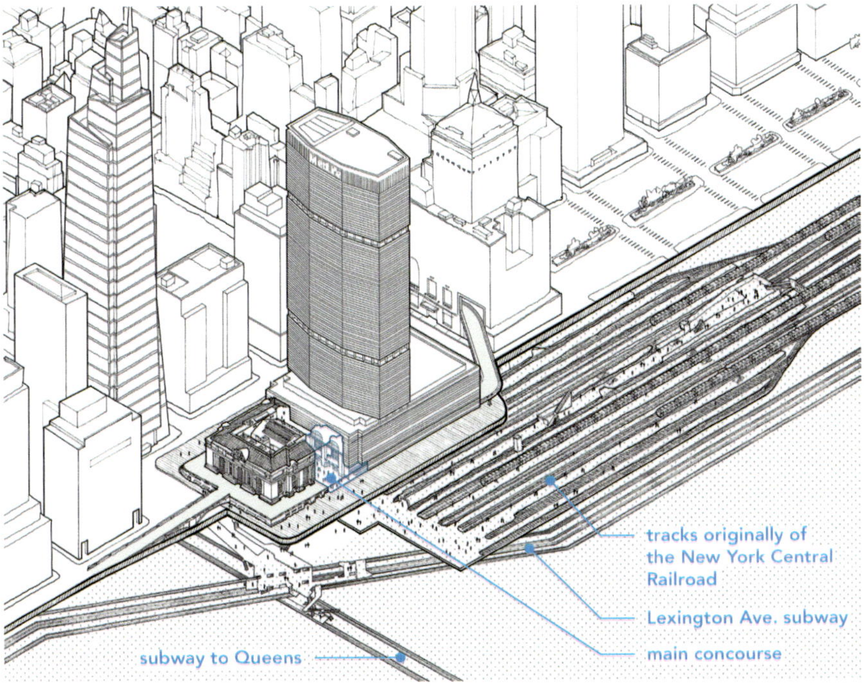

Cut-away axonometric drawing showing tracks and platforms under Park Avenue. The terminal building itself, seen at the lower left of the drawing, that seems large to the visitor with its large concourse, is very small compared to the entire system of which it is a part. Drawing: Erik Larson.

Main concourse of Grand Central Terminal, New York. The arches at the Left lead to the train platforms, except for the second one on the left that leads to escalators for the MetLife building just to the north. The clock mentioned in the reflection can be seen on the right

Grand Central than there once were, the concourse is always full of people, going in all directions to and from the MetLife Building (built as the PanAm Building) at the southern end of Park Avenue, three subway lines below (the Lexington Avenue line, the shuttle to and from Times Square, and the No. 7 train to Queens), and the busy streets around, including 42nd Street—as well as the lower concourse and train platforms themselves.

The concourse is a great urban room, with its unique vaulted ceiling painted with golden stars against a blue sky, stairs leading up toward Vanderbilt and Lexington avenues, and sunlight streaming in through the tall arched windows. Finished in 1913, the building was one of several optimistic additions to the city, affirming New York's role as a principal economic and cultural center of the United States, and of the world.

But that building is only a part of what has captured my attention and imagination. As large and complex as the building itself is, it is small compared to the urban system that it anchors, a large part of which was built at the same time as part of the same urban intervention. The terminal was really the "jewel in the crown" of a mammoth set of construction projects that included burying the tracks of the New York Central Railroad coming from the north. The trains on that line, that had been recently installed with electric engines, replacing those of steam, no longer needed to be above grade, and could now be put under the wide expanse of Park Avenue.

So since 1913, the tracks from the north along Park Avenue have gone underground at about East 97th Street. And where the tracks got closer to the terminal, they divided to be able to serve the individual platforms, therefore needing to occupy land wider than Park Avenue itself. That land was acquired by the New York Central Company and could then be used for what became a huge project of real estate investment, above the newly-underground tracks—including land under buildings on both sides of Park Avenue. The two miles of Park Avenue north of Grand Central Terminal now represent some of the highest-value land in New York City.

Entrance to platforms from main concourse.

As I learned about this, I became fascinated by the entire network of terminal, underground tracks, and buildings and their basements, in which the individual elements are connected through ownership, the realities of urban economics, and a powerful scheme

View of train platforms under Park Avenue.

of urban design. The station itself has multiple connections to streets outside, multiple levels of long-distance trains, commuter trains, subway trains, cars, and buses, below and above it (including the splitting of Park Avenue itself where it is raised above other streets to go around the terminal building), and historic connections to a post-office building. Altogether it is like a living organ connected to the rest of the body—a concentrated demonstration of the ways that the city itself is a giant system of interdependent parts.

Elsewhere in this book I have written about another New York landmark—how the main reading room of the New York Public Library (a short walk from Grand Central) cleverly brings together a technological system (the book storage, request, and delivery spaces and systems) with an architecturally beautiful room that expresses the importance of books and the building's connection with libraries of the past.

A similar thing is true for Grand Central Terminal. Around 1900, the technological innovations of the previous two centuries were becoming more a part of daily life. But there was still a social reluctance to make that technology visible. That visibility waited for the architectural modernists. As with the library, the combination of the railroad, land development, and the architectural symbolism of the great human place that is the terminal itself, is an always strong reminder of the extent of the city's complexity.

TINNGÅRDEN, HERFØLGE, DENMARK

A prototype for modern housing

IN 1999, I spent three weeks in Copenhagen where I wanted to begin to understand why the Danish building culture seemed to consistently produce such good results. I took the advice of local colleagues to visit a project by the firm Vandkunsten Architects, who were (and are still) regarded as one of the leading Danish firms designing housing. One of their projects was "Tinngården," in the suburb of Herfølge, south of Copenhagen. The original project consisted of 78 houses (later doubled) intended to support a strong community life, and providing flexible dwelling units that

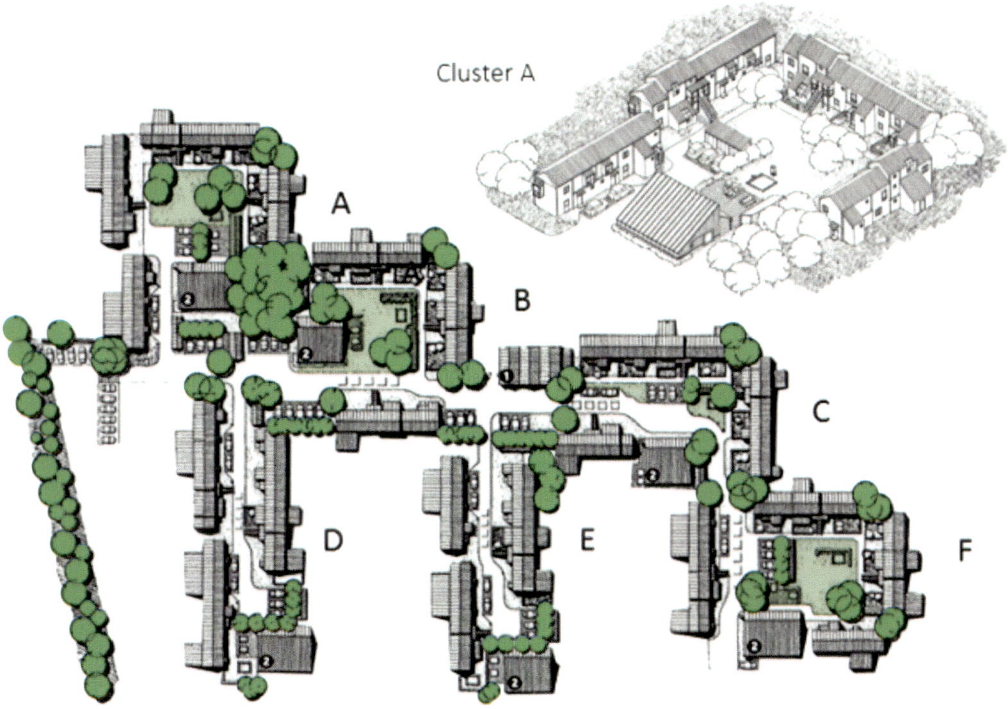

Site plan of Tinngården. Drawing: Vandkunsten Architects, Copenhagen.

could be used a variety of ways and house different sizes and kinds of families.

What I found on my visit was a place very different from typical, contemporary housing developments. There was, first of all, a sense of relaxed, ordinary life about it. There was not a lockstep, rigid industrial repetition to the buildings. They were ordinary, with variety and informality in their design. The buildings had a strong relationship to the outdoors; there were common areas and gardens; the buildings were not blocking views or light of their neighbors. Likewise, the visible materials were ordinary and likely not expensive or special, and had the ability to be easily shaped during on-site construction. It seemed like a good armature for daily life. And it visually connected well with the traditional vernacular architecture of Denmark.

The Vandkunsten firm sees the Tinngården project as an early model for contemporary low-rise, high-density housing in Denmark—an alternative to either the high-rise model or the one-free-standing-house-per-lot suburban model.

The project uses a combination of prefabricated/standard parts for the basic structural and core elements, and materials shaped specifically on site for the exterior façades and interior finishes. It has a variety of common rooms, and rooms in between adjacent dwellings that can be part of either one. That flexibility worked in concert with the efficiency of repetition of the core elements.

An original idea, not carried through, was that the residents would have a larger role in the design of the project, but that turned out to be too difficult. So one criticism of the project: that it projected an image of something that the architects thought users would want, but that it really turned out to be nostalgic and picturesque.

In fact, there was apparently a difference between what professionals said and what the users said. The Vandkunsten office website, in 2024, is candid in summing up the reaction to the construction: "Prefab, painted wooden façades and water-scoured brickwork. Grey Eternit roofs. Cowboy Town and Swedish children's book architecture were some of the criticisms from contemporary architects at the time. The residents were more appreciative."

A balanced explanation is that of Jorn Orum-Nielsen, another important Danish architect of the period: "Certainly the work was in some ways nostalgic…but, in fact, the projects that resulted were more humane, more supportive of community life,

Floor plan of Tinngården. Note the variety of dwelling unit plans and the common spaces including workshops, in yellow.

Photographs of Tinngården, Herfølge, Denmark.

more 'appropriate' with regard to their construction technology, and more suited to the Danish climate than their modernist counterparts. That works like Tinngården implied relationships between cause and effect that were not real is true … but on balance these projects were moving in a positive and fundamentally important direction."[1]

When Jorn Orum-Nielsen taught at Oregon in the early 1990s, he talked about how Danish architects saw a responsibility to look carefully at each other's work, including making visits to exhibitions of top entries in competitions that they did not win. Contemporary architects, in places where there is a need for new design solutions to housing problems, might take a lesson from this, and give another look at projects like Tinngården that recognized the need for new housing models including the balance between housing quality and higher density.

1 Jorn Orum-Nielsen (in collaboration with Mike Pease), *Dwelling: At Home, In Community, On Earth: The Significance of Tradition in Contemporary Housing*, p. 223.

1999

PATI, PATAN, NEPAL

Taking care of the community

IN NEPAL in 1999, following a two-week visit the year before, I spent a month in Patan (also known as Lalitpur), one of the three main cities of the Kathmandu Valley (the other two are Kathmandu and Bhaktapur), doing research on the changing building culture of the city. I was visiting a graduate student at Oregon who did his master's thesis based on work in Nepal[1] before returning to Sydney where he now leads an architecture firm.

As with many cities of the Global South, the Kathmandu Valley cities were in a state of transformation, including the replacement of old brick-and-timber buildings unique to Nepal with buildings with reinforced concrete frames, typical of cities all over the world.[2] What I found with my observations and interviews was a hybrid between the "old" and the "new." On one hand, materials were changing, but at the same time, the plan organization of houses was being maintained. And although a high level of craft was no longer as common as before, it was still present, maintained largely through conservation efforts on temples and other important buildings.

1 Nick Seemann, "Mapping the Mandala: An Approach to Community-Based Architecture in Kathmandu, Nepal". M.S. thesis, Department of Architecture, University of Oregon, 2000.

2 This was perhaps more true of Kathmandu and Patan than it was of Bhaktapur, in which architectural conservation efforts, financed by Germany, had essentially preserved the entire city, or at least the main central area of it, rather than only select landmarks.

Patis in Patan, Nepal.

Traditional ideas and techniques were also being maintained through the construction and restoration of *patis*. The *pati* is a community-owned rest house, and may be one of a variety of specific types, ranging from a simple covered porch attached to the side of a building, to a freestanding, one-story structure often located at a street intersection, to larger structures with enclosed second-story rooms used for sleeping.[3]

I found the *pati* unique as a building type, and saw it as representing a strong and natural community life in the town. The one-story freestanding structures were ubiquitous in the old part of Patan. They were well used, for a variety of purposes during the day—early morning prayers and chanting, places for women with babies to meet and chat, places for old men to do the same. Sometimes they were full of people, other times they were almost empty with just one or two people in them. These freestanding buildings were made with a heavy timber structure and roofed with fired clay tiles; their bases were stone and brick.

I came across one *pati* that had been in place for a long time, being rebuilt by a young carpenter, and financed through an NGO that provided money for community-based projects in Nepal. These projects included water infrastructure, education, and other socially-important efforts. I asked the leader of the community group that was rebuilding the *pati* why they decided to spend money on this, rather than, for example, on a school or improving their water supply. His reply was that the *pati* is an essential part of their community, necessary for daily life, and was seen as the most important thing the community needed to do at that time. A building type that most places don't have at all, and that might be the "first to go" in some cost-cutting measure, was of primary importance in these towns of Nepal.

[3] Thanks to Matthew Stoll for a clear explanation of the variety of buildings that belong to this typology.

Pati in process of rebuilding.

NEWARI HOUSE, PATAN, NEPAL

Taking care of the gods

DURING MY VISITS to Nepal, I came to appreciate the local, traditional houses—but one particular conversation brought that appreciation to another level.

Typical Newari[1] houses are four-story buildings with a rectangular plan and a single pitched roof, with the ridge and eaves parallel to the street. The functional organization is the same in all houses, and the same in either the country or the city. The ground floor is for service functions: storage, or the economic work of the family: a shop in the city; agricultural tools or crops in the country. The second floor is for sleeping. The third floor is the main living/reception room, with an elaborately-carved set of windows that projects from the building and faces the street. And the fourth/top floor is for the kitchen, and next to it, the prayer room. There are individual variations and adjustments, but the basic plan is always the same.

[1] The Newari are the predominant ethnic group of the Kathmandu Valley.

Three typical, four-story Newari houses in the Kathmandu Valley.

The construction system also follows a typical arrangement. The outer walls are brick. There is often an interior brick wall, parallel to the street façade, that divides the plan in half on the ground and second floors. It is topped by a row of wooden columns on the third and fourth floors that go up to the roof ridge. Otherwise, interior partitions and floors are wooden, with floor beams spanning from the interior wall to the brick exterior walls from the second floor to the roof, and the elaborate windows at the third floor are also of wood. The ceilings are low: traditionally people sit on the floor and not on chairs. The low ceilings were accompanied by low doors, and people would sometimes have to bend to get through them. And when they did that, there was often a small religious symbol on the door lintel, that a person would honor when passing under it.

The construction of a modern, new house maintained the functional organization of the traditional one, with a shop, storage, or agricultural uses on the ground floor, bedrooms just above that, the main living space on the third floor, and the kitchen and prayer room on the top floor. But the new buildings were concrete instead

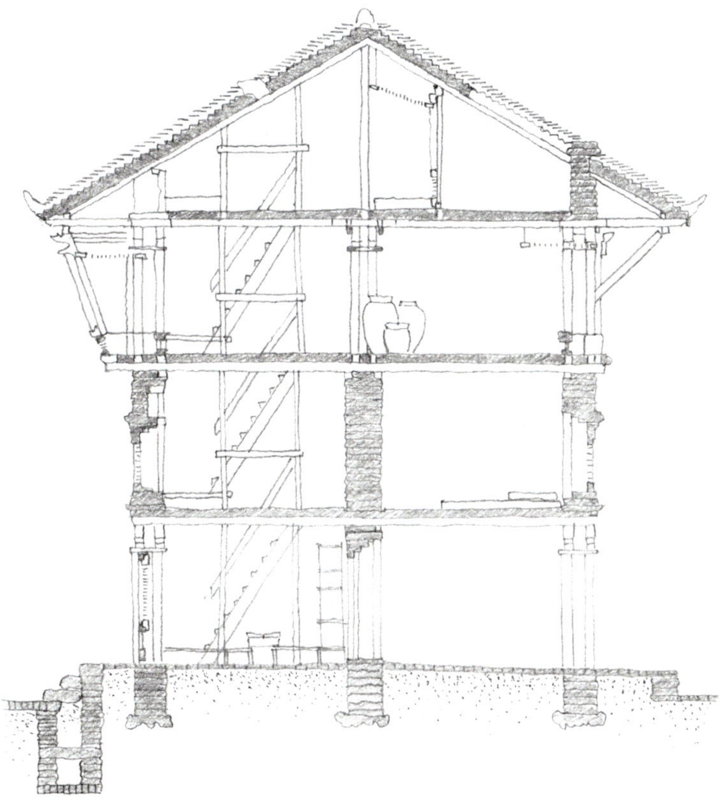

Section through typical Newari house.

of timber and brick, and the ceilings were higher, as people wanted to sit on chairs rather than on carpeted floors. And the elaborate carved-wood window of the third floor, the "signature feature" of the traditional house, was not part of the new one—the cost of that window alone, with the craft skill that it required, was the same as that of an entire new story in the house. To the extent that traditional crafts were being maintained in local building, they were also happening with specialist craftsmen working on the restoration of temples, including the elaborately-carved wooden struts that helped support the deep overhanging eaves, and the brickwork.

We went to visit a man who owned one of these houses and lived there with his family. He worked elsewhere, as a chicken butcher. Talking about his house, we asked him if he would consider building a new house. He immediately said no, explaining that if he were to do that, he would disturb the gods in the house, and he did not want to disturb the gods. This was a matter-of-fact statement that, once again, helped change my understanding of the meaning of a house to people. A house is, for him, not just a "house," but a building that he shares with its gods who turn out to have precedence in it, a framework of sacred places each of which demands its own respect.

On another visit to a different house, my interpreter and I were invited into the top-floor prayer room, to hear a woman with a hauntingly beautiful voice sing as she played the harmonium. She was the interpreter's aunt, and listening to her performance was as close as I came to that spiritual world.

TRAPEZOIDAL BRICKS, KATHMANDU VALLEY, NEPAL

Keeping out the rain

Trapezoidal bricks and brick form at brickyard.

DURING MY 1999 stay in Nepal, while researching the emerging building culture In the Kathmandu Valley, I was attracted to some walls that were completely smooth, without roughness and imperfections. They were brick walls, but with very thin joints, that seemed like single lines rather than observable mortar joints with thickness between the bricks. They seemed to be present mostly on temples and larger buildings. I had not seen anything like this before, but they made for a very elegant wall, helping the building they were a part of seem stately and important—and often helping to emphasize the carved wood of important windows.

These brick walls had an unusual construction technique, with a special kind of brick. Its largest face was a rectangle, the size of ordinary brick, seen on the face of the wall, and other views were trapezoidal. The brick tapered toward the inside of the wall in both plan and elevation view.

This is a brick fired at very high temperature, resulting in a smooth and impervious surface. It allows cementless mud mortar—the traditional, local mortar—to be placed in a way that prevents water from getting through the face of the wall to the

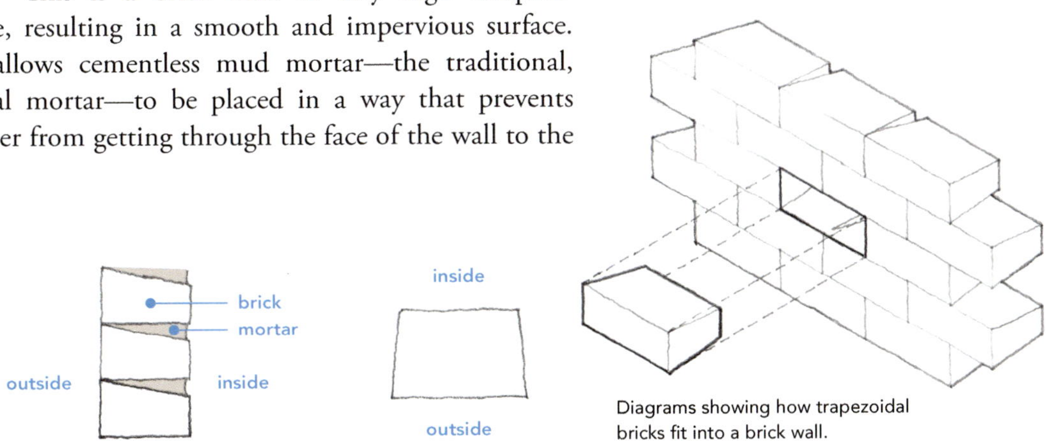

Diagrams showing how trapezoidal bricks fit into a brick wall.

Building and walls made of trapezoidal bricks.

mortar joints.[1] The joints, in other words, are completely behind the plane of the wall, with no mortar showing where the joint comes forward—and ends just before—the plane of the wall. The construction of such a wall clearly requires a very high level of skill, since successive courses of brick need to be on the same vertical plane, the verticality of which is not helped by the shape of the brick itself. Since the outside, visible plane that is supposed to be

1 Vanicka Arora and Manas Murthy, "Inventing Tradition in Bhaktapur, Nepal: The Trajectories of Lime in Heritage Reconstruction," pp. 34–51.

vertical does not have, on the brick, a perpendicular horizontal surface, there is nothing in the brick itself that easily helps the wall become a vertical plane.

The result is a wall where successive courses of brick actually touch each other, with no exposed mortar joint, preventing, as much as possible, water from entering the joint between two bricks. I had never seen a brick wall like this before, and was impressed by what seemed to be a high level of ingenuity within the local building culture. I visited a brick factory where these bricks were still being made, and noticed more walls built like this after I initially saw them and inquired about them. These bricks have a name: *dachchi apa.*

In a recent article about the evolution of different mortars in Kathmandu Valley buildings, Vanicka Arora and Manas Murthy write about these bricks in relation to the question of types of mortar. In recent decades, preservation communities all over the world have seen it as important to understand that lime mortar is "traditional," used on older buildings, and needs to be recognized in the buildings' restoration, so that the problems that have arisen in the last century with the use of cement mortar will not occur. (Cement mortar does not "breathe," and can trap water that can freeze and damage the wall.) But Arora and Murthy point out that, by far, mud mortar was used much more than lime mortar, particularly before the twentieth century, and that the development of the trapezoidal brick is most likely connected to the common use of mud mortar. The precision of the trapezoidal brick, that essentially allowed the joint to disappear on the surface, protected the mud mortar.

Learning this has given me additional insight—not only into the detail itself, but also into the idea that mud and innovation are not incompatible with each other. It's not clear who invented that brick in the first place. The Kathmandu Valley was on an important, early trading route between India and China, and the detail might have originated someplace else. But originally Nepalese or not, the brick and its detail help show that local, vernacular building cultures have talent, identity and creativity.

Paris

Left to right:
Tinos, Greece
Chandigarh, India
Punjab state, India

PART FIVE
2000–2004

These years immediately followed publication of *The Culture of Building*. My teaching continued, and I began research on the book *Living Over the Store: Architecture and Local Urban Life*, that helped foster a growing interest in the relationships between buildings, urban form, and the local urban economy. The reflections here are varied compared to other multi-year parts, and represent deeper understandings of the relationships between the vernacular and "non-vernacular" and perhaps a further breaking down of unhelpful boundaries between them. The reflections include one about my evolving view of vernacular architecture, one prompted by the work of seventeenth-century Dutch painters, and two about contemporary buildings, in Canada and Scotland, that are particularly strong in their relationships to local places.

Left to right:
Tinos, Greece
Amritsar, Punjab state, India
Punjab state, India

2000

CHAPEL OF ST. IGNATIUS, SEATTLE

Tilt-up light

St. Ignatius Chapel, Seattle.

A FEW OF our students, who frequently make the five-and-a-half hour trip to Seattle, first told me about the Chapel of St. Ignatius, on the campus of Seattle University, a Jesuit institution. The chapel's architect was Steven Holl, who is himself a graduate of the architecture school at the University of Washington, also based in Seattle. So I was eager to see the building and did so on my own next trip to Seattle.

I had seen some pictures of the building beforehand, but I was not prepared for the striking and beautiful interior I found when I walked in the door and toward the sanctuary. The interior volume is very simple, but my first experience of the interior was dominated by the several sources of daylight that were mostly located on the upper parts of the walls, with baffles and reflectors coloring that light.

In many historic churches, of most periods, windows and clerestories are located above eye level of the ground floor. These windows, either clear or with stained glass, allow the light to enter directly. This chapel is different, as the most beautiful light is reflected off colored baffles that are put in front of the window opening, on the inside of the building. This creates multiple areas of colored glow that make the space come alive. They are also of symbolic importance. The account of the building that is on Holl's office website provides a rationale for the colors that is connected to worship and the role of the building with respect to its surrounding community:

> Each of the light volumes corresponds to a part of the program of Jesuit Catholic worship The south-facing light corresponds to the procession, a fundamental part of the mass. The city-facing north light corresponds to the Chapel of the Blessed Sacrament and to the mission of outreach to

Interior of St. Ignatius Chapel showing colors of reflected lights. Photos: James Givens.

> the community. The main worship space has a volume of east and west light. At night, which is the particular time of gatherings for mass in this university chapel, the light volumes are like beacons shining in all directions out across the campus.[1]

But the other remarkable aspect of the building is that its basic construction is formed by tilt-up concrete, in which thin slabs of concrete are poured and finished on ground and then "tilted up" into place in the building. This construction material/technique is often used for warehouses and other inexpensive commercial and industrial buildings, in which repetitive wall elements can easily be used to very quickly build the shell of the building, keeping construction costs low. What is remarkable about the chapel, which was built with a fairly low budget, is just that combination of a straightforward and inexpensive basic structure, with its strong sense of "spiritual light" that comes from the reflectors in front of the windows, which themselves are quite simple.

The building achieves a lot with a little and is another example of a way of making buildings that rely more on looking toward the vernacular than toward the "great works" of architecture. In this case the vernacular is a simple, cheap, modern technique. Where does this fit in Nikolaus Pevsner's division of the world of buildings between architecture—"Lincoln Cathedral"—and "buildings"—those that are like a bicycle shed?

[1] See https://www.stevenholl.com/project/st-ignatius-chapel/

INDIA INTERNATIONAL CENTRE, NEW DELHI

Bringing tradition into the modern

IN 2001, I spent a month in Delhi as a visitor to the architectural conservation program at the School of Planning and Architecture (SPA). I was hosted by the then-director of the program, Nalini Thakur, whom I occasionally joined for lunch at the India International Center (IIC) near Lodhi Gardens, part of Edwin Lutyens' famous extension to the city.

The IIC building complex was designed by Joseph Allen Stein, an American architect from the San Francisco Bay Area who migrated to India in the early 1950s and spent virtually his entire career there. He recognized the beauty of the traditional brick and stone detailing on historic and vernacular Indian buildings, but also experimented with the idea that some aspects of those details could be realized with modern techniques of construction. Stein was a "regional modernist," arguably part of the architectural movement that developed in the twentieth century in northern California, which included such architects as William

Courtyard of India International Centre (IIC), New Delhi.

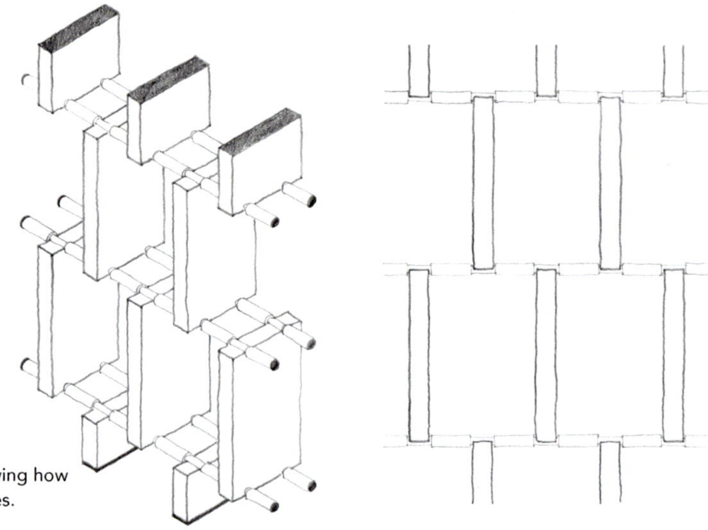

Diagrams of jali wall, showing how bricks slip onto metal pipes.

Closeup of jali wall.

Wurster, Joseph Esherick, and William Turnbull, who tried to bring together contemporary techniques and details in ways that could respond well to the climatic and social manifestations of places in California. In India, the 1950s were a time when, following the assassination of Mahatma Gandhi in 1948, the country was developing cultural and economic ties to the West, and Stein was perhaps ideally placed to further that internationalist vision in architecture.[1]

One thing that struck me at the IIC was a brick screen wall, built with a very simple detail. It requires only a specially-but-easily-formed brick, with a half-circle cut out at each end, slipped over a steel pipe. The spacing between the bricks can be easily adjusted to yield different patterns and amounts of light inside the screen. The result is a pattern of sun and shadow on the inside of the wall, seen in the right-hand picture above, that has some of the same

1 For the authoritative account of Stein's career, see Stephen White, *Building in the Garden: The Architecture of Joseph Allen Stein in India and California*. White writes that "Stein attempted to balance Nehru's ideal of an industrialized, modern India by providing workers with dignifying housing of a timeless quality which he believed possible even, if not especially, at low cost" (p. 38).

India International Centre, New Delhi, showing modern "jali wall".

qualities as the pattern of traditional *jali* brickwork. (A *jali* is a stone-carved screen. See p. 99 for a beautiful example in India.)

My visits to the IIC came at a time when my own attitudes toward modern buildings and modern details had shifted. I was always attracted to the hand-crafted vernacular, and still am. But I realized that it is also important to maintain an openness to the "new"—not because it's new but because it may be effective, appropriate, and even beautiful. This detail was appealing to me for a number of reasons. It provided a simple way to provide a detailed pattern of sunlight and shadow. It helped break down the visual scale of the wall. It suggests alternatives within its own technique (alternating spacings of bricks and steel pipe, for example; imagine bricks of two or three different lengths, with varied spacings between them) that do not add much to cost but that would introduce spatial variety and subtlety. The screen wall is a construction experiment that suggests further experimentation and variation—made even more possible today with digital techniques of design and fabrication.

COURT GARDENER'S HOUSE, POTSDAM, GERMANY

A marriage of room and garden

Court gardener's house entrance.

AFTER A CONFERENCE in Dresden, I went with a few colleagues to Berlin and Potsdam. I had been to Berlin once before, when it was still divided, but this trip was about 11 years after the reunification of Germany. Berlin was active with construction, from urban design projects like that at Potsdamer Platz to new government buildings like the 1.3 kilometer project that spans the River Spree in two places, intended to symbolically reunite East and West Berlin, to Norman Foster's renovation of the old Reichstag—which by the time I was there, had been completed.

My strongest memory of that trip is not that of a large new building, but of a small one built in the nineteenth century. In Potsdam we visited the Charlottenhof Palace. Within it, the Court Gardener's House, part of the Roman Baths, was an important building. It was designed by Karl Friedrich Schinkel, one of the great German architects of the early nineteenth century.

We walked into the trellised garden that was adjacent to the house itself, and I immediately found myself in a beautiful outdoor room, with the plants and built architectural elements in balance. My time in the room was short, but in that limited time I felt myself in a place of refinement, different in design and feeling from either outdoor gardens or interior rooms. It combined the shelter and enclosure of an indoor room with the nature, light, and air of a garden. I was with a small group, and we passed through it quickly on our way to the house itself, but I remember staying behind so I could experience it more fully, and—still too quickly—photograph it.

Drawing of entrance to court gardener's house. Karl Friedrich Schinkel.

Drawing by Schinkel of vernacular house in Sicily, 1805–06.

Court gardener's house and plan. Karl Friedrich Schinkel.

Building at Charlottenhof.

This space represented the union of architecture and landscape architecture, so strongly intertwined that the individual identity of each was lost. On one hand the room had a strong architectural order, with a visible structural frame made up of vertical and horizontal elements, providing a rectilinear framework that was not only an elaborate trellis for the plants, but an ordering device for the space. The trellis and supporting columns gave the whole room a geometrically-ordered architectural armature.

But at the same time there was no question that it was also a garden. We were still outside; if it had been raining we would have experienced the rain; the light was an outdoor light; the plants were copious—in the ground and in containers and pots; there was not a weather enclosure around the space. This was an outdoor space that had the lines and spatial order of an indoor space.

Schinkel worked with a landscape architect, Peter Joseph Lenné, and also had traveled in Italy, appreciating its vernacular buildings and landscapes: one of his drawings is "anchored to the landscape by outside staircases and the simple regular rhythm of trellises."[1] And there was a strong connection between the design of the covered garden with his experience of the vernacular landscape from decades before: "The view of the park from under the pergola is visually structured by the geometric grid of the wooden beams above, which functions like a coordinate system for the perception of the surrounding spaces. As a transitional room, this pergola leads into the park, into the courtyard, and onto the roof. Its geometric grid prepares for all these impressions. In Schinkel's view of the Traunsee of 1811, a grid of wooden beams is suspended between an Austrian village house and a large tree, framing and defining the view of the Traunsee in the distance in a similar way...Here we have two versions of a universal vocabulary of architectural vernacular."[2]

The possible connection of this beautiful outdoor room with Schinkel's experience of the vernacular architecture of Italy came as a surprise to me when reading about Schinkel, whose architecture I have usually connected with academically-understood precedents. But it makes sense. Part of my own attraction to vernacular buildings is often a simple aesthetic one. Their straightforwardness and visibility of structural materials work together to make for visual clarity and strength. This room has those qualities, making a link between vernacular Italy and the classical tradition that Schinkel also helped to further.

[1] Barry Bergdoll, *Karl Friedrich Schinkel: An Architecture for Prussia*, p. 22.

[2] Christoph Martin Vogtherr, "Views and Approaches: Schinkel and Landscape Gardening," p. 74.

SHOP/HOUSES, NEW YORK

A re-encounter leading to a big decision

A FEW DAYS before 9/11, in early September 2001, I was in New York, enjoying walking the streets of the city. One of the things on my mind during the walks was developing an idea for my next book project. I wanted to continue writing about the building culture, and in the preceding couple of years I had done some exploratory research projects with that in mind.

In 1999 I spent three weeks in Copenhagen, talking to architects and bankers, looking at buildings, interested in why the Danish building culture seemed to reliably produce good results. Later that year I spent a month in Kathmandu, talking to builders, craftsmen, leaders of NGOs, architects, and materials suppliers, trying to understand how the building culture in Nepal that had produced the beautiful brick-and-wood houses and temples of the Kathmandu Valley was changing. One of the criticisms of *The Culture of Building* was that it did not focus enough on contemporary large-scale production, on the large economic forces that had a major role in our built environment. So should I research and write about that?

Many interesting possibilities were churning in my mind, but nothing had yet clearly gelled. So it was a sudden realization on that late-summer New York walk, when I re-encountered an architectural phenomenon that was all around me, and had been with me for my entire life. It was pervasive not only in New York but all over the world, yet had never been written about as its own topic. Once the realization came it began to gather coherence, and by the end of the day I had decided what to write about: the buildings that combined commercial and residential uses.

That was a very general, preliminary idea. At that point I had not yet made the distinction between buildings where the same people occupied the stores and the dwellings, and those where the occupants were different. I had not yet realized the full scope of the phenomenon, or its historic antecedents, or the variety of

Variety of shop/houses in New York.

architectural forms that manifested this same social/economic phenomenon. I had not yet understood the ways in which the changing economy precipitated by the Industrial Revolution eventually led to the demise of these buildings in many places. But I knew that I had something, and I was familiar enough with the literature about urban vernacular architecture to know that while this phenomenon was mentioned, it had not been written about as a central topic.

I liked these buildings as buildings, as physical works of architecture, appreciating the fact that they neatly resolved functional complexity within a single architectural package. They were "foursquare": just what they needed to be, and no more. They often represented a functional way of composing a classical façade: the open structure of the commercial space at the lower floor(s) acted as the visual "base" in the tripartite, vertical ordering system of the building. At the same time, the façade often did not reveal the complexity within. Somehow, they represented aspects of architecture that I thought were important.

These buildings were all around me, a part of my own past. Growing up in Brooklyn, they were ubiquitous in every shopping street in every neighborhood. Near the corner of our block was a laundry where the family who owned it lived not upstairs, but in the back—close enough. I never got farther in than the service counter, but always wondered how it worked.

It was only later that I realized that these buildings were essentially a socio/economic phenomenon. They were a neat architectural strategy to make urban land use three-dimensional: architectural space at the street was valued differently from space at upper levels, resulting in different uses. They allowed families to profit—economically and socially—from living and working in the same place. And they brought people together.

My first encounter with these buildings was when I was very young. But they were so ordinary, so much a part of daily life, that—like a "fish in water"—I did not think about them at all. The re-encounter happened just when it needed to, and when I was in a much better position to notice, and to act, on my re-encounter.[1]

1 Howard Davis, *Living Over the Store: Architecture and Local Urban Life.*

AMERICAN FOLK ART MUSEUM, NEW YORK

A tiny architectural gem, destroyed

ON ONE OF the visits when I brought architecture students to New York, in 2001, we happened to be present for the opening of the new building of the American Folk Art Museum, adjacent to and just west of the Museum of Modern Art on West 53rd Street. We were lucky in two ways: admission that day was free, and it turned out to be a gem of a building—on a tiny site, with very particular spaces that were quite suited to the kinds of art works on display. The building was designed by Tod Williams/Billie Tsien Architects.

Contemporary museums often have two kinds of space: first, the galleries themselves, with "neutral" space, white walls, a high level of control over daylight and electric light, flexible and manipulable by the exhibition designers and curators; and second, public space of circulation, movement, and often space that gives a visible architectural "signature" to the building. Examples are Rafael Moneo's San Francisco Museum of Modern Art, with a dramatic atrium in front of functional galleries, Richard Meier's High Museum in Atlanta, with its visible stair system that weaves in and out of the main space, with galleries set away from it, and Norman

Photos showing how art is placed relative to circulation. © Michael Moran/OTTO.

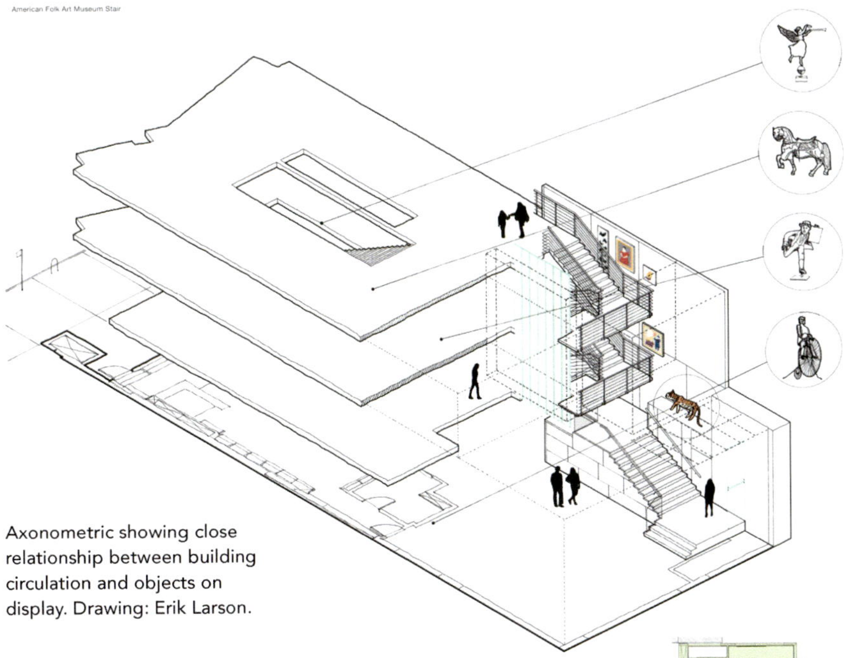

Axonometric showing close relationship between building circulation and objects on display. Drawing: Erik Larson.

Foster's central atrium at the British Museum, with an enormous glass roof over what was a glass roof over the Great Court, that was originally a courtyard system that surrounded the old British Library reading room. These designs give the exhibition designers a lot of latitude in layout, wall color, and lighting.

But that split between public circulation space and exhibition space was not present in this museum. It could not be: the building was too small to devote much space to "circulation" where art would not be on display. The site was 40 feet wide and 100 feet long—only 4,000 square feet for a museum!—smaller than the minimum area required by law for a freestanding house in many American cities, and under twice the size of a historic lot (25' × 100') in most of Manhattan. So virtually all the space needed to be exhibition space. The Williams/Tsien architects' website calls the building "an idiosyncratic museum for idiosyncratic art," and one aspect of its idiosyncrasy was a very deft, efficient plan that did not make a strong distinction between major circulation space (centered with an open stair that itself is visible in most of the building, whose landing acts also as exhibition space), and gallery space, and that would recognize the potential importance of small display spaces which would help

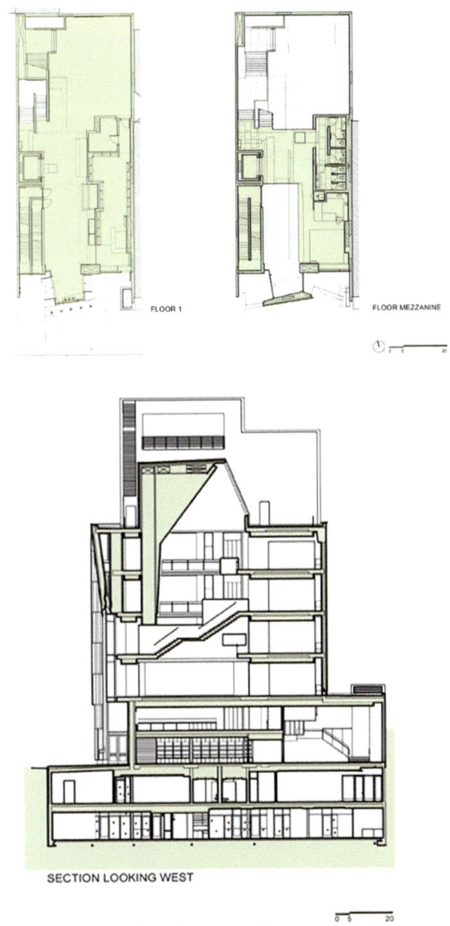

Section and plan drawings of museum. Courtesy Williams/Tsien Architects.

showcase the small, singular objects and paintings that are so characteristic of much folk art.

My experience of the building, beginning on my first visit, included the general sense of the building itself as a carefully crafted object—not a piece of folk art, but certainly not a typical art museum with what often seem to be acres of undifferentiated white walls acting as a *tabula rasa* for the curator or exhibition designer. Instead, the building was crafted so that every square inch was considered, and the objects on display, put there by skillful exhibition designers, seemed to have places in the building made just for them, but at the same time not detracting from the attention the visitor could give them.

It turned out that neutral white walls were not necessary, and that in fact, a more "crafted" surrounding for the art might have helped suggest the non-neutral surroundings of the art when it was first made or displayed—much of it in earlier times. Indeed, the architecture of this museum could have acted as a model for others, raising the more general critical question of the nature of the immediate space within which works of art may be displayed.[1] Likewise, the façade of the building, made up of sand-cast metal panels, all individual and different, added to the sense of human hands in the making of the building—contemporary folk art.

But this story does not have a happy ending. Every ten years or so, the Museum of Modern Art expands after swallowing up a little more of the island of Manhattan. And in 2014, in only its thirteenth year, the American Folk Art Museum was in the path of one of these expansions, and was demolished to make way for another incarnation of MoMA.

[1] The first paper on architecture I ever wrote, done in high school, concerned reactions by art and architecture critics and museum curators to the newly opened Guggenheim Museum in New York. If I remember correctly, I reported—based on articles in newspapers and magazines—that the consensus was largely negative—the exhibition space was not neutral enough. But this was before decades of exhibitions in the museum, some of which took advantage of the helical circulation system and the central space. This included, for example, an exhibition in 2011 of the Italian artist Maurizio Cattelan, all of whose work was on a single structure hanging from the roof dome.

ARNADOS, TINOS, GREECE

Modern additions to the traditional vernacular

ONE FOCUS of many of my trips has been buildings, neighborhoods, and settlements that fit a definition of vernacular building that excludes modern construction techniques. They are built with "traditional" techniques involving hand craft, minimally-processed local materials, and buildings that I imagined could have been built one or two hundred years ago. These were the kind of buildings written about by Bernard Rudofsky in *Architecture Without Architects*, or by Sibyl Moholy-Nagy in *Native Genius in Anonymous Architecture*. Looking at these buildings, my photographs deliberately avoided such symbols of modern life as television antennas, cars, car garage doors, factory-made windows and other building components, and anything made of concrete, including modern building additions. I wanted to keep things "pure" for my teaching, and frankly, I also found great charm and beauty in the older buildings.[1]

But at a certain point what I was photographing in the realm of the vernacular changed and expanded. This realization began in Greece, but it was something I came to notice in other places as well. In addition to the "pure" examples of the "traditional vernacular," I found myself photographing the kinds of things I had previously avoided—concrete frame and concrete block additions to stone buildings, dish antennas on buildings that were hundreds of years old, metal farm and utility buildings, contemporary metal details or metal windows that contrasted with old stone walls. Although it wasn't a conscious decision to do this—I usually just photographed what caught my eye—after some time I realized that I was also changing my own worldview about vernacular building. Although I had written about the relationship between contemporary and "traditional" buildings in *The Culture of Building*, I was now applying the idea to my own formulations and definition of vernacular building—appreciating the idea viscerally as well as intellectually.

1 In the early 1990s I joined a trip in rural Cambridgeshire for a few days, with a group of researchers who were members of the Vernacular Architecture Forum and who had extensive experience looking at eighteenth-century buildings in Virginia, around the Chesapeake and in New England. On this trip, they had little interest in looking at buildings of those time periods, regarding them as too new to warrant their attention as long as we were in England. So we spent a lot of time looking at fifteenth-century buildings—which were indeed quite wonderful.

Vernacular buildings in village of Arnados, island of Tinos, Greece. Each building has at least one modern component, change or addition.

What is the idea? It is the appreciation of people's actual lives rather than an idealization of what those lives might be, or an ideal past. A diary entry written by Le Corbusier is a perfect example of this idealization. It describes a walk up the hill in Istanbul, getting away from what he saw as the foul environment in Galata, "with its houses drawn together in a common stench":

> And then we climb and get away. We enter streets lined with cemeteries and tombs, and we find peace behind a fountain as beautiful as a temple, guarded by a cypress. We turn into little streets sectioned off by large wooden houses, or simple dwellings, connected one to another by high garden walls. Along the curve of the street we see nothing but two high walls, as pink as salmon meat. We are nevertheless perfectly happy, reflecting on the joyful life that goes on behind some fifty centimeters of brick and stone—a life of daydreaming in carefully sequestered gardens.[2]

Le Corbusier was himself dreaming: he had no idea of what was actually going on inside those gardens. He was connecting the visual sweetness of those vernacular buildings with an ideal of human happiness.

What I began to do was the opposite: not idealizing but appreciating the realities of people's lives and relationships to their buildings, and recognizing that the life of the built world includes those realities, which need to be respected.

And I began to see a beauty in the realities of modern construction and its relationship to daily life. The buildings were adaptable; they maintained the essence of their architectural organization as they were adapted; they were suitable for modern life. And it was great to see the informality and ease with which their owners seemed to be able to work as they made the changes and adaptations. There was no attempt to maintain or revive an image of the past within an easy-going relationship to the present. My photographs were still capturing a vernacular phenomenon—but a real one, and not the simulacrum of something that no longer existed.

[2] These quotes are from Le Corbusier's account of his trip to the Balkans in 1911, published as *The Journey to the East*.

2003

CANAL HOUSES, AMSTERDAM

The beauty of the pragmatic

Houses and buildings in Amsterdam.

THE VISUAL APPEAL of Amsterdam's historic core comes about for several reasons: its gridded street system that combines canals and paved streets in the half-circle that encompasses the central part of the city developed in the seventeenth-century; the use of brick as the primary material of its façades, both on public buildings and individual houses; the large windows on small houses; and the repetitive order of the domestic façades. I have appreciated that beauty on only a small number of visits—but my times there have always left me with an attraction to the city and its buildings. Indeed, the last day of my most recent visit was, for some reason, emotionally wrought: that historic core, with its combination of water, trees, and brick, is strikingly beautiful, bringing together architectural dignity and human scale. I remember my last chilly, rainy walk along the Prinsengracht (the outermost of the three major concentric canals) as being particularly melancholy, as I was about to leave a place for which I had developed a strong affection.

Houses and buildings in Amsterdam.

The uniqueness of Amsterdam starts with its brick. The soil of the Netherlands has a high clay content, suitable for firing into brick. And indeed, the vernacular row houses of the seventeenth century, through the "Amsterdam School" buildings of Berlage and de Klerk in the early twentieth century, to some of the modern buildings of firms like Mecanoo and Architectenbureau Marlies Rohmer are all brick—giving those buildings a material consistency that helps unify the city itself.

A unique aspect of the historic canal-house façade is the relationship between area of window and area of wall. That proportion is larger than often seen in brick buildings, in which the expanse and solidity of the wall are often emphasized, and the window seen as an opening that is relatively small with respect to the solid wall around it. This is different: in these houses the window area is large—consistent with the large windows that are often seen, even in modern Dutch buildings, that allow for a strong visual connection between inside and outside. Sometimes the area of wall between windows almost seems like that of a curtain wall, emphasizing the opening and de-emphasizing the load-bearing function of the wall. Bringing a lot of daylight into the building seems important here—but the brick is still there.

The canal-house façades may also tell a lot about the buildings' organization. Sometimes they have two adjacent doors, indicating one entrance to a staircase and one entrance to the ground floor—suggesting that there may have been an independent dwelling or business unit on the ground floor. There may be a short staircase leading down to a basement. Houses located on a corner, at the end of a row, may have a door in the middle of the exposed long side—perhaps indicating a slightly different floor plan and giving a point of emphasis on the façade itself.

In the end it is not any one of these attributes by itself that leads to the beauty of the old city, but the many of them complementing each other: the almost military repetition of the façades of similar width, all made of brick, glass, and wood painted white, contrasting with the green softness of the trees and reflected in the still or rippling water; the large width of the canals with footpaths along their edges, contrasting with the narrow pedestrian streets that meet the canals at right angles; different gables and ornamental details, indicating different times of construction, on buildings that have retained their width and overall organization through several decades of stylistic changes.

And within that "picturesque" order, there is a powerful architectural pragmatism that is the most powerful attribute of all. This pragmatism includes opening the buildings up to light as much as possible, very steep stairs that save floor space, the narrow building lots that have been retained and that have allowed for multiple ownership and occupancy, the ground floor easily transformed into a shop, often metal hooks in the gables used to bring furniture and goods up into the house, in lieu of the narrow internal stairs.[1]

So this is the architecture of the ordinary—and ultimately the characteristic that has stayed with me. The houses and canals were built for purely functional and economic reasons, but within culturally-shared understandings that helped lead to their similarities. And the ordinary turns out to be beautiful, even as uses have changed over 400 years.

1 The canals were originally built for commerce, and many of the houses were also used as warehouses and workshops. Those commercial and manufacturing functions declined, with the canal houses becoming increasingly residential and institutional.

SEVENTEENTH-CENTURY HOUSE INTERIORS, THE NETHERLANDS

Connections of space and light

EVEN BEFORE I studied architecture, I had a particular architectural idea in my imagination. It included my workplace with a desk, arranged in a way that allowed me to have a longer view than just a wall at the back of the desk. I wanted to be able to see farther than the desk itself, to be able to look up from my work to see another room, extending my view outward. This idea returned in the encounters described here.

I visited the Netherlands for the second time in 2003 in connection with research for *Living Over the Store*. On that visit, I spoke to historians at the Hendrick de Keyser Association, an Amsterdam-based research and architectural conservation organization. They guided me to seventeenth-century buildings in Amsterdam and Dordrecht, and later, I also began to look at

"The Bedroom." Painting: Pieter de Hooch. National Gallery of Art, Washington.

"Woman with a Child in a Pantry." Painting: Pieter de Hooch, Rijksmuseum, Amsterdam.

paintings by Vermeer and another seventeenth-century artist, Pieter de Hooch. This reflection is based on encounters with both the buildings and the paintings.[1]

Many of the de Hooch paintings illustrate the settings of domestic life. They show the continuity of architectural space, and the ways in which room adjacencies are emphasized and used to reinforce views, take maximum advantage of daylight, and lead the eye from room to room. In a book about the paintings of de Hooch, Peter C. Sutton elaborates on this idea:

> No other artist has ever equaled De Hooch's achievement in the evocation of the contiguity of indoor and outdoor space. Despite their rigorous order, his interiors are never confining. As the walls promise shelter, so the doors and "doorkijkjes" connote release.[2]

In de Hooch's "The Bedroom," the doorway and glazed window adjacent to the doorway are on axis with an outer window

[1] This is a different kind of encounter. It was actually seeing the de Hooch paintings for the first time that reminded me of my experience with the buildings, and particularly the ways in which each small room could be opened to the next, taking maximum advantage of daylight.

[2] Peter C. Sutton, *Pieter De Hooch*, p. 19.

in the front wall of the house, in the next room. This is the case even though there is a window in the wall of the room itself that brings in daylight. The sleeping alcove, on the right side of the painting, is dark and not directly opposite any of the openings. The painting shows four spaces: the bedroom itself, the sleeping alcove, the room between the bedroom and the outside, and the outside space in front of the house. His painting "The Pantry" is similar, except that both of the adjacent rooms have windows on their far walls, taking the viewers' eyes to other spaces beyond.

[3] Seventeenth-century Dutch paintings did not only illustrate domestic life. The book by Linda Stone-Ferrier, *The Little Street: The Neighborhood in Seventeenth-Century Dutch Art and Culture*, shows how the life of neighborhoods was also illustrated in paintings.

Plan of historic house at Dordrecht.

This idea is illustrated in the plan of a long, narrow house in Dordrecht. Although the rooms are all accessed from a common corridor, interior windows connect them to each other, providing a similar sequence of spaces as that seen in the de Hooch paintings.[3]

There are several related ideas suggested here. One is the idea of continuous space: that there is something beyond the immediate room. Second is that of multiple sources of daylight, which might enter a room directly from a window to the outdoors as well as from an adjacent room that itself is directly connected to the outdoors. And the third is the idea of a sequence, or chain of rooms, and the possibility of moving directly from room to room rather than through (or in addition to) a corridor.

HD house, view from study through interior window to living room.

In the design of my own house in Oregon, built in 1990, I developed two spatial sequences, in addition to connecting doors—finally providing for myself the "real thing" that I had imagined many years before.

TOWN HALL, HILVERSUM, THE NETHERLANDS

Ambiguity and order

DESIGNED BY Willem Marinus Dudok and completed in 1931, the town hall in Hilversum, the Netherlands, is an important work in that school of architectural modernism that attempted to retain traditional ideas of architectural ordering and composition while at the same time introducing modernist ideas of space, materials, construction, and ornament.

I visited the building in 2003, during a two-week stay in Amsterdam. I had been introduced to Dudok's work by a colleague on the Oregon faculty, and took advantage of my time in the Netherlands to take the short trip to Hilversum to see the building. On seeing and entering it for the first time, I was immediately comfortable, with a feeling of lightness and informality. Even as a stranger

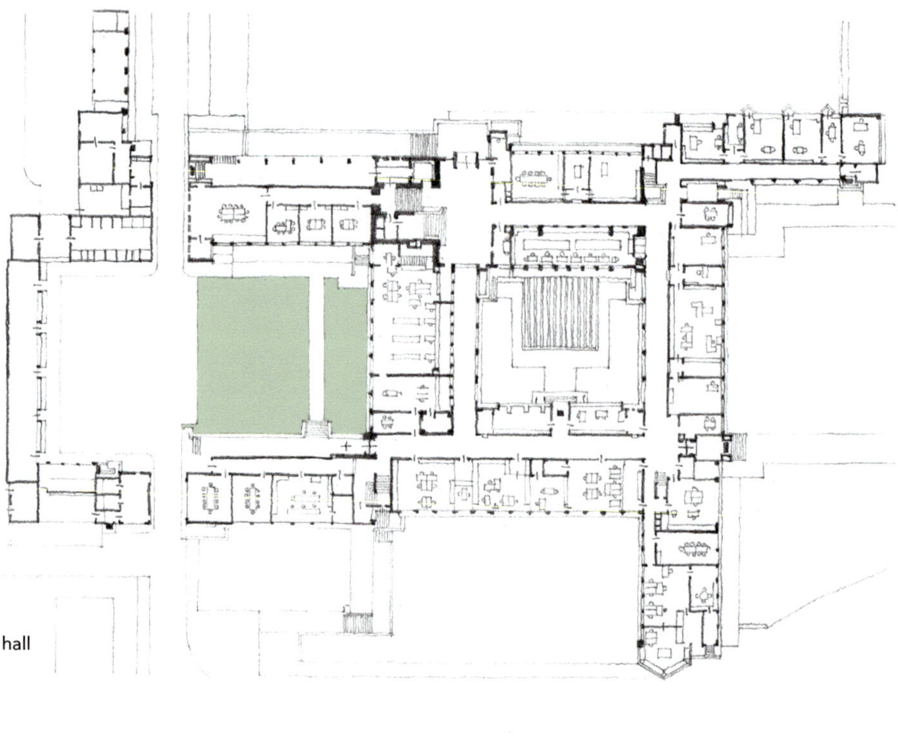

Plan of Hilversum town hall ground floor.

Views of Hilversum town hall. The corridor described below is seen in the central picture on the bottom of the photo array.

I felt welcomed, able to just enter and walk through it. It had none of the heaviness or formality that institutional or governmental buildings often have. It was made for ordinary people.

The town hall is a courtyard building, organized around a large, square, roofed central space, and with building wings partly surrounding an adjacent, open courtyard space. The entrance led me directly to an edge of the covered square space, after passing through a vestibule with the foot of a main stair leading to the second floor. It is a classic plan, giving the building a strong center, clear circulation, and the potential for good daylight. The spatial order of the building is familiar, logical, and efficient. It uses a known type as a starting point (rooms arranged around a courtyard and a large interior space) and organizes the program elements according to that type. On the other hand, it is a modern building, with ornament that does not make historical references, and with kinds of spatial continuities and ambiguities that tend not to exist in pre-twentieth-century buildings.

I was particularly struck by the corridor along the edge of the community hall on the upper floor. A colonnade, made of relatively thin columns, forms a clear boundary between the room and the corridor. But at the same time, that boundary is not a wall. The space of the community hall continues to the wall of the corridor, allowing people walking in the corridor to be seen by and interact with people in the community hall. The corridor has an almost continuous row of benches along that wall. And finally, the floor itself straddles the boundary of the colonnade, helping to make an ambiguous zone between the two spaces. The openness, the spatial ambiguity, the metal columns—all of these are modernist ideas, used in this case to help make the hybrid between traditional and modernist ideas of building.

My affinity for these buildings can be traced back to the differing ideas that I was trying to reconcile, beginning in architecture school. I appreciated the twentieth-century architecture that had been the basis of education and practice of many of our teachers; I appreciated the work of Chris Alexander, who was developing understandings of how buildings could maintain important relevance to everyday life; and I appreciated the work of many architects of the Bay Area school, ranging from that of Maybeck and John Galen Howard to that of Wurster and Joe Esherick, all of whom stayed clear of the International Style but were trying in their own ways to reconcile modernism with place. I saw the work of people like Otto Wagner in Vienna, Gunnar Asplund in Sweden, and Willem Dudok in the Netherlands, who were popularly fit into different "schools," as all helping to build a helpful bridge between different architectural epochs. Seventy years after its construction, the town hall felt like a human and welcoming place, with lightness and spatial continuities, strongly fitting into these intentions.

ARTISTS' HOUSES AND STUDIOS, HAMMERSMITH, LONDON

Light at the top

St. Paul's Studios, Hammersmith, London. Photo: Frances Holliss.

UNTIL 1998, when the Heathrow Express train connection between the airport and Paddington Station began operation, I traveled between Heathrow and central London by bus or coach. On one trip, near the eastern end of the Hammersmith Flyover, I was looking out the window, toward the south, when the quickly-moving bus passed a row of houses that caught my eye as being quite different from the endless Victorian terraced houses that are all over London. I was immediately attracted to them because of their unusual big windows on their upper floors. But they came and went very fast. After a few more quick sightings like that, I learned that those buildings were well-known artists' houses built in the 1890s. And finally I went to look at them on foot.

Like many English houses, these are party-wall, terraced houses, with a basement, ground, and first floors. The main floor is two rooms deep. The dwelling functions are split between the

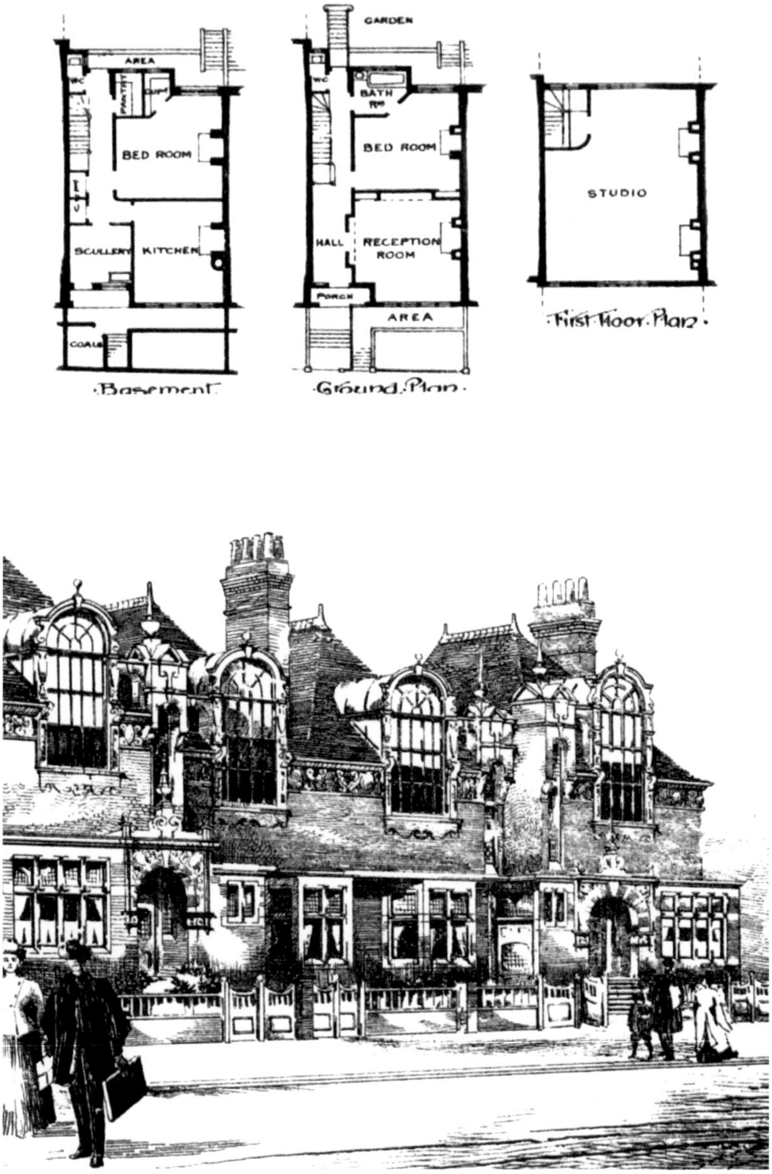

Early drawing of St. Paul's Studios showing floor plans. Illustration: *The Building News & Engineering Journal*, vol. 60, no. 1 (1891), p. 401. Public domain.

basement and ground floor, with the kitchen and a bedroom on the basement level, and the living room and another bedroom on the ground floor. The studio occupied the entire first (upper) floor, largely within the hipped roof and with the large north-facing window on the front of the building. A second, narrow vertical window in the studio, also on the front façade, allowed for large canvases to be brought in and out. An area to the south of the basement bedroom allowed light to be brought into that room.

Why was I attracted to these buildings? They were, first of all, designed for both living and work. They are similar to the houses by Philip Webb (see p. 282), built as dwellings and workshops, but with the "workshops" on the upper rather than the ground floor. But more specifically, the large, north-facing upper-floor windows, lighting the studios that are just under the roofs, strongly contrast with the more typical and expected ground-floor window and doorway. I appreciated that contrast between the size and industrial nature of the studio windows and the load-bearing-wall and smaller windows below. Here, modern construction techniques exist in contrast to older architectural ideas.

Ozenfant House, Paris, designed by Le Corbusier. Photo: Pierre Jeanneret © 2025 Artists Rights Society (ARS), New York / ADAGP, Paris.

The composition of the façade combines symmetry and functional pragmatism. The studio window, facing north, is centered on the façade as whole, on axis with the ridge of the roof; each of the sides of the large window is the same distance from its side wall. But the brick walls on either side are different widths, because of the narrow vertical window, making the big window seem off center. And like in many small, terraced houses in London, there is a lack of alignment between the windows on the ground floor and those on the first floor.

The studio window is dominant enough on the façade to hold its own in the context of those mismatches and discontinuities. It emphasizes that the principal purpose of the building is its studio and not the domestic functions below.

And the studio takes full advantage of its top-floor position. It has a taller ceiling, that spans the width of the building providing as much space as possible. Its large window, the glazed top of which projects slightly from a slanted gable end, brings in plenty of light. The buildings are like Le Corbusier's Ozenfant house and studio in Paris, built about 25 years later. The studio in that building also takes advantage of its top-floor position, but perhaps even more strongly as the studio takes advantage of the light from two large windows that meet a horizontal skylight at a corner.

These buildings, that I originally saw as a quick blur from a coach, combine the very typical organization of the London party-wall, terraced house with large studio windows on the upper floors, that draw one's attention to them immediately. Those windows, with their distinctive round tops that project slightly from slanted gable ends, say everything. These are not typical Victorian terraced houses, but places filled with daylight, that use their prominent glazing to begin to connect the observer with the idea that inside, something other than ordinary domestic functions is taking place.

SEABIRD ISLAND SCHOOL, AGASSIZ, BRITISH COLUMBIA, CANADA

Anchoring a native community

Sq'éwqel Community School, building and mountains. Photo: Patkau Architects.

IN 2004 I made a visit to Vancouver to carry out interviews with architecture firms in connection with research for *Living Over the Store*, still in its beginning stages. But there were some other buildings that I was also interested in seeing. I had known about the architects Patricia and John Patkau's school project for a community of First Nations people in the region, about an hour's drive east of Vancouver.[1] I was familiar with the architectural design and siting of the building, but also wanted to see it in the context that had apparently influenced the design very much. Getting there was an easy drive on a sunny summer day.

My visit supported and reinforced the reasons I was attracted to the school in the first place. The building, with a prominent set of roofs, formed the northern edge of a large, open space,[2] with mountains behind it, to the north. Other buildings around the space were much simpler, often with basic walls of corrugated metal, plywood, or concrete block. In the far distance, to the north of the building, were strongly-profiled mountains. Visually, the

1 The school is now known as the Sq'éwqel Community School.

2 I have not been back to the school since my 2004 visit, but the current (January 2024) Google aerial view shows a building parallel to and south of the school at a distance of about one-quarter of the site's long dimension. This essay is based on what I saw and felt in 2004.

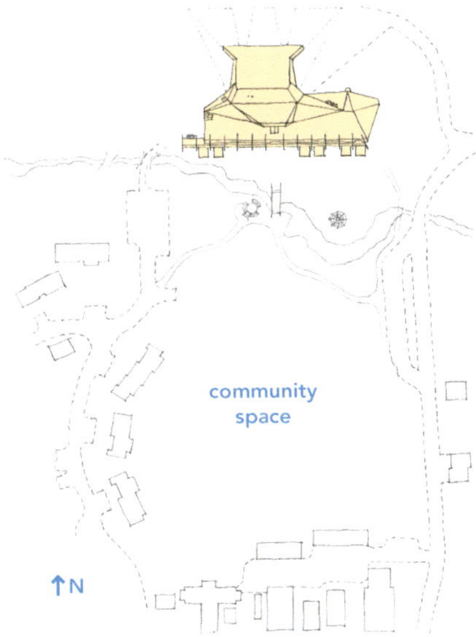

Sq'éwqel Community School (formerly called Seabird Island School) site plan showing building at north of large community space.

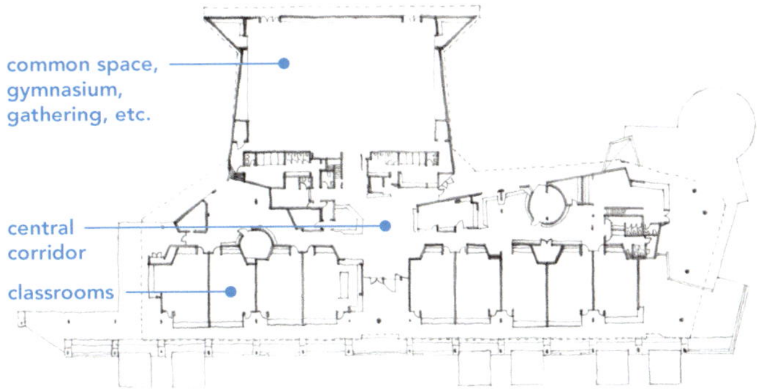

Sq'éwqel Community School, plan. Courtesy Patkau Architects.

building strongly connected to its place with both "ordinary" buildings as well as a rather spectacular natural backdrop.

There are three features of the building's design and construction that have attracted me.

First is the overall setting, and particularly the relationship of the building to the mountains. The topography of the immediate area is flat and there are no high buildings nearby, so the mountains to the north and east are prominent, and seem as if they are strongly connected to the site, even though they are miles away.[3] The bold massing of the building, and particularly the huge roof over the large room that acts as a gymnasium and a room for varied common activities, helps also to anchor its connection to the past and reinforces, with architecture, the continuity of the local culture over long periods of time. That very-large roof is critical, but its position allows the south-facing classrooms to also be visible from the large community outdoor space.

Second is the role of the building as the primary structure in the large open space that forms the center of the community. Thinking about the program for the school, it is a modest institution, that in another place might be one of several public or community facilities. Here it has pride of place—at the head of the open space, with the principal façade of the building facing

[3] The reflection in this book on the Entsu-ji Temple in Kyoto (pp. 143–144) discusses the idea of the "borrowed landscape," or in Japanese, *shakkei*. The mountains discussed here help form such a relationship in the landscape.

that open space (and thereby also providing sunlight to all the classrooms), and through that location and its design, supporting the idea of the importance of education to the future of the community.

And third is the fact that the school was built with local construction labor, much of it from the community itself, solidifying the school's ownership by the community, and strengthening, in another way, the unity of the community, the school, and the landscape in which they exist.

Now in 2024, about a quarter century after the construction of the school, "indigenous architecture" is gaining in importance, and this school is in many ways an early exemplar of that movement. My own continued reaction to this building only partly comes from what can be seen of its physical relationship to its landscape, but also from the knowledge of the meaning of that landscape to the people who have inhabited it for centuries, their continued connection to it, and how the building may help reinforce that connection.

SCOTTISH POETRY LIBRARY, EDINBURGH

Connecting to the geology of a place

Scottish Poetry Library looking toward Arthur's Seat. Photo: Keith Hunter, with thanks to Malcolm Fraser.

IN 1983 I spent a term teaching design in the architecture department at Edinburgh University. My studio consisted of about a dozen or so good-natured and talented fourth-year students, who fortunately were intellectually generous toward an instructor who was learning the history of Scottish housing design from them. One of my students was Malcolm Fraser, who eventually became one of Scotland's leading architects, and who has remained a good friend. Malcolm draws beautifully, kept a sketchbook filled with diagrams, sketches, colors, words, facts, and ideas, and most importantly, loves Scotland and Edinburgh, the city where he was born and grew up. He committed himself to designing buildings for Edinburgh, and took pride in a map that showed how close his projects were to his office, which itself was in the center of the city, just steps from the main railroad terminal, Waverley Station.

When I visited Edinburgh in 2004, Malcolm took me to see the Scottish Poetry Library, a small new building he had designed a few years before. Such a "guided visit" was unusual: I visited most of the buildings and places mentioned in this book without accompaniment by their architect. But nevertheless, my reaction to this building was strong: what inspired me was that the building is a powerful example of how architecture and place can fuse together.

This building recognizes and supports Scotland's strong oral tradition of storytelling[1] and poetry, through its program, contents, and its architecture: particularly the way it relates to the city and landscape. The building is on a narrow street that visually connects the Royal Mile with Holyrood Park and the outcropping that includes Arthur's Seat, important in the identity—and geology—of Scotland and Edinburgh. This connection is reinforced by the façade of the building, which features an outdoor staircase, facing a lectern, that was used for poetry readings—an important function of the building, which was not only a repository of books and pamphlets. The idea was to keep the tradition of Scottish poetry alive, by bringing it out to the street in a way that visually links the heart of the city with the distinctive geography of the landscape in which the city is located.

When Malcolm talks about Scottish towns and Scottish architecture, he begins with the millions-of-years-old geology of Scotland, and never lets that get too far from his explanations. But that connection to geology also happened through Scottish poetry itself, at least in one instance. The Scottish Poetry Library's website includes some important poems, sometimes interpreted. For example, Robert Burns' poem "The red, red rose" includes two verses about how long love will last:

As fair are thou, my bonie lass,
So deep in luve am I;
And I will luve thee still, my Dear,
Till a' the seas gang dry.

Till a' the seas gang dry, my Dear,
And the rocks melt wi' the sun:
I will luve thee still, my dear,
While the sands o' life shall run.

[1] Based on the success of this building, Malcolm later designed the Scottish Storytelling Centre, also near the center of Edinburgh.

And on the website, the poem is followed with a geological analysis by the contemporary poet Colin Will:

> My second reaction to the poem is rooted in my geological training. The lines about all the seas going dry, and rocks melting with the sun, suggest to me that Burns must have had a grasp of what we now call 'deep time', of an almost infinite length of time through which his love, and the world, would last. Yet geology as a science was brand new at the time Burns was writing; this is a very modern poem. And where was his inspiration? I submit that he got these ideas either directly from James Hutton, the Berwickshire farmer sometimes called the 'Father of Modern Geology', or from Hutton's friend Sir James Hall of Dunglass. The two men in a boat discovered the famous unconformity of Siccar Point, near where I live, where an ocean going dry formed a sandstone which was eroded and folded upright, then overlain after an unimaginable interval by another ocean, which also ran dry. Hutton and Hall were among the distinguished men and women of Edinburgh society we know Burns met during his time in the city.
>
> COLIN WILL,
> *writing on the Scottish Poetry Library website,*
> *https://www.scottishpoetrylibrary.org.uk/poem/red-red-rose/*
> *(accessed Jan. 14, 2024)*

This bringing together of poetry and geology, and of the distant past with the time of Robert Burns in the eighteenth century, may also be useful to an approach to architecture that is anchored in place and history. But this is not always the responsibility of the architect to undertake alone. In this case, writing a brief for a library of Scottish poetry is itself an act of suggestion, which could lead to a useful synthesis of place, history, and building. Malcolm Fraser's design represented one version of such a synthesis.

Torino, Italy

Lisbon

Left to right:
Vicenza, Italy
Porto, Portugal
London

PART SIX
2006–2014

During these years, I finished *Living Over the Store* and began new research in Guangzhou and London, concerned with urban districts and the ability of people at lower rungs of the economic ladder to make their way in the urban economy. This work contributed to another book, *Working Cities: Architecture, Place and Production*. A byproduct of the work in London was learning about Gillett Square, a new public space that was developed over 20 years, that brought together people of all means, in a place that included small vendors' spaces, rooms for the use of local community groups and organizations, a jazz club, and a large space for daily use as a public square as well as performances of all kind. In Hamburg, I first encountered the "stolpersteine," stumbling stones, that are a remarkable way of memorializing people who were deported and killed during the Holocaust.

Several of the reflections here were written on the basis of encounters that occurred after several visits to a particular place that had remained more or less the same over the years. My visit to Chartres in 2014 was different: until I entered the building then, I was unaware of the cathedral's cleaning and restoration of its original colors and luminosity.

Left to right:
Venice
Porto, Portugal
Vicenza, Italy

2006

EQUITABLE BUILDING, PORTLAND

A well-composed modern façade

Equitable Building among Portland buildings. Photo: SW 6th Ave. looking towards SW Oak St. The Equitable Building is the modern building on the right, about two blocks in front of the camera. Portland City Archives, AP/28280.

SINCE I MOVED to Oregon, I have spent a lot of time in Portland, its largest city, particularly in more recent years when I lived there for several months each year while teaching. The Equitable Building (built in 1948 and now named the Commonwealth Building) is commonly recognized as one of the first modern glazed, tall buildings built in the United States after the Second World War.

In years when I was more focused on smaller, vernacular buildings, I didn't pay much attention to the building, but at a certain point, I remember looking at it carefully for the first time, and began to appreciate it quite a bit. I liked the geometric order of the façade, and realized the care that had been put into its design—more complex and pleasing than many façades of contemporary high-rise buildings constructed around or after the same time.

Pietro Belluschi, the architect of the building, took particular care with the two-dimensional organization of the façade.

Equitable Building, Portland.
Photo: Peter Keyes.

Equitable Building façade.
Photo: Peter Keyes.

There are three kinds of horizontal elements on the façade: the aluminum cladding of the concrete, the large glass panes, and the dark cast aluminum spandrels between the glass and the horizontal elements of the aluminum cladding. Although Belluschi wanted the façade to only show the glass and the concrete cladding as an expression of the frame, the spandrels, four inches thick, were required by the fire code. But they turned out to play an important role in the design. By giving the modules of each of the elements different lengths, the spandrels have a different rhythm from the glass windows above them and the cladding covering the concrete below. There is also a difference in the dimension of modules between the short and long façades of the building. And the dark color of the spandrels still allows an emphasis on the structural frame.

These ideas allowed Belluschi to make the façade more lively and appealing than it would have been if the horizontal dimensions of all three elements had been the same, without differences between the adjacent short and long façades. The façade thereby avoids the monotony of square or rectangular grids that sometimes characterize contemporary curtain-wall buildings, or other buildings like this one with flat façades. The architectural historian Meredith Clausen wrote that "It was this sense of visual order-[Belluschi's] classic sense of balanced scale, rhythmic harmony, and carefully measured proportions-coupled with rigorous rationality that gave the building its timeless quality."[1]

That simple attention to the two-dimensional composition, the need for which was initially prompted by a building code requirement, is successful. The difference in color between the three different materials, along with the carefully designed difference in dimension and alignment, give the façade a sense of resolution along with a liveliness that it might not otherwise have.

1 Meredith Clausen, "Belluschi and the Equitable Building in History."

ST. MARK'S CHURCH, BJORKHAGEN, STOCKHOLM

Lewerentz's modern modesty

THERE ARE OVER a dozen churches and religious buildings that are the focus of the reflections in this book, and a few others that while not churches themselves, are connected to religious institutions through adjacency or affiliation of some kind. Churches, cathedrals, mosques, temples, monasteries, and other places for contemplation, prayer, and connection with the divine have long been central to the study and understanding of architecture. They have given architects and builders the opportunity for innovation in design and construction; they may occupy central places in cities and towns; they are often singular and clear in their basic spatial order and its relationships to liturgy; and they provide opportunities for often dramatic spatial features.

Church interior, main sanctuary. Photo: Sébastien Corbari.

I have been to Stockholm two or three times; once in 2006 when I was there for the meeting of the International Seminar on Urban Form. I had heard about the work of the architect Sigurd Lewerentz, so I took the opportunity to take the short tram ride out to Bjorkhagen to see his important project there, St. Mark's Church.

Many of the religious buildings in this book have some feature that left me spellbound: the angelic lighting at the church at Vantaa in Finland; the complex spatial order given to the church of Santa Prassede in Rome by the straightforward structural additions in the thirteenth century that kept the building from collapsing; the powerfully beautiful landscape at the Ise Shrine in Japan that has been developing for 1,200 years; the simple strategies for colored light at St. Ignatius Chapel in Seattle, designed by Steven Holl.

This building is different, but strikingly beautiful and memorable in its own way. It does not have the emotional intensity of many of the other religious buildings. What I found were two things: modesty of approach to architectural space, and an emphasis on the architectural materials themselves as expressions of the visual order of the building.

The church is composed of two long, low-slung buildings, one containing the main sanctuary and related spaces, and the other offices. They are separated from each other by a long, linear outdoor space, that I found to be quite relaxed in feeling without a strong sense of symmetry or symbolism that would suggest the formality of a church. It was a welcoming space, not intimidating, not putting any burdens on its guest.

But what affected me the most was the brickwork, inside and out, particularly the exaggerated mortar joints and seeming

Church exterior emphasizing outdoor space between buildings.

Church exterior emphasizing entrance.

informality of the details of the brick coursing. Lewerentz himself spoke to this informality. The chairman of the building committee, Nils Roth, reported that "One day the architect was discussing a task with a tile-setter, who maintained that if he did it as Lewerentz wanted, he wouldn't 'get it straight.'" Lewerentz responded: "Straight, straight. Why does everything have to be straight? It can be beautiful even if it's crooked." [1]

The "crookedness" and informality of the brickwork, combined with the low scale and asymmetries of the building's composition, seemed to me to be an important expression of the architect—and his understanding of the possibility that a building like a church could be an everyday building, supporting everyday life at the same time as being a place for contemplation and prayer. In the words of Janne Ahlin:

> Windows are located near the floor in the nave, an exception being the asymmetrical opening near the vault at the rear section of the southern wall, through which during the summer months a beautiful beam of light is directed to the altar. The low windows frame the trunks of the birch trees outside, forming lovely pictures for the space within; from time to time, someone passes by: a dog nosing around at the window, a few children dancing around their mother's shopping bags. With the passing of the seasons, the background to these spontaneous happenings changes, and enlivens the ritual of the service.[2]

[1] Janne Ahlin, *Sigurd Lewerentz, Architect: 1885–1975*, p. 155.

[2] Ahlin, p. 159.

CANTONAL LIBRARY OF TICINO, LUGANO, SWITZERLAND

Modernism and human comfort

Cantonal Library of Ticino. The main book stacks are on the left and the main reading rooms are behind the columns on the right. Photo: Ryan Arreola.

LUGANO is the largest city in the Italian-speaking Swiss canton of Ticino, and the location of this building, designed by the architect Rino Tami in the late 1930s and completed in 1940. I have visited it twice: once in 1989 with friends who then had a house in Lugano; and again in about 2013 as part of a four-day excursion with our architecture student group based in Vicenza.

The building is in a park that is right on Lake Lugano. The strong concrete form of the building helps connect it to a view of the rugged Alps. But it is really the building itself, and the experience of being in it, that have attracted me to it. It is an exemplar of the humanistic side of modern architecture.

The building is "L"-shaped, on three floors. The ground floor is largely below ground, allowing the main (second) floor to have only about eight steps up from the entrance door, making the main reading room on that floor the building's architectural and human

Main reading room of Cantonal Library of Ticino. Photo: Ryan Arreola.

Façade showing main reading room with outdoor terrace on right. Photo: Ryan Arreola.

center. That large room has a window wall that faces the park and the lake beyond. An outdoor terrace is accessible at the south end of the room. The north wing of the building is for bookstacks and storage; it has daylight that enters through a screen-like wall, but otherwise blank walls that contrast with the more open walls of the north–south wing.

It is a straightforward plan that gives clear precedence, in siting and design, to the students and others who use the building for research and writing. Being in the building, it seemed like a place I would like to work: good daylight, a room with a beautiful view that itself evokes peace and quiet, a clear and simple overall plan efficiently organized.

Hallway in building. Photo: Yash Akhouri.

Detail of main reading room. Photo: Ryan Arreola.

And the details have been carefully thought about as well; the height of the windowsills, the wood where hands can reach it, the hint of ornament where the ceiling meets the window wall, the depth of the west wall, including the railing, the round columns, the window wall itself—all of these things add up, in the main reading room, to a sense of being anchored in a comfortable place.

This adds up to two aspects of this building that work together in my appreciation of it.

First, as a work of modern architecture, it is expressive of frame, structure, and materials; it has clean and simple lines with a minimum of applied ornament. Views and access to daylight were clearly major factors in its design.

But second, at the same time, it does not reject the spatial order of older buildings, particularly the spatial hierarchy/scale relationships of façades and the subdivision of interior spaces. Rooms of different sizes are well and simply formed.

The result of the application of these attributes to the building's design makes it a comfortable place to visit and work. The interior space is soft and calm; the placement of work tables and chairs seems like a logical elaboration of the plan; daylight and views are naturally provided.

The building has a quiet, settled confidence, representing a "situated modernism" where it is strongly tied to its place. The building does not exist for its own sake, but to support and serve the ordinary life of students, scholars, and researchers. It is remarkable that the building is 85 years old (in 2025)—in this case its modernism seems to have worn well.

2009

COMMERCIAL EXTENSIONS TO HOUSES, LONDON

Pragmatic urbanism

BEGINNING IN 1992, I often stayed with friends in Peckham, south London, whose house was convenient to many bus lines that go to the city center. Sitting at the front of the upper deck of the bus, I became aware of the commercial extensions to terraced houses on the major streets that the buses use. Construction of these extensions began at least as far back as the middle of the nineteenth century, and their construction continued into the twentieth century. Many were built onto the fronts of houses that originally had gardens between the front façade and the street. Riding on the top deck of a bus, ones' eyes are just high enough to have a glancing view of the roofs of these extensions.

Commercial extensions in London. Photo at lower right of Kentish Town Road by Matt Brown.

The extensions are almost always one story high, the full width of the site, with their length varying from just a few feet to 20 feet or more. Their flat roofs allow daylight to enter the front rooms on the first floor (the floor above the ground floor). In many cases the shop extends back into the original house—the shop would have obscured daylight in the original front room. There are often two doors: one in the center, leading into the shop, and one at a party wall, leading to a passage into the house behind, through the original door opening. Unlike New York brownstones built after the Federal period around the beginning of the nineteenth century, the ground floor of London terraced houses remained at the level of the street or one or two steps above—making it straightforward to align the level of the passage and the new shop with that of the ground floor of the existing house.

As London was growing rapidly, it is likely that the front extensions were added when the streets became busy enough to support commercial activity, and built by contractors who may have done either one shop or several adjacent shops at a time.

These commercial extensions are ubiquitous in London; part of the ordinary urban fabric that people experience every day. They interested me as a completely pragmatic, visible representation of making the most out of a piece of urban land, a natural response to the changing land values that come from streets carrying more traffic. They represent yet another way through which the row (terraced) house can transform—not only with the flexibility of the interior, or with the clever ways back extensions add interior space, but by obscuring the one wall that was arguably the most important in showing status—the front façade.

These commercial extensions are found all over London, and help give the city a particular character that is quite different from other cities, like Paris or Vienna, which also combine commercial and residential uses in the same street. In those cities the design of the building façade often incorporates commercial uses from the start, so is strong enough to accommodate shopfronts at the ground floor without destroying the overall architectural composition, and the buildings work together to make beautiful streets.

This is not necessarily the case with London. What is most characteristic of London is just its pragmatism, and the ways in which hundreds of thousands of individual decisions about building and the economy turn out to have their own order, unique to the city.

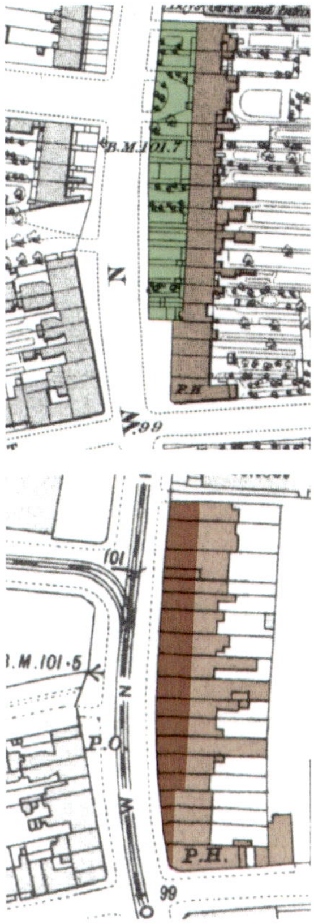

Ordnance Survey maps of a section of Kentish Town Road in London, indicating how front gardens became the sites of commercial extensions to houses. Top map 1870, bottom map 1913. The bottom map includes tram tracks in the middle of the street. Color added to original maps.

STOLPERSTEINE: HAMBURG AND OTHER EUROPEAN CITIES

Stumbling stones of memory

I FIRST CAME across a *Stolperstein*, or "stumbling stone" when I was walking in a neighborhood of Hamburg in 2010. The "*Stolpersteine*" are thousands of brass plaques set in pavements all over Europe, by the German artist Gunter Demnig. They are individually made, 10 cm × 10 cm (a little under 4" × 4"), fitted to stones, and permanently set into the pavement next to houses in cities in Germany and other European countries. Each commemorates a person who lived in the nearby house during the Second World War, and who was arrested, taken away, and likely murdered in a Nazi death camp.[1] Some of them memorialize people who fled and

[1] *Stolpersteine* are usually placed where the named people lived, but may also be installed at workplaces, schools, or other places where the people spent time.

Four stolpersteine outside house in Rome.

Stolpersteine in Vicenza, Italy. They read similarly. "Angela Caivano Orvieto lived in Vicenza; born 1893; arrested 1943; deported to Auschwitz; murdered 1944".

were later killed, or people whose fate was unknown. Sometimes there is just one of them in the pavement, sometimes several marking a number of unrelated people, sometimes an entire family.

Embossed into the metal are simple inscriptions, giving just a few facts. It usually begins with the words "HERE LIVED" and continues with the name of the person, their year of birth, the year they were arrested and taken away (or fled to escape), and finally the year, place, and means of death, if known.

Two adjacent *Stolpersteine* in Hamburg told the story of a married couple:

HIER WOHNTE	HIER WOHNTE	{ HERE LIVED
HEDWIG KRACAUER	ROSETTE KRACAUER	ROSETTE KRACAUER
GEB. OPPENHEIMER	GEB. OPPENHEIMER	BORN IN OPPENHEIMER
JG. 1862	JG. 1867	1867
DEPORTIERT 1942	DEPORTIERT 1942	DEPORTED 1942
THERESIENSTADT	THERESIENSTADT	TO THERESIENSTADT
ERMORDERT 26.9.1942	ERMORDERT 26.9.1942	MURDERED 26 SEPT. 1942
TREBLINKA	TREBLINKA	IN TREBLINKA }

In addition to the Auschwitz death camp, near Krakow, I have been to various museums and memorials that keep alive the memory of the atrocities of the Second World War: the Holocaust Museum in Washington, the Holocaust Memorial in Berlin, the Jewish Museum in Berlin, the Museum of the History of Polish Jews in Warsaw, Yad Vashem in Jerusalem, and several others. Each is powerful in its own way.

But apart from Auschwitz itself, for me the *Stolpersteine* are the most powerful memorial. My grandmother, whose mother was an immigrant from Poland, was born in New York in 1895. She was brought back to Warsaw by her mother in 1901 after her father died, and returned to New York in about 1912 with her new husband, leaving her mother behind in Poland. During the Second World War, the letters from her mother stopped coming, and it is likely that her mother, my great-grandmother, was murdered at Treblinka.

When I first saw the *Stolpersteine* on the pavement outside houses in Hamburg, I realized their importance as memorials and works of art: *this is where these people lived.* I subsequently saw them in other European cities, some more familiar, where they added another layer to my understanding of the city. The association of the murdered people with their houses, their streets, their places, gave a reality to the world that they inhabited and that was destroyed. This was very different from the world that might be evoked by photographs or artifacts. This was not an exhibit in a museum, but something with a palpable reality, part of everyday life. The *Stolpersteine* strongly emphasized the power of place itself in giving understanding to human history. They are tiny things—among the smallest described in this book—but they had a large role in the "sense of place" I experienced while in their presence. I stopped walking, immediately focused on the place and the lives—and deaths—of those who lived there.[2]

[2] Another artist, Ruth Sergel, developed a New York version of the *Stolpersteine* project. Every year, on the anniversary of the terrible Triangle Shirtwaist fire of 1911, in which 146 young, immigrant garment workers died when they jumped out of ninth-floor windows because the stairs were locked shut, the tragedy is commemorated in an organized act. People chalk the names, addresses, and cause of death of those who died in the fire on the pavement in front of the tenement buildings in which they lived, many of which are on the Lower East Side. See Ruth Sergel, *See You in the Streets: Art, Action and Remembering the Triangle Shirtwaist Fire.* I participated in this project, using a big piece of chalk, on a rainy day in March 2023.

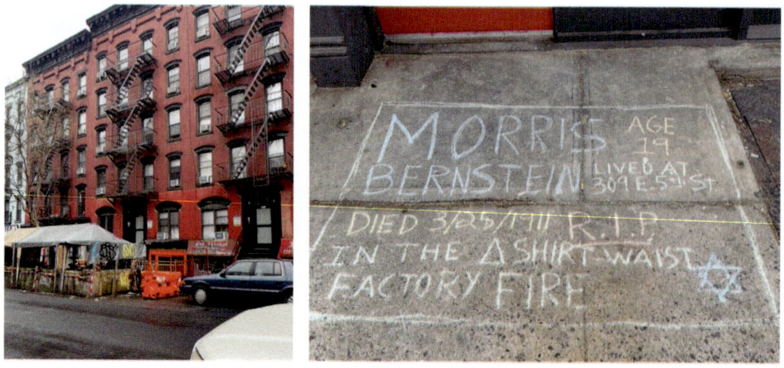

Inscription in chalk outside tenement building in Lower East Side, Manhattan.

HOUSING PROJECT, LINDENSTRASSE, BERLIN

Human scale in space and construction

Lindenstrasse housing.

I HAVE VISITED several projects of the Dutch architect Herman Hertzberger: the office building of the Centraal Beheer office building in Apeldoorn, the Vredenberg music center in Utrecht, and the Montessori and Willemspark Schools in Amsterdam. These projects are all, in one way or another, buildings of human scale, where structural and construction details were not hidden but expressed, and where explicit attention was given to the smallest details of human/neighborly interaction and privacy. On a visit to Hertzberger's housing project at Lindenstrasse in Berlin, I was immediately impressed by the livability of the building, expressed not only in its architecture, but in its daily use. It was clearly a building in which people felt at home; children's toys were scattered around, and terraces and gardens were occupied spaces. The place was clearly theirs.

Some of the relevant attributes of the design included:

- Multiple entrances from the surrounding streets to the courtyard at the center of the project give people the ability to use stairs that are directly associated with their own dwelling units, without common passages or corridors on the level of their dwelling.
- The access stairs have good daylight, and large landings—suggesting that they might act as social space as well as for circulation.
- Each dwelling unit has outdoor space. That outdoor space faces the common garden, giving people the opportunity to see and call out to a neighbor in the garden.
- Balconies are not lined up vertically but shift, allowing users of the balconies the choice to be more private, under the balcony above, or in a position where they can see and communicate with neighbors above or below them.
- These features, as well as balconies and round columns that are freestanding, help break up the overall scale of the building.

Placement of balconies to give people choice in Interacting with neighbors above and below.

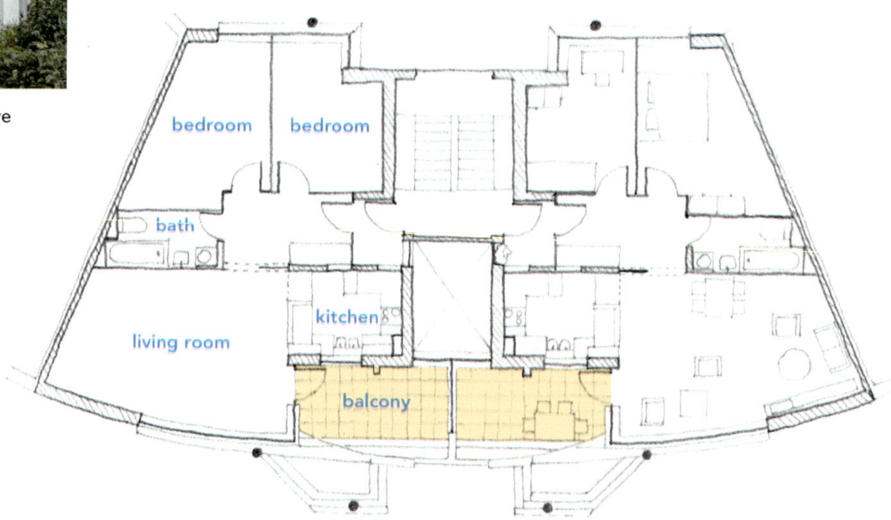

Plan of Lindenstrasse housing.
Drawing: based on original provided by Office of Herman Hertzberger, Amsterdam.

- In the dwelling units themselves, most rooms have light on two sides, and the balcony is pulled into the plan of the unit rather than only projected outward, making it like an outdoor room that is very much a part of the unit. This adds to the sense of livability and ample space.
- The floor plan suggests that rooms may have multiple uses—perhaps a carryover of Hertzberger's Diagoon housing in Delft.[1]
- The ground-floor garden is itself partly subdivided in a way that suggests individual places rather than a large, undivided outdoor area, making it comfortable for planting and use by individuals, families, or small groups.

[1] Hertzberger's Diagoon housing project was an attempt at an extreme architectural flexibility. In the drawings documenting the design, Hertzberger showed multiple possible uses of rooms, and multiple kinds of relationships among them.

It is not a very large housing project, and has an intimate scale. But at the same time, the design elements suggested how to ensure a human scale and human places in larger projects. Hertzberger does not see dwellings primarily as abstract repetitive elements of large conglomerations, which is the case in much modern housing. Instead, he is insistent on seeing them as places of human habitation. And this is a very subtle matter, requiring thought about each individual element of people's experience and specific ways of turning that thought into architectural results.

People using project's outdoor space.

DUNBOYNE ROAD HOUSING, CAMDEN, LONDON

Flexibility and efficiency

Façade of part of project showing pedestrian walk and entrance leading to dwelling unit. Photo: Martin Charles/RIBA Collections.

IN LONDON in 2012 I stayed for a few nights in a maisonette (two-story flat) that was part of a development designed by Neave Brown, one of the best-known postwar architects who specialized in housing in the UK. This house was part of the Dunboyne Road development in Camden, a scheme that has 71 units, mostly two-story maisonettes, organized in an arrangement that maximizes daylight and outdoor space to each dwelling.[1]

This turned out to be a place designed with people and their daily lives in mind. It has been 12 or 13 years since I stayed there, but I remember my reaction to it at the time as being a very positive one.

Like many London maisonettes built in postwar housing projects, as well as older working-class, party-wall, terraced housing, the dwelling has two floors, and is two rooms deep, allowing for good daylight in all the rooms. The exterior public walkway that provides access to the dwelling is pulled away from the front façade

1 The history and design of this project is described in Mark Swenarton, *Cook's Camden*.

by several feet. This increases the privacy of the front room, and also helps bring daylight to the dwelling below.

The overall organization of this maisonette is simple. The front door is accessed over a short bridge from the public walkway. On the other side of the walkway is a garden, one of two outdoor spaces that belong to the maisonette. Inside the front door, a small entry area gives four choices: left to the kitchen, right to a service room with a washing machine, or ahead to either a stair leading to the upper floor or to a passage along the stair leading to two bedrooms and a bathroom. The upper floor has a living room, bedroom, and bathroom—as well as a terrace outside the living room.

The maisonette has small spaces, but I was impressed with several features of it:

- Good daylight.
- Privacy with respect to the public realm.
- Flexibility of use.
- Provision of outdoor space.

The maisonette was occupied by a couple who used the upstairs bedroom, and two independent renters were in the two downstairs bedrooms. Clearly, the maisonette could also have been occupied by a single family unit, by the couple renting to related people occupying the two downstairs bedrooms, or by the couple using either the upstairs or downstairs bedrooms for home-based work.

The existence of one common room downstairs (the kitchen) and one common room upstairs (the living room) gave the couple the ability for privacy even when the lodgers were using the kitchen. A bathroom on each floor, and a laundry room near the front door, were in positions that gave each group easy access to those rooms. The position of the stair gave the lodgers privacy as anyone going up the stair avoided their doors. And the upstairs terrace gave the couple a private outdoor space that was removed from the lodgers.

View of entrance to unit showing short bridge from pedestrian walk. Photo: Tim Crocker.

The organization is therefore quite sensitive to details of layout

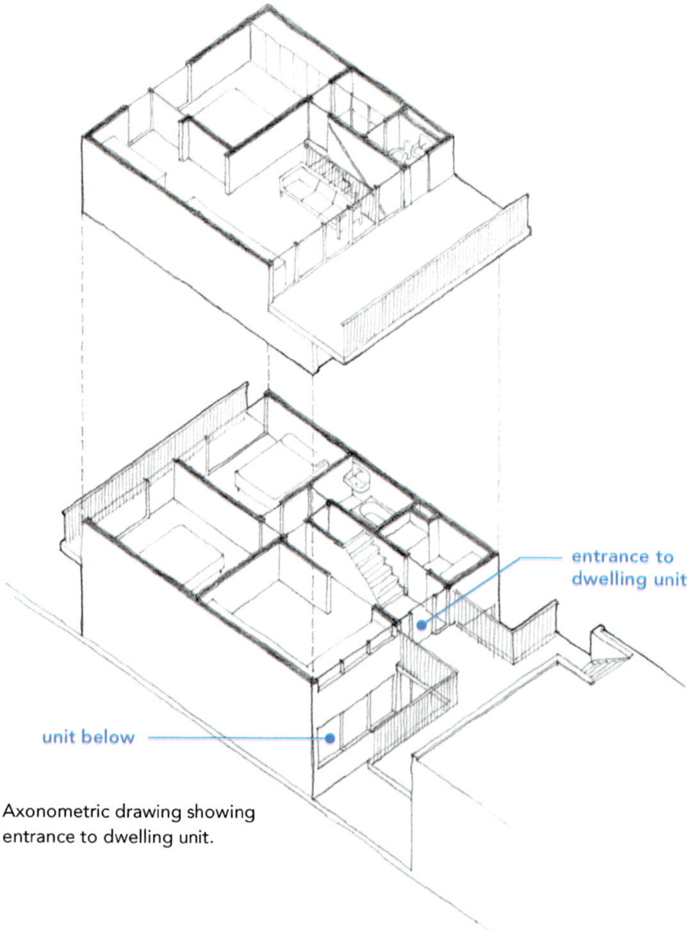

Axonometric drawing showing entrance to dwelling unit.

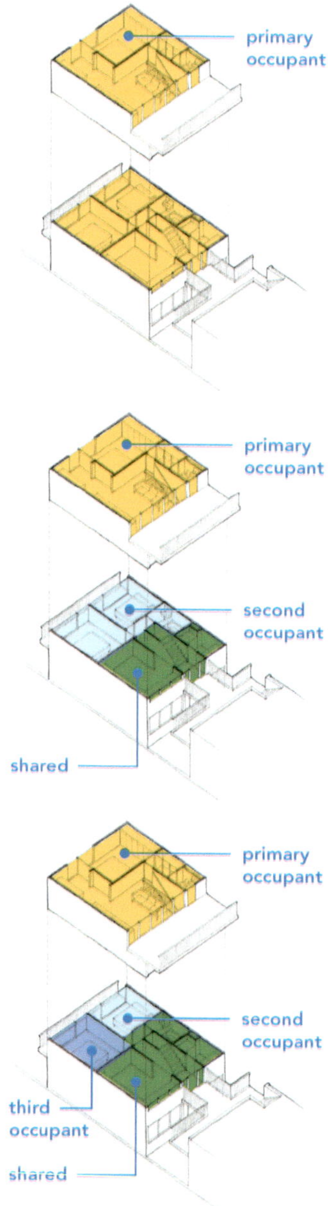

Diagrams showing flexibility of dwelling unit among different groups of residents.

that support flexibility of use. It is a very good example of how a two-story layout may maintain the privacy gradient that prompts a two-floor layout in the first place, but also allows each floor, when desired, to be used independently by unrelated individuals.

My reaction to this example took a few days to develop. Spending a few days there, seeing how people used the space, and talking to them, helped me appreciate the care and thoughtfulness that had gone into its design, and the architect's serious attention to the way people live. This was a building that appeared simple and ordinary when I first encountered it, but which I appreciated more and more as I became more familiar with it.

GILLETT SQUARE, DALSTON, LONDON

Enterprise, performance, and respect

GILLETT SQUARE is in Dalston, a neighborhood of Hackney, one of London's most ethnically diverse boroughs. (Eighty-nine languages are spoken there, according to one count.) The square is near two stations of the Overground, a major outdoor market, a community-run public garden, a stage theater in a converted paint factory, and a diversity of housing types. The result of a 20-year grassroots project, Gillett Square brought together local residents, a community organization, and civic government to develop one of the most successful new spaces, a public square, in London. I first learned about it and visited it through Dalston-based friends, one of whom, Adam Hart, spearheaded the project and led it over the years.

Gillett Square is different from the quintessential London square. That is the residential square, surrounded by terraced houses, green and parklike in the center, perhaps with locked gates making it accessible only to nearby residents. A quiet haven in a busy city, it exacerbated class differences by putting that haven away from commerce and the working class. Gillett Square is more like many European squares in its diverse social makeup and stronger connection to busy streets—and designed to bring people together rather than keep them apart.

The project involved the transformation of a car park on the site of demolished terraced houses, along with surrounding buildings, into a lively public place that incorporates a variety of community and cultural activities. The newly renovated and designed spaces include a jazz club, a flexible outdoor venue for a variety of kinds of performances, terraced houses converted into spaces for local organizations, prefabricated pods for tiny businesses, and workspaces for artists and small craft-businesses.

It was built incrementally, beginning with the renovation of the terraced houses fronting on Bradbury Street, and including, in separate phases, the renovation of an old garment factory to

Map of Gillett Square.

Prefabricated business units at edge of public space.

New galleries on Bradbury Street houses providing access to rooms in renovated terraced houses, overlooking square.

Looking up Bradbury Street with renovated terraced houses on right.

Shops on Kingsland Road in Dalston near Gillett Square.

Standing in front of coffee house looking toward Vortex Jazz Club.

Enjoying Gillett Square on a sunny day.

Watching a performance in Gillett Square.

become a venue that was partly occupied by the Vortex Jazz Club, ten prefabricated business units for rental to tiny, fledgling businesses that might start with very small investments, the paving of the square itself, and an entrance building giving access to the rear galleries of the terraced houses that would overlook the square.[1]

The square is open to everyone, respecting them and supporting diversity and tolerance. On a typical day, there are people gathered informally in front of the business pods (including a café run by an Ethiopian immigrant, a tailor, a money transfer office, a local radio station, a place for cell phone repairs, a barber, and others); parents pushing strollers with youngsters attending toddlers' jazz classes; young children playing in the square; people crossing the square on foot; people setting up for musical performances in the evening; and people without another place to

[1] For an account of the formation of the square, see Howard Davis and Adam Hart, "From the Bottom Up: Gillett Square in London."

be, some of whom are experiencing substance abuse, who gather around a wooden platform shaded by four trees in the eastern part of the square. It is really a place for everyone.

I have experienced that social mixing in the square, in different seasons, different days of the week, and different times of day. It varies in the intensity of activity and the number of people who are there. But I always feel welcome there, and looking around see that other diverse users do as well. It was fitting that Gillett Square was one of the sites at which the handover of the Olympic Games from London to Rio de Janeiro happened in 2012, helping to celebrate the global diversity of Hackney and of London.[2]

[2] But Gillett Square also changes in uncertain ways. A £1 million grant from the London government has resulted in an addition to the backs of the terraced houses, and the movement of the business pods from the base of those buildings to the north side of the square. There is also talk about expanding the square across what is left of the car park to the south side of the old factory building to the north. Only time will tell whether those changes will be successful in maintaining the diverse social makeup of Gillett Square.

Diverse activities at Gillett Square.

THERMAL BATHS, VALS, SWITZERLAND

Moving from the cave to the mountain meadow

ONE OF THE highlights of our architecture department's spring term program in Vicenza is a trip to Switzerland, including a visit to the thermal baths designed by Peter Zumthor. The baths are at the village of Vals, in a mountain valley in the southeastern part of the country. I joined the group several times for that visit, each time being a highly sensual architectural experience.

The building that contains the baths is on a hillside, and partly underground. The hill has a stream at its bottom, and from the baths one can see the hill and meadows on the other side. A powerful ten minutes in itself, the sequence of entry to the baths is a gradual "opening up": from closed to open, from inside to

View of exterior showing outdoor pool and building embedded in hill. Photo: Donald Corner.

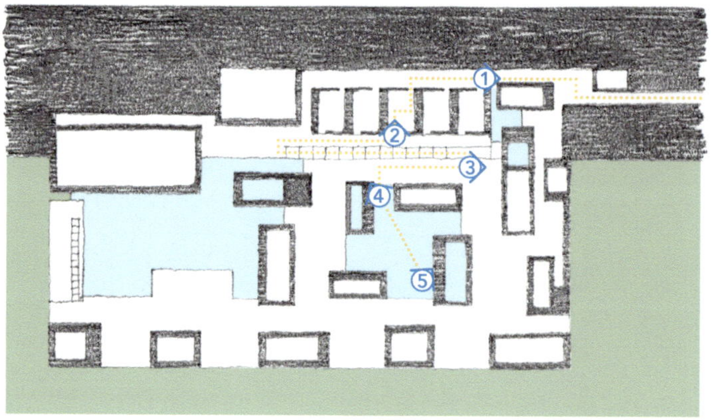

Diagram showing layout of building. Numbers indicate locations of sketches that show sequence of steps following entrance to the baths.

1. Entrance passage with dressing rooms on left.

2. Looking out from dressing room toward the balcony and pool beyond.

3. Looking back toward stair and balcony above.

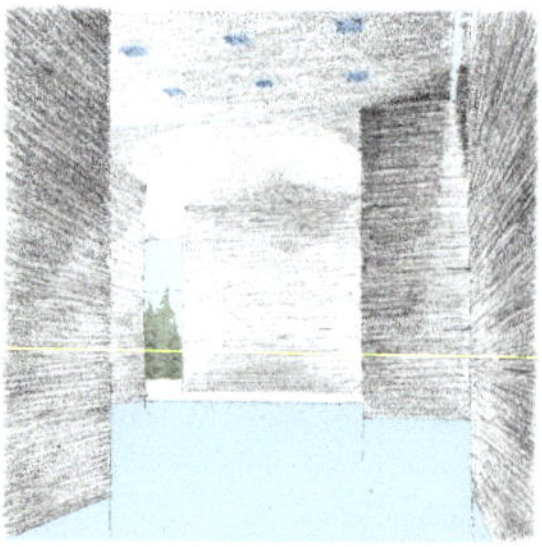

4. Central indoor pool.

5. Window toward valley and meadow.

outside, from dry to wet, from clothed to unclothed, from dark to daylight, from building to landscape, from cave to meadow and sky.

I start out in a room to check in and obtain a towel, then pass through a turnstile, and turn left into a long, low-ceilinged corridor [1] with stone and smooth concrete walls, dimly lit with only electric light, with a small bubbling fountain on the wall. On the left side of the corridor are five rooms in a line for changing and storing clothes in lockers. Each room has two doorways (but no doors)—the first from the corridor, at one corner of the room, and the second leading out toward the waters, diagonally opposite the first. While changing into my bathing shorts, I am still in a room with no direct daylight, but now have a glimpse of light and space and the indoor pool below, through the outer doorway [2].

Above, balcony and stair. Below, central interior pool. Hackenberg Photo Cologne/Alamy.

After passing through that doorway, I am on a narrow balcony overlooking the interior complex of baths, and a staircase, parallel to the balcony, leading down to those baths. The light is still relatively dim, but the space now has a sense of openness and the clear hint of ways to move through and around—but not yet a view through to the outside. To get to the head of the stairs, I turn right, and come close to two shower rooms and toilets. After using those rooms, I go down the stairs, parallel but opposite in direction to my path along the balcony, to the main floor of the baths. I am walking barefoot, feeling the hardness of the floor, sometimes dry and sometimes wet. At the bottom of the stair, I look back [3]. Now at the lower level, I walk back along the stair, and look to my left into the central pool [4]. I am aware of more daylight but not yet the full view of the valley and opposite hill. Lines of daylight are coming down from above, powerfully formed by thin gaps where the roof slabs almost meet. They do not connect me to the outside as much as give me a hint of the sky.

Almost there. I turn back again, and enter the central pool through the opening in the concrete walls directly opposite the stair. Gentle steps lead down to the water, at the perfect temperature of 32°C (89.6°F)—very slightly cool, but close enough to body temperature to be neither hot nor cold. A very gentle and comforting welcome to the thermal adventures ahead. And when I swim

[1] Peter Zumthor, *Thinking Architecture*, pp. 86–87.

or walk to the far side of the pool, nearest to the outer wall facing the valley, I see the valley at diagonal views [5], on either side of the concrete that forms the wall of the space. The valley is green and lush, finally achieving the connection to mountainous place that started in the dark and closed corridor, underground, a few minutes before.

This sequence of entry has engaged all my senses: tactile with the concrete and stone walls and floor and eventually water, felt through bare skin, and the humidity from the water; aural with the echoes of voices transformed into an almost single low-pitched tone, and eventually the gentle lapping of water and ringing of the cowbells in the valley; smell of the water; perhaps a little taste of it when I am finally in the pool; and visual, with controlled and suggested movement achieved through the subtle and not-so-subtle arrangement of solid and void, human movement suggested and supported by the concrete itself, the pull of daylight in between the concrete masses, and the lines of light in the ceiling.

There is more to the experience beyond: the tiny bathing rooms—one very hot, one icy cold, one fragrant, one with drinking fountains, the outdoor pool and its remarkable approach through a chain doorway and three giant "faucets" at the far end, and finally the strong connection to the green valley once outside. Movement to and within these places is equally experientially intense as the entry sequence. But perhaps because I was coming from the outside world, the entry sequence was particularly powerful and strongly felt. The entry sequence is a perfect example of Zumthor's own statement that "Architecture is the art of space and it is the art of time as well…following a path and discovering a path of our own wandering…I give thought to careful and conscious staging of tension between inside and outside, public and intimate, and to thresholds, transitions, and borders." [1]

CATHEDRAL, CHARTRES, FRANCE

Not a monument to melancholy

IN 2013 I spent a few days in Paris after a longer stay in London. I stayed in Versailles at the home of a friend, an architect and architectural historian. He suggested a visit to Chartres, but I was hesitant as I had been there a few times before, and preferred to spend my few days in historic Paris. But I agreed with my friend, and off we went.

What I expected to find was the cathedral as I had known it before: dark, mysterious, and showing the blackness of hundreds of years of burning candles, with the stained-glass windows in great contrast to the blackened walls. And as we had always learned, seeing the light through the stained glass was one of the main reasons for the structural evolution of Gothic cathedrals, particularly the use of flying buttresses that helped to "dematerialize" and open up the wall.

What I found was that the building was in the middle of a restoration. The soot was being removed and the walls, columns, and fluting were being painted. The walls that had been restored were a pale ochre and the columns and fluting were white. By then, parts of the narthex, transepts, and choir had been painted, but not yet the nave.

My reaction was first one of surprise, but then great delight. The parts of the building that had been restored were indeed luminous. The building glowed, the stained-glass windows had not lost their power (they could not), and I had the feeling that if the ochre and white were the original colors, they would have helped make the religion joyful and uplifting. The feeling was different from what it had been before, but no less powerful, and no less spiritual.

At the time, I was not aware of the controversy surrounding the work, with some experts claiming that history was being erased, and others arguing that the work was bringing back the original color, luminosity, and spirit of the building.

One of the critiques came from the American architecture critic Martin Filler, who began his article with an account of his visit to the building, including the following:

> "Carried away by the splendors of the moment, I did not initially realize that something was very wrong...The belief that a heavy-duty reworking can allow us to see the cathedral as the makers did is not only magical thinking but also a foolhardy concept that makes authentic artifacts look fake." Filler went on with some specifics: how the electric lighting had already changed the interior; how the exact chemical composition of the historic paints was unknown; and finally that "One can only pray that by some miracle this scandalous desecration of a cultural holy place can be reversed."[1]

[1] Martin Filler, "A Scandalous Makeover at Chartres."

Chartres Cathedral in process of renovation, 2013.

View toward altar, 2024. Photo: James Givens.

View toward rose window in west/entrance façade. Photo: James Givens.

A reply came from two other scholars: Madeline H. Caviness and Jeffrey F. Hamburger. They wrote about the care with which the work had been carried out, the initial cleaning of grime that was "centimeters thick" that could have destroyed the cathedral if it caught fire, the work of archaeologists to uncover the original colors, and even the painting of false masonry work that was typical in medieval churches. "Exposed stone may appeal to a modernist aesthetic…but has little to do with medieval conceptions of sacred space."[2]

Filler's sentence, "Carried away by the splendors of the moment, I did not initially realize that something was very wrong" implies that Filler has made a choice between two ways of understanding the building: first, experientially, and second, within the discourse of architectural conservation. The difficult question of what to preserve from what period has been central to preservation practice since at least the time of Viollet-le-Duc in the nineteenth century.[3] There is not a single answer, particularly to complex questions that usually

[2] Madeline H. Caviness and Jeffrey Hamburger, "Reply to Filler."

[3] Viollet-le-Duc was responsible for a nineteenth-century restoration of Notre Dame in Paris, including the design of what was then a new spire, the destruction of which, in the 2019 near-catastrophic fire, has itself led to much discussion and debate about preservation and reconstruction. Coincidentally, I was editing this reflection on the day of a TV news story about the success of the Notre Dame rebuilding, with images of its beautiful, newly-restored interior.

attend buildings like Chartres—almost 1,000 years old, built in the first place by sequences of different bands of masons coming and going,[4] and subject to disasters, restorations, and everyday wear-and-tear over centuries. Multiple interpretations of appropriate practice will always be present.

My experience of the cathedral, and apparently that of at least one prominent architecture critic (and probably many other people), was a strongly positive one, at least as strong as the three or four times that I had visited the cathedral before, with its interior darkened by several hundred years of soot from candles and oil lamps. The new paint along with the old stained glass made the entire interior luminous, strongly enough to suppress, at least for the moment, any thoughts about the pros and cons of particular modes of restoration.[5]

So, I am partial to the view of Prof. Hamburger that "there is no reason to be nostalgic or romantic about the dirt…The association of Gothic buildings with 'dark, brooding gloom' is fundamentally misguided; they are not monuments to melancholy."[6]

4 John James, *The Masons Who Built Chartres.*

5 I returned to Chartres in November 2022, on a cloudy day, and found that a good deal of progress had been made with the painting. Large temporary structures associated with the restoration had been erected in the interior, making it more difficult to experience the full space itself. But I still saw the repainting as a powerful and delightful development, and I'm looking forward to my next visit, which hopefully will show the work completed.

6 Benjamin Ramm, "A controversial restoration that wipes away the past." *The New York Times*, Sept. 1, 2017. https://www.nytimes.com/2017/09/01/arts/design/chartres-cathedral-restoration-controversial.html

PIAZZA DEI SIGNORI, VICENZA, ITALY

Balancing the monumental and the vernacular

OVER MANY TRIPS to Vicenza, the Piazza dei Signori, the city's central square, was part of my day, every day. I often walked through the square, or sat at a busy café in it with a Campari-and-soda, talking to friends and looking at the buildings and people. One opportunity to photograph it was very early one Sunday morning in late June 2022, when the piazza was quite empty except for a few people walking their dogs.

Long and narrow, running from southwest to northeast, the piazza is best known for the Basilica, one of the masterworks of the Renaissance architect Andrea Palladio. The Basilica forms much of the long southeast side of the piazza. It is distinguished by a white-marble façade that includes a ground-floor loggia, with Doric columns, topped by an Ionic first-floor loggia; both with repetitive "Palladian openings," each composed of a central arch flanked by smaller openings. The outer wall and stacked loggias of the building are an addition to buildings on the inside that were built centuries earlier.[1]

The piazza has other important buildings, including the Palazzo del Monte di Pietà, housing a charitable religious institution, the Loggia dei Capitaniato, and a tall clock tower near the northeast end of the Basilica.

Finally, two free-standing columns topped by sculptures of Christ the Redeemer and the Lion of St. Mark help separate the main part of the piazza from its northeast end (which is also the northwest end of the Piazza Biade). It is this space at the end of the piazza that caught my eye, and particularly the relatively narrow, five-story vernacular buildings that are on its short, northeast edge. The buildings are of different heights, different colors, and with different floor levels. Some of them have a Venetian window pattern, with windows at the corners of rooms. A few of the buildings are joined by an irregular arcade, the columns of which are different from each other (apparently *spolia* taken from earlier buildings).

1 The small side openings have different widths, allowing for the main openings to line up with the existing old buildings.

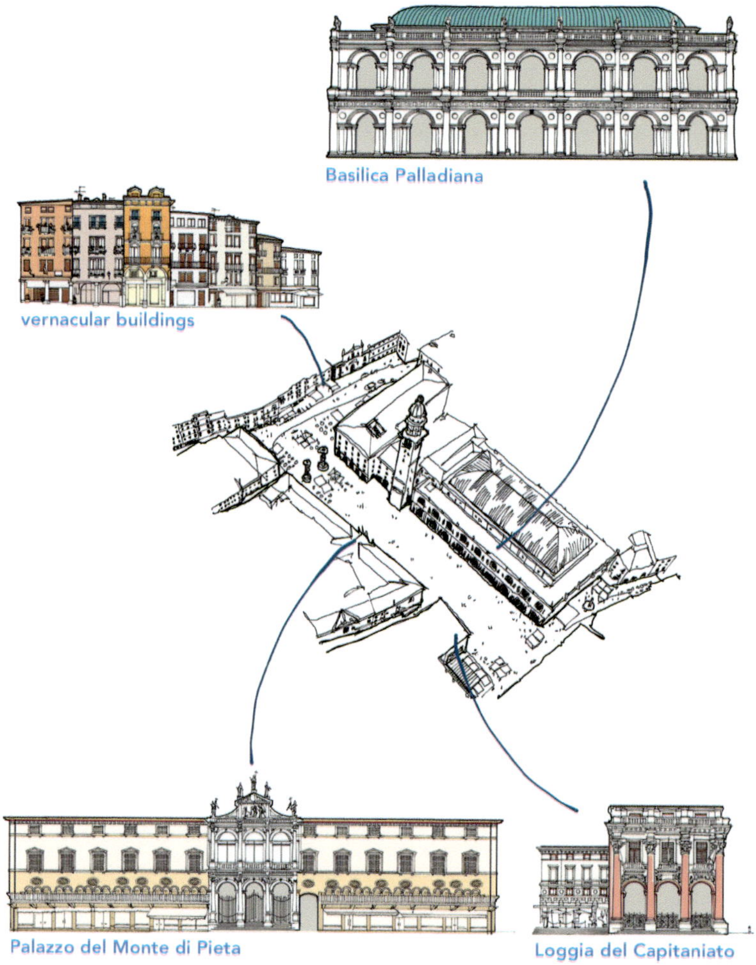

Piazza dei Signori, Vicenza. Map/diagram: Erik Larson.

Together these features emphasize the difference between that "vernacular end" and the main part of the piazza, where most of its building edge is made up of monumental buildings, emphasizing its civic and religious importance.

This strong difference between the variety of the vernacular and the regularity of the monumental helps unify the overall piazza rather than visually fracturing it. In the overall composition, consisting of the civic and religious buildings, the vernacular buildings, and the columns, the vernacular and the civic, support each other in the overall ensemble. Why is this the case?

The pair of columns is critical, and helps define the larger space as a major civic space. They are white, helping to "connect" them more to the large civic space than the vernacular end. Although one can see the vernacular buildings beyond the columns, the columns establish a vertical plane, an implied wall, that

Both photos show the two columns marking the end of the main part of the piazza with the vernacular buildings beyond. In the foreground on the right of the photo on the left is the Basilica Palladiana.

has something of the same civic character as the large civic buildings. The columns are strong enough visually so that they and the plane they define have a presence similar to that of the major buildings in the piazza, helping to give an "end" to that main part of the piazza—at the same time that that end allows a view of the vernacular buildings beyond it.

The contrast between the columns (as major civic objects) and the vernacular buildings (as more minor façades) itself helps reinforce the strength of the columns. The shafts of the columns are strong and repetitive, contrasting with the vernacular buildings themselves, that emphasize the individual façades, the windows, the separate pieces, the different colors. And this piece-iness of the vernacular buildings is reinforced by their contrast with the strength of the columns. Large scale in front of small scale, monochromatic in front of polychromatic.

The large and small working together helps give the end of the piazza a strong harmony, visually highly balanced. It also symbolizes a city and civic space in which the individual and the civic are in balance with each other. One can also see this kind of balance in such places as the Piazza Farnese and Piazza Navona in Rome, the Piazza delle Erbe in Padua, and many other urban places in Italy. Although it takes different forms in different cities, the balance between the small and the large, the everyday cheek-by-jowl with the monumental, is a strong characteristic of much traditional Italian urbanism.

Close-up of the vernacular buildings.

SWIMMING POOL, MATOSINHOS, PORTUGAL

Concrete, rocks and water

WHILE ATTENDING a conference in Porto in 2014, I visited several buildings designed by the Portuguese architect Álvaro Siza: the school of architecture, two or three housing projects, a tea house on the beach at Matosinhos (a suburb of Porto), and the swimming pool complex, also on the beach, about a ten-minute walk south of the tea house. A native of Matosinhos, Siza designed buildings within a modernist approach to construction, that were compatible with, and at the same time enhancing of, their contexts.

The cluster of buildings that serves the pools is to large extent a work of landscape architecture that includes a few buildings for service—locker rooms, snack bar, and service rooms. What I found beautiful in its connection to the landscape was the transition from the long boulevard overlooking the sea down to the bathing complex and the bathing complex itself. From the sidewalk on the ocean side of the boulevard, I entered through an opening in a long, horizontal concrete wall, to find a gentle ramp leading down through two concrete walls, and then passed through an opening leading to the large area that finally presents a wide view of the ocean. This was a version of the architectural technique of moving through a confined space ("compression") before entering a much more open space ("expansion") as a strong contrast. And it effectively removed the bathing complex itself from the boulevard and its traffic.

But what was most striking was the relationship between the concrete construction and the natural, rocky part of the beach. Coming down the ramp, almost completely surrounded by concrete, I felt strongly connected to the landscape, and the concrete seemed a natural part of it.

Although used by the Romans, concrete is usually considered to be a "modern" material. But at this place on the edge of the Atlantic Ocean, it took on a different, timeless quality. Apart from buildings like the Louis Kahn-designed Salk Institute in California,

Views of the swimming pool on the beach at Matosinhos.
Photo of concrete ramp leading to beach: LusoArchitecture/Alamy.

concrete rarely has the kind of visceral relationship to its immediate, natural surroundings as it does with this Siza building. Indeed, it often seems as if its use is deliberately making the point of being *different* from earlier buildings and more "historic" materials, rather than helping to extend and intensify the existing order of the place. With this building, the major "design move" was the use of concrete itself, and its power in reinforcing the context of the Atlantic Ocean and its Portuguese coastline.

SÃO BENTO TRAIN STATION, PORTO, PORTUGAL

Beauty in an understated building

São Bento train station, Porto, main hall.

São Bento train station, Porto, looking through door toward platform where people transfer to buses and cars.

I HAD KNOWN little about Porto before my 2014 visit—its location on the Douro River, its hilly topography that led to wonderful views, its historic buildings covered with azulejo tiles, its housing projects and other buildings by the modernist architect Álvaro Siza. The combination of human scale, white-and-blue tiled façades, and tightly-organized streets, helped give the sense of a most appealing and livable city.

These attributes, bringing together history and the present, craft and technology, ceramic tiles and modern steel, all came together for me in the São Bento train station. The station was designed by architect José Marques da Silva and opened in 1916. It is at once monumental and human-scaled, special and everyday, inside and outside, ornamented with techniques that go back to the Arab occupation of the Iberian peninsula alongside the railroad technology of the nineteenth and twentieth centuries. This all co-exists comfortably in what is, in the end, a modest structure with well-resolved spaces and details.

São Bento train station, Porto, tile mural.

The main lobby/waiting area of the station is based on a simple, overall rectilinear volume divided by a horizontal line that marks the top of all the doors and connecting passages. It has good daylight, provided by high, ground-glass windows. And within this simple organization, it was built with a variety of materials, including stone, glass, and *azulejo* tiles, that are characteristic of many other buildings in Porto. The ground-glass windows have a softness that acted in contrast to the hardness of the stone and tile. The "modern" and the "traditional" worked together: tiles and stone, plus electronic signs, steel, and iron. All of this together provided an overall sense of ease in a building that one would typically encounter only for a few minutes.

Looking through a doorway to the outside, I could see a line of cast-iron columns at the edge of an outdoor space that is the place for buses, cars, and taxis to drop off and pick up passengers, very near the tracks. (Some railroad lines end at this station, a terminal, allowing for access and train changes without passengers needing to use stairs or lifts. This single-level organization also helps give the station its modesty.)

I particularly enjoyed the view of that outdoor area, a place for the everyday activities of travel. The open doorway was flanked with blue-and-white tile murals, ground-glass windows above, along with simple stone walls. At the far end of the outdoor area, I could see a hill rising up with houses at the top and railroad tracks emerging below. The view shows how the symmetries, craft, and formality of the train-station building are brought together with the contingencies of the landscape and city outside it. And the relationship makes wayfinding easy for passengers, helping them move easily from one transport mode to another—one of the important functional requirements of transportation stations of any kind.

Petajavesi, Finland

Left to right:
Petajavesi, Finland
Bergen, Norway
Lahti, Finland

PART SEVEN
2015–2024

The final group of reflections includes my first trip to Finland in 2015, a research trip to India two years later, various encounters in Europe, a strongly-felt re-encounter in Mexico, and, finally, a visit to a major street along with an informal settlement in São Paulo. I included it because it is particularly characteristic of what has emerged as a major theme in my 100 reflections. The world of building is one world. It is not "architecture and building," or the "global north and global south," or any of the binaries that are often used to describe and classify buildings. My intention has been to demonstrate, through my reactions to buildings of every stripe, size, and purpose, the importance of all of them and the relationships among them.

Left to right:
Ainola, Finland
Seinajoki, Finland
Porvoo, Finland

PIAZZA DELLA MADONNA DEI MONTE, ROME

Public outdoor life in an ordinary place

I VISITED this Roman piazza for the first time with two friends, in 2015. We didn't set out to go specifically to this place; we were walking along the Via dei Fori Imperiali, turned up a street to find a café, and found one at this square. It turned out to be an ordinary but appealing piazza, in the Monti neighborhood, just halfway between the Colosseum and the Quirinale. From one point of view it is an ordinary place, lacking the important fountains of the Piazza Navona, or the monumental palazzo of the Piazza Farnese. Although located near some of the main touristic areas of Rome, it is not a well-known piazza like some of the others. The church associated with the piazza shows its side wall rather than main door to the piazza; the fountain, while pleasant enough, has little distinctive about it; likewise with the other buildings.

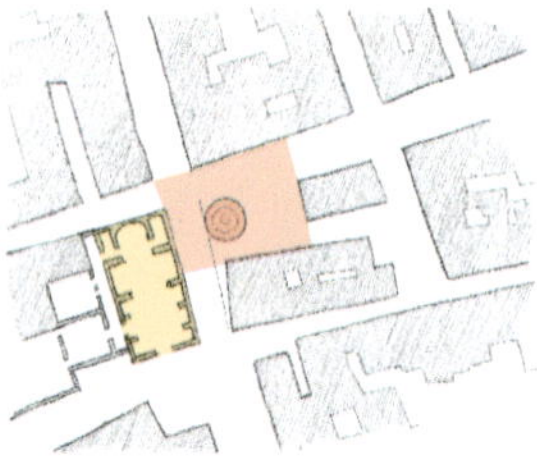

Map of Piazza della Madonna dei Monti. Drawing: Jonah Nees.

Piazza della Madonna dei Mont.

But at the same time, we realized after sitting down that the piazza had a wonderful sense of life—a variety of people, sitting on the fountain, in cafés, walking through, entering, and leaving the buildings on its edges, in cars passing through on the streets that enter. (Surprisingly, the piazza is lined on two sides by through streets that together take up the majority of its area.)

The physical elements of the square include:

- Streets on two edges of the square that continue into the neighborhood and city.
- An enclosed and roofed area of a café which is located in a building that is on one of the short sides of the piazza, opposite the side wall of the church.
- The side wall of the church, on the other short side of the piazza, immediately adjacent to one of the through streets.
- A large fountain, off-center, between the café and the church.
- The façades of two larger buildings, along the long walls of the piazza.

Façade of church of Madonna dei Monti. The façade does not face the piazza.

And these physical elements seemed to add up to a place of active human use. During our visit, we experienced activity and busy-ness. The piazza was active with people—local people, tourists, old people, young people, small children, people sitting in the café or on the fountain edge, people just walking through, and cars and other vehicles on the boundary streets. There was a lot going on, but it was not overwhelming. And the cars did not detract from the positive experience of the piazza, but added to it: they gave the piazza more of a sense of life.

Piazza della Madonna dei Monti. Photo: Jenny Young.

In the 1920s, the piazza housed a small market: a photo from that time shows several market stalls sheltered by umbrellas. Since then the Monti neighborhood has undergone a lot of change, transforming from an ordinary, small, neighborhood with a market square to a place with a mixture of local people and tourists. The anthropologist Michael Herzfeld writes about the gentrification of the Monti neighborhood in *Evicted from Eternity: The Restructuring*

Piazza della Madonna dei Monti.

of Modern Rome. He writes that the piazza was the main social place of the neighbourhood, a place of gathering where local political events would take place, a place of religious and everyday observances—"Some participate in the ritual activities associated with the annual Feast of the Madonna to whom the parish church is dedicated…several thousand elderly former residents and their families crowd around the sixteenth-century fountain dominating the square. But many come at other times as well, to sit and chat in the spring or autumn sunshine with the few remaining residents of the old population, the Romanesco cadences, languorous reminiscences, and salty jokes contrasting with the clipped, fast diction of mostly younger people walking straight across the square with determined steps and briefcases in hand."[1]

By 2015, the Monti neighborhood had already experienced considerable gentrification that had driven out many long-time residents, along with their occupations and businesses. What we experienced on our visit was apparently quite different from what was there before. But what had persisted the most was the piazza itself which maintained its life, at the same time that its history continued to give it meaning. The framework for public daily life persisted even as the social fabric of the neighborhood changed—and as it continues to change, that physical framework will hopefully persist.

[1] Michael Herzfeld, *Evicted from Eternity*, pp. 20–21.

WINKLEY ESTATE, BETHNAL GREEN, LONDON

Mixed-use and flexibility

ONE OF THE most remarkable historic examples I've found of projects specifically designed for "mixed use"—in this case bringing together craft-based industry and dwelling—is in the London district of Bethnal Green, designed and built around 1900. My growing interest in urban industry, including the historic transformations from craft-based to factory manufacture, led me to this project, the "Winkley Estate." I was introduced to it by a London colleague who lived there, and our common interests led to a research investigation that we carried out together.[1]

The Winkley Estate consists of four small blocks of buildings built by local developers, Charles and Henry Winkley.[2] There is little documentation of the Winkley brothers or this project, but the brothers were ahead of their time in their respect for the historic vernacular. In a sense they were recreating that vernacular—and

1 Howard Davis and Ashley Dhanani. "The Winkley Estate."

2 Charles Winkley became the mayor of the London Borough of Hackney in 1913.

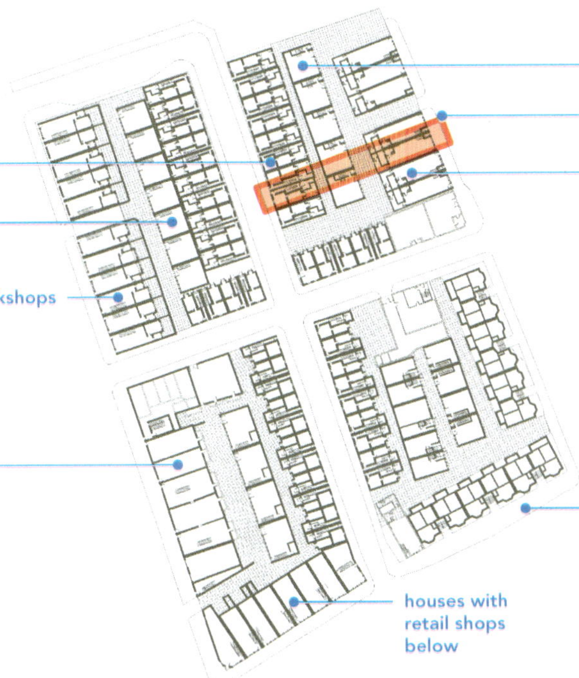

Overall plan of Winkley Estate showing variety of functions Housed in the four blocks.

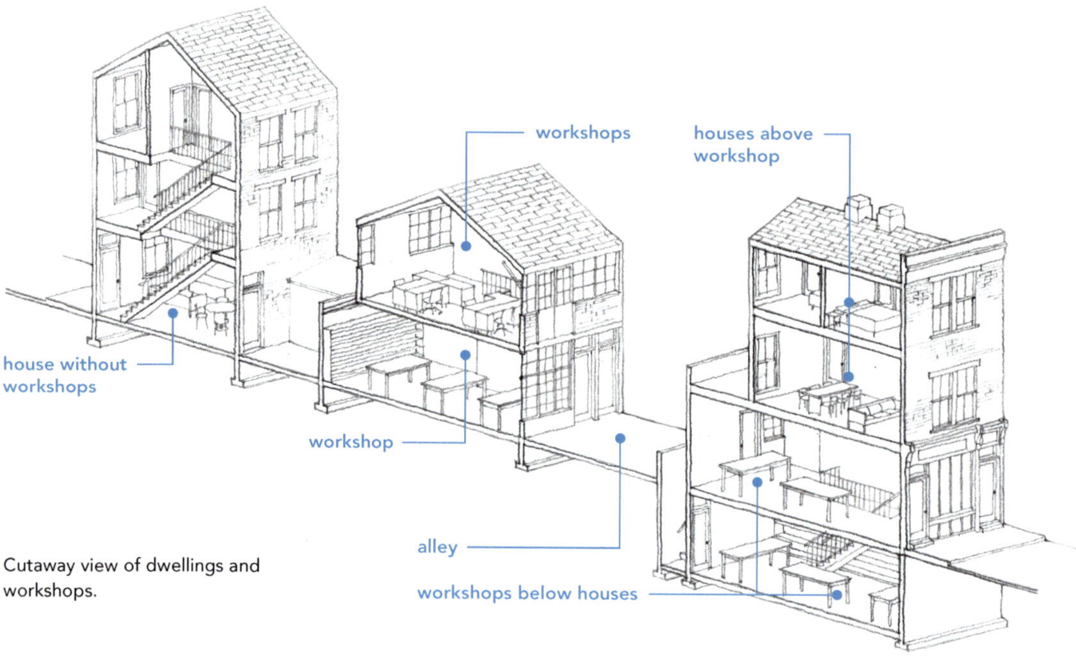

Cutaway view of dwellings and workshops.

there are very few projects in London, built as a single project, that approach the same variety and distribution of functional types.[3] It is not clear why the Winkley brothers did this—it seems like some kind of Utopian ideal combined with a prediction, based on contemporary life in east London where craftspeople lived close their workshops, that the buildings would be financially successful for them.

The Winkley Estate buildings are of six different types:

- Four-story buildings—with one story below sidewalk level—consisting of two floors of workshops and two floors above (the floors above essentially making up a single-family terraced house).
- Two-story terraced houses without workshops.
- Three-story terraced houses without workshops.
- Two-story workshop buildings, with varying connections to the houses, on the interior of blocks.
- Four-story workshop/factory buildings facing a street.
- Three-story houses with retail space at the ground floor, facing Old Bethnal Green Road.

The fact that they were all designed and built at the same time is by itself unusual, because by the end of the nineteenth century

[3] One is Pullens Yards, in south London, which combines artists' studios, workshops and dwellings. Thanks to Frances Holliss for showing this to me, and who wrote about it in her book *Beyond Live-Work: The Architecture of Home-Based Work.*

Rear view of building with workshop(s) below and terraced house above.

Workshop in the interior of block. One door leads to a stair and the other directly into the ground floor. The foot of the stair may be accessed from the inside, allowing the two floors to be used either separately or together.

Part of Winkley Estate facing Old Bethnal Green Road.

Street view. The ground floor is the upper floor of a two-story workshop and the top two floors are a dwelling.

much large development involved the repetition of single building types, particularly terraced houses. The Winkley Estate buildings were occupied largely by people in the furniture industry: cabinet makers, wood turners, upholsterers, polishers, and other related craftspeople.[4]

But equally striking is the flexibility built into the designs. The buildings could have different and changing spatial connections with each other. The back workshops could connect to houses facing one street or the other. The workshops could be used together or separately. The workshops in the lower floors of the building that had two-story terraced houses above could be independent of those terraced houses, or connected to them. And although the buildings have changed their function over the years, many

4 This is verified by entries in the Kelly's London Post Office Directories in the first decades of the twentieth century.

of them still incorporate workshops and workspaces that are connected to the dwellings in varying, changing relationships.

The Winkley Estate has had a large impact on the way I think about spatial flexibility, as well as the relationships between dwelling and other functions in urban environments. The variation is facilitated not by strategies such as the use of moveable walls, but by the combination of proximity and the use of doors that can be either open or closed.

Around the time this project was built, there were still blocks in London that incorporated a rich mixture of dwellings and workshops. The map from about 1895 shown below is at what is now the northwest corner of Hampstead Road and its intersection with Euston Road. It includes the following businesses: a japanner (varnisher), a furniture warehouse, a sawmill, a cabinet factory, a carpenter, an ivory turner, a nickel plater, an oil and color shop, various small woodworkers, a brass foundry, and a piano factory. In the four adjacent blocks that included this one, there were 46 separate types of business involved with furniture making. These blocks were eventually eliminated in various kinds of slum clearance. The Winkley Estate represents an understanding of the importance of small spaces, flexibility of use, and the mixture of dwelling and workplace.

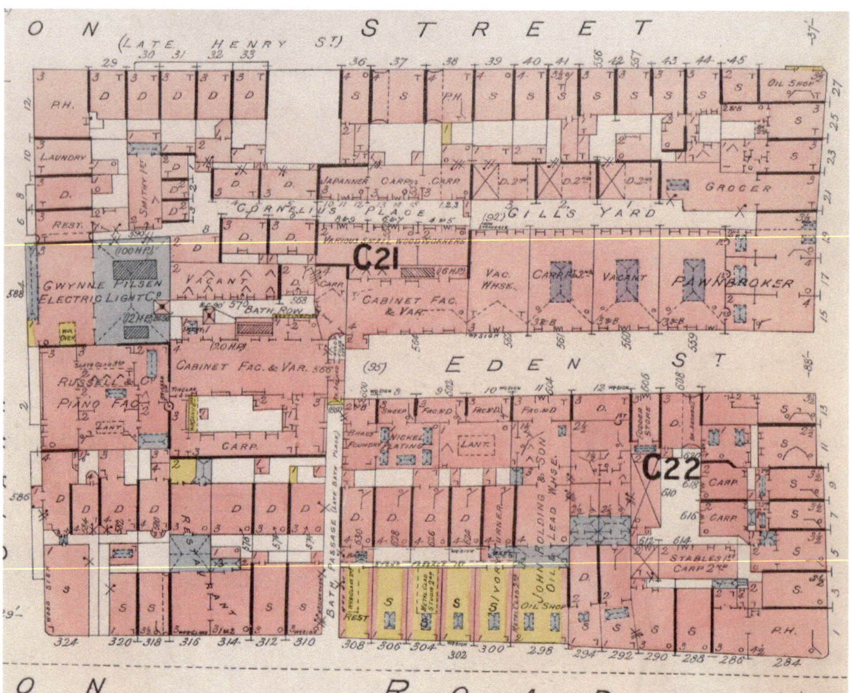

Goad's map from the 1890s showing the variety and mixture of workshops and dwellings in a typical London industrial block.

MYYRMAKI CHURCH, VANTAA, FINLAND

Angelic incandescence

BEING IN THIS CHURCH, which I visited with a Finnish architect friend on my only trip to Finland in 2015, was a spiritual experience of light. Designed by Juha Leiviska, the church came close in spiritual feeling to my visits to two other religious places described in this book: the Ise Shrine in Japan, and the monastery of Simonas Petras at Mount Athos in Greece. In this case, it seemed not only as if the purpose of the light was to illuminate the church in a beautiful way, which it certainly did, but that the purpose of the architecture of the church—its physical structure and materials—was to provide an armature for the light.

Hanging lamps in church at Vantaa.

A few architectural moves intensify the power of light in the experience of the church. The principal one is the position of the altar—not at the end of a long nave-like axis, or even on the side of a square space, but in the middle of the longest wall in the building, making the principal axis toward the altar into the short rather than the long axis. The long wall behind the altar is very high, and admits light reflected near its top, providing what is essentially a hidden source of daylight. The daylight, somewhat cold, reflected off the white walls, provided an appropriate, contrasting background to the warmer electric light that came from the delicately-hung fixtures, almost angelic in their presence. The light fixtures themselves were supported by thin wires, and floated in space, almost alive.

Interior view looking along altar wall, including skylights.

The English architect Sir Colin St. John Wilson wrote, a little wordily, about the relationship between architectural space and light in this church: "The most extraordinary spatial result of this parti is that the axis towards the altar is not the conventional long axis but the short cross axis. This device results in the altar wall gaining dramatically in intensity of focus from the pews that press towards it in shallow space. Furthermore since the wall is very high, an extraordinary suggestion of spatial pressure is evoked, animating the wall's surface with a pronounced upward directionality. This apparent weightlessness is derived from the veiled modulation of light created by the vertical and horizontal overlapping of planes which makes a space of luminous resonance evoking a trance-like experience of levitation. The aesthetics of light become transformed into the metaphysics of light."[1]

Interior view of Myrmakki church at Vantaa, looking toward altar.

A major result of the church's architectural design is the provision of the framework, described by St. John Wilson, in which the hanging lights are seen and experienced—altogether providing a powerful feeling, that on my short visit led me to the edge of a spiritual experience.

[1] Colin St. John Wilson, "Leiviska at Myyrmaki," pp. 63–67.

TOWN HALL, SÄYNÄTSALO, FINLAND

The modest center of a masterwork

ON MY FIRST TRIP to Finland in 2015 the town hall in Säynätsalo was high on my list of buildings to visit. This building, more than any other, exemplifies the work of Alvar Aalto, one of the canonical architects of the twentieth century. Set in the woods, the building houses the governmental center of a tiny farming town. The day I visited in early August was gray and drizzly, the kind of day, without shadows caused by sunlight, that allows the details of buildings to be emphasized. Whereas bright sun and shade emphasize the overall form of the building, gray yields a soft light where details are clear.

The building is organized around a courtyard, that has on one side a small tower containing the town-council chamber, on another a two-story wing containing the library, and on the remaining two sides, two-story office wings. There are several features to the architecture that are often described: the grass steps leading up to the courtyard, symbolically connecting the building to the landscape; the asymmetrical balance on the façade that shows both the library and the council chamber; the spatial sequence leading up to the council chamber; and the council chamber itself with its exposed wooden roof structure as a culmination of the spatial sequence.

Although the courtyard itself is less commented on for its architectural innovation, it also captured my attention. It did play the essential role of a courtyard, in bringing together all the parts of the building. At the same time, it was modest—one story in height, fully glazed, providing a simple outdoor view for the single-loaded corridor that connects the offices around it. The "tower" containing the council chamber is on axis with the grass staircase, and gives the courtyard a larger scale order than the one-story building around it.

It was perhaps this modesty, combined with a knowledge of the central role of the courtyard in the building's organization, that drew me to it. Although the tower of the council chamber is on

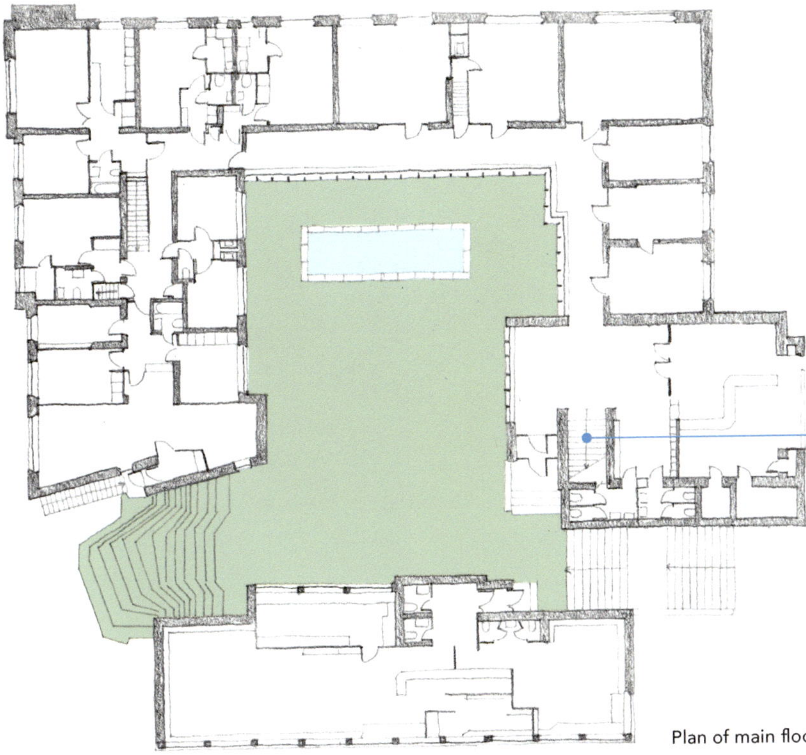

Plan of main floor.

In the corridor around the courtyard.

View of courtyard corridor from lobby at bottom of stair leading to council chamber.

axis with the grass staircase, and thereby arguably gives the courtyard a larger-scale order than the one-story building around it, even that was not very strongly emphasized in my experience. It was very small details that I noticed: the low scale of the corridor around the edge, the ledge at the sills of windows that lit that corridor, the grass in the courtyard, the simplicity and uniformity of the windows, the

Grass steps leading to courtyard.

Entrance from courtyard.

uniformity of the brick. And I did keep coming back to the courtyard, even as I visited the more iconic parts of the building.

One of the well-known attributes of Aalto's buildings is their architectural restraint. Rather than overly-exaggerated spatial moves, Aalto designed in a way that allowed for a balanced purposefulness—buildings that did not over-emphasize or flout their functional attributes. In another Aalto building, the Mount Angel Abbey Library in Oregon (one of only two buildings that Aalto designed in the United States, see page 21), the prominent main section through the building is a brilliant device for reflecting and distributing daylight, but even it is just what it needs to be and no more.

The courtyard at Säynätsalo does not have the symbolic role of the grass staircase or the loftiness of the council chamber. Nonetheless it is essential to the plan and to the functional/social organization of the building. It speaks to its role and importance with its scale, and the care of its details, rather than through a large formal intervention. Iconic moves are reserved for the grass stairs and the council chamber, and even those are carefully calibrated so as not to overwhelm the scale and position of the building.

HVITTRASK, KIRKKONUMMI, FINLAND

Incorporating the vernacular

Hvittrask. View of exterior.

IN FINLAND, I was taken to visit Hvittrask, designed and built in 1901–1903 as a house/studio for the first architecture firm of which Eliel Saarinen was a part: Gesellius, Lindgren and Saarinen. It later became the home and studio of Saarinen.

The building is an example of the "National Romantic Style" of Finland, which is related to similar styles in Scandinavian countries. The style is characterized by steep tile roofs; materials like brick, stucco, stone, and large darkened wooden boards; and reference to buildings from historical eras. Every northern European country had its own version of the style, sometimes referring to important events in the country's history. But like the Arts-and-Crafts movement in England and the United States, the buildings of that style often included modern conveniences like indoor plumbing, and the beginnings of other modern approaches like the openness of rooms to each other.

Hvittrask. Outside corner.

Hvittrask. corner alcoves.

At Hvittrask, I particularly wanted to see the studio, a large workroom which joined the two dwellings that were part of the building. It has a gable ceiling—flat on top and walls with slanted upper parts, revealing the shape of the roof, that join the flat ceiling with the vertical walls below. High windows emphasize the slope of the roof and provide daylight to the drawing tables that were just below them. This is an appealing modern room, simple in form and detail.

The building also incorporated "modern" features. In addition to the clean lines of the studio and some of the other rooms, the building's plan took advantage of views and the aesthetic pleasures of the site; it had inside bathrooms. The building was very much a hybrid, incorporating features of an imagined past as well as the use of modern materials and spatial ideas.

But it was the connection to the vernacular architecture of northern Europe that caught my attention during my visit. On a number of previous trips to Denmark, Sweden, and Norway, I had visited many vernacular wooden buildings, some of which were hundreds of years old. Some were preserved in outdoor museums and some were still in place, even in larger towns like Trondheim and Helsingor. Usually based on log construction, the houses included a special place in the main room, bounded by a low ceiling, walls, and windows, in which the main table was placed. The table had benches on its sides near the walls, and chairs on the

Hvittrask. corner alcove.

other two sides. The "master" of the house had a place at the end of the table facing across the room to the door. The table was the principal piece of furniture in the house. The transparency and light of the small windows contrasted with the darkness and thickness/heaviness of the walls and ceiling. These attributes together gave the spaces both light and a strong sense of enclosure and protection.

So the traditional vernacular of the Scandinavian countries was brought into the design as well. My immediate attraction to those spaces at Hvittrask was at least partly due to their architectural/sensual qualities and the sense of enclosure and warmth they evoked. It was only later that I thought about those spaces as part of a particular architectural movement, or even their connection to the traditional vernacular of northern Europe. What might be considered the most important part of the hundreds-of-years-old vernacular was brought into a building which was part of a movement that was bridging between the past and the twentieth century. It was not the log construction itself, but the room that was symbolically and functionally the center of family life.

DINING ROOM, AALTO HOUSE, HELSINKI, FINLAND

Simplicity and connection

House seen from garden.

MY VISIT to Finland in 2015 was largely organized to visit places with buildings designed by Alvar Aalto. The trip was too long in coming; Aalto's work had long helped support my interests in the diversity of twentieth-century architecture, and how that diversity included buildings that were responsive to their culture and place. My trip included a variety of buildings designed by Aalto, from the large and civic Finlandia Hall in Helsinki, to the small experimental house in Muuratsalo. All demonstrated a modesty of self-conscious expression and a corresponding sense of simple human comfort.

I strongly felt these two attributes in Aalto's own house and studio in Helsinki, built in the mid-1930s. It is a building with a complete lack of pretense, but careful

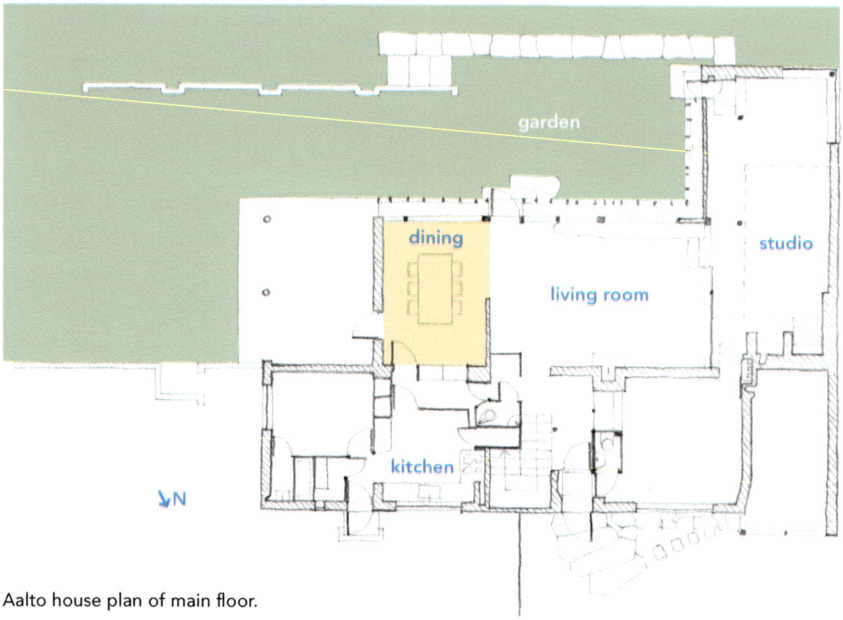

Aalto house plan of main floor.

in its details—in ways that made it into a place to live rather than a demonstration or showpiece of architectural ideas themselves. It seemed like a house where one could come home, and easily be comfortable, and where guests could do the same thing.

The ground-floor plan is composed of two lines of rooms: three large rooms facing south and enclosing a south-facing garden, and a line of smaller rooms facing north and including the main entrance. These smaller rooms include the kitchen, but also the library, office, and servants' rooms. In plan, the dining room is the end space of the living room, bringing the two rooms together into a single large space on the south side of the house, which along with the studio helps to form a large, indoor light-filled room as a kind of edge to the garden.

The dining room has its own clear spatial identity at the same time that it is strongly connected to the living room, the garden, and the kitchen. The four sides of the room are different from each other: a wall covered with fabric secured by wood slats on the east, a large window to the garden on the south, a large opening next to a full wall on the west (toward the living room), and a door and half wall with openings on the top toward the north and the kitchen.

Dining room showing window toward garden.

Dining room looking toward kitchen.

Living room looking from dining room.

Living room looking toward dining room.

Although the lack of continuity of materials on these four walls might have made the room spatially and experientially incoherent, the design at different scales helps tie it together. The top of the cabinet on the living-room wall corresponds to the line separating the wooden panels from the openings above them on the kitchen wall. The top of the opening of the door on the east wall corresponds to the top of the opening between the dining room and the kitchen. But these are modest continuities, which do not necessarily include horizontal lines that span a full wall. Indeed, the overall composition is quite informal. The surrounding surfaces include plaster, glass, fabric, wood slats, and wooden panels. It is in fact a wonderful variety, almost like the brick walls at Aalto's experimental house at Muuratsalo.

The Finnish architect Juhani Palaasma had his own explanation of the house: "Aalto's collage-like use of materials and details relieves the formal coherence of the architectural entity and the feeling of a single creator or time of construction; the setting seems to be the result of a long process of occupation by several generations rather than of an uncompromising aesthetic and deliberate design. This is 'deep' time in contrast to the 'flat' time of modernity. This is architecture conceived for comfortable and integrated life rather than visual design aimed to impress as pictures on the pages of architectural journals."[1]

Palaasma is offering one way of describing much vernacular architecture: an architecture that is rooted in time and place, and done to support "comfortable and integrated life." I did not have the sense of what I understand as the traditional Scandinavian vernacular when I entered the house and spent a little time there. But I did have a sense of ordinary human comfort, that the house would be a place to spend a lifetime, maturing as the people living in it were themselves growing and changing.

[1] Juhani Palaasma, "Rationality and Domesticity," p. 80.

TRIPOTAMOS, TINOS, GREECE

A village as a theatre

IN 2016 I made my second trip to the island of Tinos, one of the lesser-visited islands of the Cyclades. It is an extraordinarily beautiful place, with white-plastered villages that have splendid views of the sea. Stone quarries produce different varieties of marble and granite. A variety of landscapes ranges from cultivated to wild. And beaches and restaurants help organize one's days. I was staying at the house of a friend in the village of Arnados that looks over other villages to a view of the sea to the south, a view that encompasses Mykonos and Delos, a house where my friends and I enjoyed long evening conversations and late breakfasts.

One evening we were invited by a friend to his vineyard—one of many enterprises that had been established relatively recently as part of an emergent new economy of local food and wine. After we had visited the vineyard, we sat at a table at the edge of a landscape terrace, under a big Aegean sky, and enjoyed wine, bread, olives, and cheese; it was a peaceful and pleasant hour.

After we left the vineyard—by then it was probably nine or ten o'clock—we went to a nearby village, Tripotamos, for a very different experience. It was the night of a festival, with music, singing, dancing, and food, with people from the village and other places on the island all enjoying the event and the place.

The character of the event was strongly influenced by the spatial characteristics of the place in the village where it took place. It can be best described as a cone-shaped space, with the apex of the cone at the bottom, and the walls of the space moving upward and outward from the apex. At the apex was a very small horizontal space; it was too small to be a village square,[1] but large enough for a small ensemble of musicians, including a singer, a keyboardist, and a

[1] I cannot verify this, but a commercial website <https://www.greecehighdefinition.com/blog/tripotamos-tinos> (accessed Nov. 6, 2021) calls Tripotamos "perhaps the only village in Greece where a village square does not exist."

Musicians at the bottom of the common space. Photo: Artemis Anninou.

Celebration on terraces, porches, steps and landings. Photo: Artemis Anninou.

violinist. The sides of the cone expanded and rose up to include several levels of public stairs and landings, private terraces and entrances, and rooftops that accommodated people who were listening, singing, and dancing, and enjoying snacks and drinks bought from a couple of vendors who had set up their "pop-up" businesses at one or another level of this inverted public space. Every level space had people on it.

Many good buildings and towns are not fixed in their roles: they act as a flexible armature for human activity, accommodating to gradual or cyclic change. In Tripotamos, the space of the festival is usually a place of ordinary daily life. On an ordinary day there are a few people outside, walking up or down the stairs, chatting with neighbors, hanging laundry, or enjoying a cool drink together. It is peaceful; one can hear a barking dog or a car passing on the road, or music coming from someone's house. But on the night of a festival, the configuration of the space remains the same, but its shape allows for it to be transformed into a theater. And it may seem as if the space were actually made for that purpose, as well as it was for the ordinary day.

EVERYMAN THEATRE, LIVERPOOL

People first

THE ARCHITECTURE of theaters has always helped support my interest in complex buildlings: they need to be organized to accommodate multiple functions that require very different sizes and configurations of spaces, in three-dimensionally efficient ways. The stage itself is the transition zone between the audience/what the audience can see, and the "back-of-house" spaces that are the zones of production. A comedy by Michael Frayn that I particularly enjoyed when it came to Broadway, *Noises Off*, was a humorous commentary on the stage/audience relationship itself. In the play, the stage was turned around so that the audience was supposedly in the backstage looking out in the direction of where the audience should be, making the "back of the set" into the set, while various funny backstage mishaps with the actors and stagehands were taking place.

On my first trip to Liverpool, with London friends, I was happy to see the newly-rebuilt Everyman Theatre, in a building renovated by the London architectural firm Haworth Tompkins.

Everyman Theatre on street in Liverpool.

The building, very near the Liverpool Cathedral, was originally in a converted chapel on its same site. The converted building, which won the UK's Stirling Prize in 2014, is deftly designed, with a thrust stage that can be adjusted to different configurations, ample lobby space on the ground and first floors, and what seem to be efficiently-designed back-of-house spaces.

But what most struck me about the building is its remarkable façade, and the façade's relationship to the street, the interior of the building and the population of Liverpool. The theater has a strong connection to its community, and its façade is probably the most powerful possible expression of the people in that community.

The façade at the first floor, between the ground-floor entrance lobby and the rotating panels above, has clear glass, providing light and views for the lobby bar just outside the main theater space. This space is completely open to the street, helping to connect the theatre with the daily life of the city.

It is the upper three floors that have a unique appeal. They consist of 105 photographs of Liverpudlians, chosen from over 4,000 photographs, collected while the rebuilding of the theater was in progress. Each one is etched onto an aluminum panel, making the word "everyman" real to theater-goers and other

View of theater bar on first floor (ground + 1).

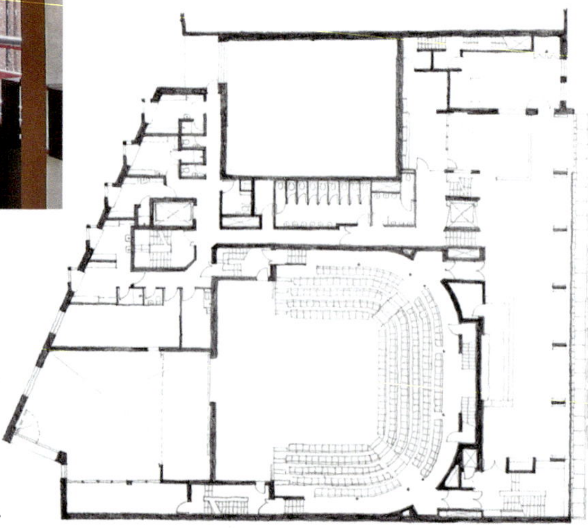

First floor (ground+1) plan of theater. Plan: Haworth Tompkins.

Close up of façade.

citizens alike. Each of these panels rotates around a vertical axis, allowing the airflow through the building to be adjusted, which along with the high thermal mass of the concrete help the building achieve a high level of passive thermal control.

The panels bring to mind other examples of visual art at some famous performance spaces—the Marc Chagall murals at New York's Metropolitan Opera, or the Charles Garnier ornament at the nineteenth-century Paris Opéra. Many modern stage theatres are more neutral with respect to art that is not the theater itself, and emphasize the particular performance—photographs and information about which are seen against a neutral architectural background, without any representational art at all.

But these portraits in Liverpool are of people who may actually be recognized by visitors to the building, connecting the building to the ordinary life of the city. And visually, the panels give scale to the façade. They are the same dimension as the height of the people themselves. According to its website, the mission of the Everyman Theatre is "to use the power of theatre to inspire, entertain and nurture positive social change." Beginning with the representation of the people of the community, the theater brings the visitor face-to-face with the reality of that mission. It happens in a theatrical way, almost analogous to the reversal of roles in Michael Frayn's play, where ordinary people from the community, just walking by and living their lives, become the stars of the show.

HOUSES, WORSHIP STREET, LONDON

Arts-and-Crafts architecture for furniture makers and craftspeople

Houses designed by Philip Webb on Worship Street, London.

THE ARCHITECT Philip Webb is best known for the design of several Arts-and-Crafts buildings, particularly the Red House that he designed in 1859, together with William Morris, for whom the building was designed and who lived there for a few years. Webb is less known for a project of six connected houses in central London. Although I have visited the Red House, it is those London industrial/residential buildings that I became quite attracted to, during my research on workshops and factories in cities.

Located on Worship Street near the district of Shoreditch, now amongst tall, modern office buildings, these buildings are essentially terraced (row) houses. They consist of workshops for craftspeople in their ground floors and basements, and dwellings on their three upper floors. The ground floors project slightly from the floors above, and have large, glazed windows that contrast with the more solid brick walls. The first building of six, at the left, had a portal that allowed access through to the back of all six buildings, a place intended for use as a timber yard. These are appealing buildings, partly because of the contrast between the ground floor of glass and upper floors which were of brick punctuated by windows.

The buildings were designed in 1862, soon after the Red House, and represent a very early example of projects involving multiple buildings specifically to combine dwelling and work. (Others in London include the Winkley Estate [see pp. 261–264] and Pullen's Yards.[1]) These buildings are near the furniture-making neighborhoods of Shoreditch and Bethnal Green, and their dwellings and workspaces were intended for craftspeople involved with that industry. The glazed fronts would have brought daylight in to support crafts of various kinds, ranging from cabinet-making to upholstery to polishing.

The buildings are rather plain in their detail. But the ground floor does have carefully-crafted windows and entrances, hinting at their connection to the Arts-and-Crafts Movement. The façades are thoughtfully designed, relying for their overall appeal on three things: the stone stringcourses that act as continuous sills below the row of small second-floor windows, the arches over the first-floor windows (similar to the arched windows at the Red House), and the contrast between the ground-floor glazing and the brick above. My own architectural attraction to them has largely to do with this visual contrast, and how it gives the buildings a sense of liveliness and activity, hinting at the craft-based activity inside the ground floor.

These buildings are connected to my research concerning the London furniture industry, and the fact that as early as 1862, there was a conscious attention to how the furniture making industry, one concentration of which was still near the center of London, might be supported by its buildings—and an apparent concern for the relationship between the house and the workplace. This row of houses was built several decades before the construction of the Winkley Estate (see p. 261). A tantalizing question comes out of Philip Webb's relationship with William Morris,

1 Thanks to Frances Holliss for bringing me to Pullen's Yards.

Detail of façade of Worship Street houses designed by Philip Webb.

Entrance to a Worship Street house.

and whether these buildings are in any way connected to Morris's advocacy of the crafts, and his ideas of the connections between life and work which, as he argued, were being severed during the nineteenth-century acceleration of the Industrial Revolution. There are very few projects in London in that era that specifically brought together dwelling and manufacturing in the same building—and this one suggests an early Arts-and-Crafts reaction against the way cities were fragmenting as the Industrial Revolution proceeded.

SILKWEAVERS' WORK SPACES, KANCHIPURAM, TAMIL NADU, INDIA

Making do, and making it beautiful

AS PART OF MY research for a book on urban industry,[1] I visited the south Indian city of Kanchipuram, in the state of Tamil Nadu, where the handloom silk weaving industry is still alive. One of my architecture students, who is from Tamil Nadu and had silk-industry contacts in Kanchipuram, was my assistant, interpreter, and guide for the fieldwork visit.

Over two weeks we visited dozens of small, family-owned weaving shops, usually part of or connected to houses, along with associated businesses such as silk dyers, loom-makers, shuttle makers, comb makers,[2] and pattern designers, who based their work on sculptures in local temples, as well as retailers and agents. The industry as a whole, which must have consisted of thousands of individual firms, some as small as one person, seemed to form

1 Howard Davis, *Working Cities: Architecture, Place and Production.*

2 The comb is a moveable part of the loom that pushes the new weft threads, that have been brought through the warp by a fast, hand-powered shuttle, tightly against the already-woven fabric.

Weavers' house in Kanchipuram.

Weavers' workshop and silk sari in Kanchipuram.

This craftsman occupies a tiny space next to the stair. He makes combs for looms, seen on the left, from dried corn stalks. Each may have thousands of dents in it.

a tight network, "one great workshop,"[3] with individual shops distributed over the geography of the entire city.

What I found remarkable was the small size and sometimes clever configurations of the rooms and spaces in which the craftspeople worked. In one tiny room, I saw two horizontal looms at two different levels, where the frame of one was located above the frame of the other, so that the weavers, on different levels, were horizontally apart from each other only by the length of one loom. I saw a comb-maker using a very sharp blade to make a three-foot-long comb with thousands of dents, or "teeth" made of dried corn stalks, all cut precisely and extremely thin. He was working in a space, adjacent to and under a concrete stair, that could not have been more than eight or ten square feet in area. I saw the sizing of silk threads taking place in the middle of a street, and a dyer's workshop with six or eight employees on the roof of a house.

3 "One great workshop" is the title of a book about the nineteenth-century cutlery industry in Sheffield where, as in Kanchipuram, the different buildings and firms associated with the industry are broadly distributed throughout the city. Nicola Wray, Bob Hawkins, and Colum Giles, *'One Great Workshop': The Buildings of the Sheffield Metal Trades.*

Silk weaver at horizontal loom.

I did not delve into the complex real-estate economics of the industry, nor into how real threats to the industry were affecting its workspaces. But for then and there, everyone was "making do"—using rooms of the house, the roof, the public space of the street. The buildings were not built for this industry, but the different parts of the industry were able to adapt to the available architectural space. "Flexibility" had a vital meaning and life to it. It was dependent on people's ingenuity combined with what remained a strong desire and ability to make beautiful things.[4]

The two horiztonally-ordered looms are in the same vertical space.

[4] The scholar and activist Annapurna Mamadipudi told us how the industry is threatened by mechanization and foreign competition. (Imagine a silk sari, with local Hindu motifs, bought by a village family following their annual ritual of a shopping expedition to the retail sari shops of Kanchipuram, imported from a large factory in China.) The talented weavers whose work I complimented, and who learned their work from their parents, loved their work. But they said that they were continuing to do it only so that their children could go to university, and get a job where they did not have to do the same thing. And Kanchipuram remained using hand-looming only by common agreement not to allow machine-powered looms in the local industry. See Annapurna Mamidipudi, *Towards a Theory of Innovation in Handloom Weaving in India*.

KARAPPANKADU, TAMIL NADU, INDIA

The unity of a village: the past or the future?

Main street of Karappankadu with temple at end.

IN THE MIDDLE of our two-week fieldwork visit to the silk-weaving industry of Kanchipuram, we took a two-day detour to the village of Karappankadu in southern Tamil Nadu. This was the ancestral village of my student, informant, and interpreter, who had arranged the details and visits of the fieldwork trip.[1] The village is about 150 miles south of Kanchipuram, several hours' journey by van, much closer to Madurai and Thanjavur (Tanjore) than Chennai, very close to the coast and the shortest crossing to Sri Lanka. We spent only a part of two days there, and a night in between. So this was a very quick visit, but it made a powerful impression and raised a major question.

1 See p. 285 for another account of the fieldwork trip.

As soon as we turned off the main road into the village, I felt the calmness of the place. We saw small clusters of houses set apart from each other, rice paddies with water supplied through hand-controlled irrigation systems, a large tank (storage pond for water), planted fields, and many trees. A temple, near the center of the village, faced down a street with brick-and-plaster courtyard houses on either side, each with a shaded porch. Late in the evening of my arrival, there was a ceremony in the temple, lasting about an hour, that involved 15 or 20 people, including my student's family, with music, singing, and offerings of food.

Rice paddy in Karappankadu.

Early in the morning, I sat outside a house on one of the raised porches, watching neighbors going in and out of houses and a man leading two cows down the street, and listening to dogs barking and birds chirping. It was ordinary, peaceful, normal.

But in my conversations, I saw and heard a few things about daily habits that spurred more thinking about the "ordinariness" of the village. The front door of the house was open from at least early in the morning, and one could see through the front door to the main courtyard of the house, and through it to the back garden. The kitchen was just inside that back door. I was told that the house had no refrigerator—that the family consumed everything on the day it was cooked, with the rest given away to poor people who frequented the temple. Members of my student's family were caretakers of the temple. Neighbors were going in and out of the house without knocking at the door.

Karappankadu houses.

View through central courtyard of house to back garden.

These observations and conversations prompted me to see the village differently—not only as a collection of people living in a remote and beautiful place, in the middle of a lush and rich agricultural landscape, but also as a single entity, in which people are acting on behalf of the village as a whole. This is not a new way of understanding a village and distinguishing it from a city, but the physical beauty of the place was a stepping stone toward this understanding. We may call it "cooperation" or "shared purpose," but those terms are not enough as they still imply the idea of individuals acting on shared behalf. In fact the individual is not primary, but shares his or her identity that defines itself as part of a group.

In the introduction to his book *Villages*, first published in 1981, the journalist Richard Critchfield wrote that "the central idea advanced in *Villages* is that village life is not only vital in itself, but is also the fundamental basis of all civilized behavior, including our own."[2]

[2] Richard Critchfield, *Villages*.

Early morning.

Karappankadu is one of about 650,000 villages in India. Part of the current narrative about India is the economic and agricultural progress that has followed its economic liberalization in 1991, its technical advances, the growth of its middle class, the construction of new highways, and modern ways of business.

Most people in India still do not live in large cities.[3] And in the world, the village has attributes that are often offered, in different places, as important steps toward changes that can support a future of environmental sustainability: social cooperation, using less, recycling more, living closer to the land and the sources of food and energy. Karappankadu seems remote, in both distance and time, from big cities and urban centers. But this sense of remoteness is tied to the erroneous ideas that progress is measured by the disappearance of small-scale agriculture in favor of industry, that small-scale agriculture is necessarily primitive, that it is only in the city that real progress is made.

If the peacefulness, beauty, and humanity of Karappankadu are indeed attributes of a model for the future, it will not be to the exclusion of cities, and not to the exclusion of modern means of agriculture. It seems important not to rely on a purely nostalgic, idealized view of the village. Indeed, Richard Critchfield's book makes it clear that villages harbor the same range of human emotions and human frailties, of good and bad, that cities also do. But villages may be one starting point for thinking about the nature of a truly sustainable future. And the beauty and calm of places like Karappankadu may suggest one aspect, out of many, of this possible future.

[3] Census of India, 2011.

CASTELVECCHIO, VERONA

Harmonic meetings of the old and new

I HAVE BEEN able to easily visit Verona during my stays in Vicenza: the two cities are only about a half hour apart by train. In addition to important churches, a restored Roman amphitheater, and a beautifully connected group of squares near the center of the city, Verona is the site of two of the architect Carlo Scarpa's most important projects, the Banca Popolare and the museum of the Castelvecchio (old castle). I did not know about Scarpa until I was teaching in Edinburgh in the early 1980s, when a colleague was talking exuberantly about the remarkable buildings by Scarpa that he had just encountered on a trip to the Veneto (the region that includes Venice, Verona, and Vicenza).

When I had the chance to visit some of Scarpas' buildings myself—the Olivetti showroom and Fondazione Querini-Stampalia in Venice, the Brion-family cemetery in San Vito d'Altivole, the Banca Popolare and the museum of the Castelvecchio in Verona among them—I was very moved by Scarpa's focus on the small scale and the detail, the foregrounding of materials, the importance of the surface, the deliberate contrast between old and new.

Scarpa, who lived from 1906 to 1978, was born in Venice, spent years of his childhood in Vicenza, and did a good part of his architectural work in or near both cities. He had a deep respect not only for materials, but specifically for the historic building materials of the Veneto. For Scarpa, the ultimate "preservation architect," there was not a choice to be made between old and new, but instead the working out of how they would become equally present, inseparable and dependent on each other for their identity.

The Castelvecchio has qualities that are not present in some of Scarpa's other buildings. Because it is a large building with large rooms and spaces, it has the ability to maintain a contrast between the more intense places where different materials, old and new, meet, and the larger surfaces of walls, floors, and ceilings that are more expansive, continuous, and calm. This allows the visitor to

These photos of the Castelvecchio all show how Scarpa brought together the construction of the old building with modern materials and techniques.

the building not to be overwhelmed by its details, but to experience them individually, often at places of transition between rooms and spaces—for those details to emphasize transitions and changes of materials, as many architectural details often do. In those ways, the Castelvecchio has an ordinariness about it that provides a calm backdrop for the more intense rhythm of material transitions, temporal transitions, and details.

Materials of the traditional architecture of Venice.

Some of Scarpa's contrasts, in the Castelvecchio alone, include a modern steel stair and narrow balcony in contrast to the brick wall behind it; the wall with a square grid of stones finished differently, some smooth and others, larger, more roughly cut; the steel windows set into a stone wall but not in the same plane; the separation of a smoothly-finished stone-slab stair from a more roughly-finished stone wall. These showed not only the juxtaposition of modern and older materials, and the techniques of their construction.

All of this makes the Castelvecchio into a museum of three kinds: of the old castle itself, which is evident in the overall order and location of the building at a river crossing; of the use and shaping of brick, stone, and wood, connecting the visitor to the traditional materials of the Veneto; and finally of the use of steel, concrete, and glass, demonstrating that modern construction techniques do not represent a break with history, but are very much part of architecture's continuous evolution.

HEDMARK MUSEUM, HAMAR, NORWAY

Ancient stone and modern wood

THE TWENTIETH-CENTURY Norwegian architect Sverre Fehn worked with a deep respect for the traditional wooden architecture of Norway. After many years of looking at his Hedmark Museum in books and journals, I finally had the opportunity to visit it. After several days at a conference in Bergen, I went to Oslo, so that I could easily take the one-hour train journey to Hamar, where the building is located at the outskirts of town. It is largely the reconstruction of an old, stone barn, built in the early eighteenth century on the ruins of a bishop's manor, in which the old stone remains, in contrast with the new concrete and timber.[1]

The oldest structures associated with the project date from the middle of the twelfth century, and what's visible of those structures are incomplete stone walls. Fehn did not completely restore or re-construct those walls, but raised them and stabilized them, and introduced contemporary construction systems that contrast with them. These

Interior of museum showing old stonework and modern concrete and wood.

[1] Information about the building's history comes from Jorgen Tandberg, "Revisit: Hedmark Museum in Hamar, Norway by Sverre Fehn." *The Architectural Review*, 9 August 2021. https://www.architectural-review.com/essays/revisit/revisit-hedmark-museum-in-hamar-norway-by-sverre-fehn

Interior of museum showing old stonework and modern concrete and wood.

include glu-lam beams for the walls and ceilings/roofs, and poured concrete, largely for the second-floor slab and ramp(s) leading up to it. The beauty of the building comes from the visual presence of the glu-lam roof trusses, and from the continuity of the concrete ramps and the formwork of the low walls that frame them. Both the wood and the concrete exist in visual contrast to the historic stone walls. Like Carlo Scarpa in the Veneto (see p. 292), Fehn puts the historic and contemporary into a balance so that the beauty and importance of each is made more visible and prominent by the other—and neither is more important than the other.

Traditional wooden architecture of Norway consists of load-bearing log construction (as well as frame construction used in old farm communities on the west coast of the country, and often for porches and similar extensions of houses). The frame construction tends not to be heavy-timber framing—so although Fehn used wood to connect to the Norwegian past, it is done in a contemporary way with the material itself, but not necessarily the replication of historic details that were made with it.

In the museum, the use of daylight is minimized and carefully controlled, apparently to protect the objects of folk culture displayed inside as part of the historic collection. Despite the variety of materials and complexity of spatial relationships, the overall feeling of the building is a unified one that comes largely from the continuity and repetition of construction details, with old and new working together in harmony. All the materials are experienced at a variety of scales. The small scale in particular—including the individual wood members, the metal fittings, the formwork clearly showing on the concrete, and the ancient stones in the outer walls—help give the building a sense of complexity, accentuating the museum's role as a place for exploration. In combination with the relatively low level of daylight, the focus on construction and detail help give the building an intimacy and welcoming scale that seem appropriate for this museum in a small Norwegian town. My visit was worth the two- or three-decade wait.

Interior of museum showing old stonework, modern concrete and wood, and the reconstruction of an old board gate.

PLACE DU TERTRE, MONTMARTRE, PARIS

Three ways of seeing

Place du Tertre, 2022.

I HAVE BEEN to the Place du Tertre a few times on my trips to Paris. It is a lovely square: relatively small, with a grid of trees that provide shade and help order its space, still bounded by the two- and three-story buildings that were already there 100 years ago. It is now full of artists—and tourists who also visit the Basilica of Sacre-Coeur, the Montmartre landmark just steps away.

But unlike the other reflections in this book, the Place du Tertre has a strong connection with me only partly because I have appreciated it on my visits. I have been looking for many years at photographs of the square by another visitor, the French photographer Eugène Atget, who photographed it in the 1920s. Atget was trying to record a historic city that he saw as being threatened by demolition and new construction, and this led to a unique record of Paris, consisting of thousands of pictures.[1]

Atget took at least three photographs of the Place du Tertre in the 1920s. Together they show different aspects of the same place,

[1] Most of Atgets' pictures are held by the Museum of Modern Art in New York and three archives in Paris: the Bibliotheque Nationale, the Musée Carnavalet and the Bibliotheque Historique de la Ville de Paris. They have been published in many books, including a four-volume work, *The Work of Atget*, edited by John Szarkowski, longtime curator of photography at the Museum of Modern Art. Atget's photographs were originally brought to New York by the photographer Berenice Abbott.

bringing together the square's geometry with its potential for human life, and with the inanimate things that help the square support that life. This has helped me see and interpret not only the square, but also similar complex places in which human activity is supported by the physical frameworks of architecture and what is brought to them as benches, chairs, kiosks, trees, plants, lights, signs, paving stones, Metro entrances, bus shelters, and many other things.

The first photograph was taken on an overcast day sometime between late fall and early spring, probably in the early morning, when Atget took many of his photographs. This view emphasizes the orthogonality of the square (done through the one-point perspective that keeps the far row of buildings in a plane parallel to the picture plane), the grid-like arrangement of the trees themselves, and the emphasis on their trunks rather than what would be an emphasis on their crowns if the trees were in leaf. The orthogonality is emphasized by a view of the left-hand side of the square and the first row of trees, which together form an axis, reinforced by the roadway. The photograph shows a variety of buildings around the square: the far side has a four-story building, two two-story buildings, and a three-story building, with three different roof shapes.

When I first looked at the photograph, what also came through is what the geometry, buildings, and trees suggest *could* be there but is not, about how the square might support daily life. In this photograph, the square is a little forbidding—bare and windswept—but we can imagine it when there are people there in spring and summer: sunny, dappled light

Place du Tertre, Atget photograph, 1922. Musée Carnavalet, Paris.

Place du Tertre, Atget photograph, 1922. Digital Image © The Museum of Modern Art/Licensed by SCALA/Art Resource, NY.

Place du Tertre, Atget photograph, 1924. Musée Carnavalet, Paris.

when the trees are in leaf, in the middle of the day a rather pleasant place. In fall a little chilly, crisp leaves on the ground. People sitting and walking, babies in carriages, children kicking a ball around, old men with canes sitting and talking. Shops open, cafés and restaurants with tables and chairs in the square. There is a balance between the regular geometry of the square and what one imagines is its human life. But so far this is left to the imagination.

The second photograph is taken from a different place, and starts to illustrate what is only suggested by the first one. Although the camera is pointing in more-or-less the same direction as the first photograph, the overall geometry is not emphasized as much. The side of the square on the left of the first picture is not visible at all, and the de-emphasis on the lines of perspective gives a little more dynamism to the picture. Atget is closer than in the first picture to the buildings on the far side, and more visible are a bench (framed by two mature trees), a kiosk, tree protectors, and the signs and details on the far buildings—all the things that work at a scale smaller than the square itself, helping provide the "support" for the human life in the square.

The third photograph was taken two years later, in May rather than March, well into spring. It de-emphasizes the overall square and even its buildings. The trees are in leaf, and tables and chairs are out. John Szarkowski writes, "what in March always looked like an old town square became in May the setting for a large outdoor restaurant-café."[2] And although this picture shows the square in morning, before its human use, and it includes the fixed buildings and trees, it gives more emphasis to all the apparatus and objects needed for the people who would come later in the day.

When I was teaching introductory architecture studios at Berkeley, working under the master teacher Raymond Lifchez, Ray talked about "support, fill and activity"—the structural and spatial framework of a building, the furniture and objects that people bring to it, and the human activity that is enabled by all those inanimate things. We have no idea whether Atget was thinking about anything like this. But looked at together, Atgets' three photographs illustrate this idea rather beautifully. And together, they have helped me understand the complexity and meaning of this ordinary place.[3]

[2] John Szarkowski, *The Work of Atget: The Art of Old Paris*, p. 186.

[3] Apparently, the Place du Tertre also had an important, symbolic role in the formation of the French automobile manufacturing industry. A plaque in the square reads: "Pour la premiere fois le 24 Décembre 1898 une voiture a pétrole pilotée par Louis RENAULT son constructeur atteignit la Place du Tertre marquant ainsi le depart de l'industrie automobile Française," or "For the first time on December 24, 1898 a gasoline car driven by Louis Renault, its manufacturer, reached the Place du Tertre, thus marking the start of the French automobile industry."

GEFFEN HALL, LINCOLN CENTER, NEW YORK

Music and wood

ON A TRIP to New York with Portland friends, we went to hear Bach's *St. Matthew Passion*, in the newly reconstructed Geffen Hall. One of the original buildings of Lincoln Center, designed by Max Abramovitz, Geffen Hall was first named Philharmonic Hall and later Avery Fisher Hall. It had a troubled acoustic history since its original construction in the 1960s. The room had at least two major renovations since it was built, but none had improved the musical acoustics to the satisfaction of the public, music critics, or the musicians themselves. The newest renovation, intended to fix it once and for all, was a complete reconstruction of the building, designed by a team that included Tod Williams and Billie Tsien, along with Diamond Schmitt Architects. This renovation left only the exterior columns and walls but involved the total redesign and replacement of everything inside, including a radical transformation of the concert hall. The hall had only been completed and reopened only a few months before our visit.

Geffen Hall, Lincoln Center, NY, looking toward stage.

Geffen Hall, Lincoln Center, NY, balconies.

I had been to the previous Avery Fisher Hall numerous times. It was certainly familiar; I associated it with New York and Lincoln Center, but it did not particularly move me as an important work of architecture. And although I had read about the new project and had seen some pictures, I did not focus on them very much. So I did not really know what to expect when I entered the hall, except that the proscenium had been eliminated and the stage was now located in the same space as the audience.

Our seats were on the main floor, in the back of the orchestra section, so we entered at that level in the back. And I can only describe my reaction when entering as "stunned delight." I was immediately taken by what I can only describe as the "life of the room," the way in which the new shape of the room, the closeness of the stage and my connection to it (even though I was at the other end of the room from it), the coherence of the wood surfaces and details—including the vertical wood slats, the railings at balcony edges, the array of lights above—all came together to make a room that was bright and whole in its feeling.

The wood-covered balconies played a particularly strong role in giving the room its architectural unity, with the horizontal lines they formed, that continued alongside the stage and behind it (in front of a section of seats to be used for a chorus or for additional audience members). The smaller wood details—which had their own acoustic function—also helped provide a necessary level of scale to the surrounding surfaces. But there was also a restraint to the wood detailing; it did not seem superfluous in the context of the visual resolution of the design—and I can only assume that the same was true for its acoustic function.

An array of simple hanging lights over the stage helped give just the right amount of focus to the stage, balancing its importance with its inclusion, along with the audience, in the main space of the hall. And a deep blue light on some of the upper walls helped give an illusion of the night sky.

Bach's beautiful *St. Matthew Passion* has always seemed to me like a modern piece of music, and the new hall turned out to be the perfect place to hear it. Others may be better able to pass judgment on the detailed acoustics of the room, but I felt close to the music, and able to appreciate the full range of sound, from the piccolo to an extraordinary baritone. Here was a living example of architecture's ability to give us delight, and to set the stage for more of it.

EXPERIMENTAL HOUSING PROJECT, MEXICALI, BAJA CALIFORNIA, MEXICO

A re-encounter after four decades

THE YEAR AFTER graduating from architecture school, I was part of a team led by Christopher Alexander that carried out an innovative housing project in Mexicali. Our work had several goals: to keep building costs low, so low-income people could afford the houses; to allow people to design their own houses, to satisfy their individual needs, which made all the houses different; to respond to the extreme local climate in which the daily high temperature regularly reaches 110°F for several months a year; and to build the houses to resist the impact of frequent earthquakes in the region.

These goals led to the development of a building system that involved interlocking mortarless concrete blocks, with a component of soil in the mix, that when stacked accommodated steel rods set in concrete for earthquake resistance. The roofs were made of lightweight concrete vaults. The construction system was developed to allow the houses to be designed directly on the ground without the use of architectural drawings, and there were various agreements with the lender and local government regarding financing, building codes, and site design.

We developed these innovations through the construction of a cluster of experimental buildings. These were followed by five houses designed individually by the families. We spent over a year

Building the experimental buildings in 1976: construction work on roofs, showing walls and round columns in foreground.

Placing concrete for roof vault.

Shaping a window opening.

living near the site while working on the project. It was a difficult year in many ways, but ultimately satisfying: the families were by-and-large happy with their houses and the sense of agency that working on the houses gave them; a book was published about the project and its relationship to ideals about the design and construction of housing; and for those of us who worked on the project, it remained an important step at the beginning of our careers.[1]

Until 2023, I had last visited the project in 1982, a few years after it was completed. In 2023 I was invited to participate in an event on the site of the project. It was sponsored by INSITE, an arts organization that includes members from the region that spans California and Mexico, including the cities of San Diego, Tijuana, and Mexicali. INSITE's goal is to support art and artists for whom the landscape of the region is important to their work, and the project started to be seen as an important place in that landscape. The three-day event brought together about 200 people, including artists, architects, students, scholars, and journalists, for presentations and conversations on the site—now known as "El Sitio"—and in other places in the city of Mexicali.

Although I had not been to the site in many years, I knew that the buildings were still there, that some of the families were still living there, and that the experimental buildings were in use. But I knew little else about it. Arriving there and spending several hours a day there over three days were highly moving experiences. The project looked as we had left it, the buildings had been maintained, the houses had been altered and added to, the experimental buildings

[1] The team included Christopher Alexander, Don Corner, Howard Davis, Julio Martínez and Jenny Young. The book is Christopher Alexander et al., *The Production of Houses*.

The project after almost five decades, in 2023, at event to highlight the project: main entrance looking toward street.

View to courtyard.

were in use. When I arrived on the first day of the event, it was as if no time had passed: the project looked familiar and very much part of my life. But at the same time remarkable, knowing that much time had indeed gone by. I was heartened to hear that over several decades, the buildings remained in use and served people's needs. The experimental buildings housed, for several years, one of the professors of the local architecture school and his family—including a son who is presently an artist, and who I met at the event with his mother, who now lives in Mexico City. They both spoke highly of the time their family spent living there; the mother called it "paradise." At the time of our visit, the buildings housed a local community clinic, which has now reverted back to the architecture school that will use it as an off-campus construction laboratory. It was gratifying to know that

Main courtyard with canopy for shade.

Kitchen of Rodríguez family, originally built in 1976.

Public conversation about project.

the life of these buildings had persisted for the several decades they did, through and including the INSITE event.

The most moving experience was a visit to the house of one of the three families who were still living in the houses they built for themselves, the Rodríguez family. We were welcomed by the daughter of the couple who were the original owners. Her father, who was a happy man whose humor and optimism was essential to the project, was no longer alive; her now-elderly mother was present but said little. The daughter showed us, with great pride, the new living room they had built, the new floor and countertops in the kitchen, and a picture of her father when he was a young man, hanging on the wall with many other family pictures.

My visit to El Sitio was one of two or three "re-encounters" described in this book, and my visit to the Rodríguez house was the highlight of my visit. It reminded me of the commitment that all five families had made, their willingness to be part of this experimental project, and the work they put in, for the better part of a year, to bring the project to fruition.

People at Mexicali event.

2024

JARDIM PIRATININGA AND AVENIDA PAULISTA, SÃO PAULO, BRAZIL

A world of urban co-existence

THIS FINAL REFLECTION was written a few days after a trip that I did not expect would include places to be described in this book. I had been invited to speak in São Paulo, at the annual meeting of the International Seminar on Urban Form (ISUF). Asked to join a few post-conference excursions, I chose to visit the Avenida Paulista, a modern street in the center of the city, and the Jardim Piratininga, a neighborhood that is one of Brazil's models for successful support of informal settlements.

Avenida Paulista from one of the tall buildings along it.

Small businesses near modern art museum designed by Lina Bo Bardi.

Small businesses along pedestrian walks at edge of Avenida Paulista.

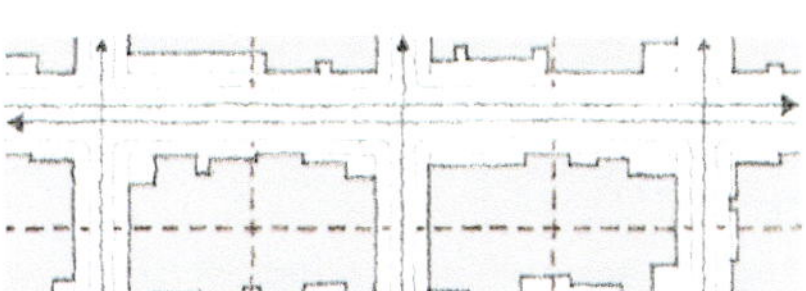

Diagram showing grids of principal streets and pedestrian walks along Avenida Paulista.

The Avenida Paulista is a wide, modern avenue, lined with high-rise buildings that had replaced old colonial mansions. The buildings are mostly mixed-use, incorporating retail, office, and residential space. Many have entrances on all four sides, setting up a secondary pedestrian grid, shifted from the main grid of wide avenue and cross streets. And some of the buildings have outdoor space—public terraces and gardens—on floors a few levels above the street. Altogether these elements give the city a three-dimensionality and variety of scale of public space that is an extension of the main, full-of-traffic avenue and vehicular cross streets. The buildings include private developments as well as public facilities, including a library and, a couple of blocks away, a modern art museum designed by the Italian-Brazilian architect Lina Bo Bardi.

By itself, that all represented an architecturally rich area of the city. But in addition, at the ground, were street vendors selling food, jewelry, clothing—filling in the gaps between buildings, making walking in the city varied in its experience, providing the kinds of goods and services that are not available inside the buildings—and providing livelihoods for the vendors. The street vendors gave additional life to urban space that was already quite complex and lively.[1]

The next day I visited an informal settlement, the Jardim Piratininga, that was quite different in its architecture and manner of formation. This was a low-rise settlement, with most buildings one or two stories tall, a few were four or five stories. Some of the houses were rudimentary, sided in plywood. Most had brick-and-mortar walls, with solid or hollow fired brick, some with stucco over the brick. All the houses were different; people built when they had the money to do so and did it in a personal way, leading to a healthy variety in the collective environment of the houses and streets.

And there was enterprise everywhere. People were sitting in their garages using sharp knives to peel manioc (cassava) to be cooked or turned into flour after its sale. One man was making kitchen countertops in his workshop in a shed next to his house. A fruit-and-vegetable market appeared in the middle of the settlement, with vendors barking their goods. Trucks parked next to houses advertised delivery services. A grocery store was open to the street, in the ground floor of a five-story apartment house. A tiny corner store sold household cleaning supplies. This seemed like a neighborhood headed for economic success.

Clearly, the Avenida Paulista and the informal settlement are quite different from each other. But not completely. In each of

1 The history of the Avenida Paulista, brought up to the present with its advanced, small-scale interventions, is described in a book by Renata Priore Lima, *The Avenida Paulista as a Linear Urban Centre: Collective Spaces, Plug-Ins and Urban Interfaces.*

Vegetable market in street of Piratininga.

Small retail business at ground floor of house in Piratininga.

Craftsperson making kitchen counters at home workshop in Piratininga.

them, small-scale enterprise is welcome; in both cases the space of that enterprise was easily available from the public realm; in both cases at least some of the businesses were just starting out; in both cases the continuity of streets and public spaces supported small-scale businesses.[2] As different as they seemed at first sight, both were contributing to the informal urban economy, giving people the opportunity to join that economy near the "bottom", thereby helping eliminate the sharp divide that is so present and typical in contemporary urbanism. I thought I was going to visit two places that were "opposite"—but it turned out that their commonalities were as visible and important as their differences.

[2] They were accessible and strongly connected to the overall street network.

AFTERWORD: WHAT I SAW

THE INSIGHTS I gained from these hundred places have played a large role in the ways I see and think about architecture. Over the years, I have thought about these places, talked about them with students, used them as case studies in my research, and sometimes revisited them multiple times. Working on the book also gave me the opportunity to revisit and remember many of the buildings and places through my large collection of slides and digital photos—re-encounters that have themselves rekindled memories that were never really lost.

It was only after the writing that I realized that there are commonalities of ideas among many of the hundred places. These ideas, shared across different categories of geography and human purpose, in different eras of history, form a complex web of connections, defying any neat arrangement into singular categories. The ideas all spring from an understanding of buildings and places as the armatures for human experience—and that a few attributes may be important in their ability to help make places with usefulness, longevity and human attachment.

These include such characteristics as spatial overlaps, continuities and connections; the importance of the small and large together; the continuity of urban public space; boundaries and in-between space as places; functional complexity and mixed uses; the importance of texture, ornament, color, and daylight; the ability of a place to evoke strong emotions.

These do not add up to an exhaustive list, as this is not a "how-to" book. I did not start working on this book with these ideas as a guide. Writing the reflections, I started with the memory, and it was through the writing, when I tried to uncover the reasons for the persistence of the memory, that these ideas emerged. Going back to Peter Zumthor's words in the Introduction, "first the emotion, and then the scientific, academic explanation," it seemed as if the memory was of something real, and that my task was not only to report the memory itself, but to try to understand what made it important enough to remember.

Sometimes the memory was clear in its lessons; other times it took more work to bring out its important points. That was often accomplished through the writing—through a conscious attempt to find explicit meaning in something that started out vague but possibly important. To me, the importance of that meaning existed in well-known buildings, in everyday places that were part of my ordinary life, and, through my travels, everyday places that were part of the ordinary life of others. I see all of these as important, and all are woven together in my experience.

But this kind of experience is not mine alone. We all experience rooms and buildings, streets and gardens, dense cities and open landscapes. We live in them, look at them and maybe wonder about them. If we engage those places with an open mind, and a generosity of spirit toward the people who inhabit them and build them, we will find that the world of buildings and cities belongs to all of us. The reader is encouraged to walk, to wander, to travel, to look and to wonder at what they see—and may find, as I did, that the built world is infinitely rich with the products of human creation and the physical armatures of human life.

In the course of a typical day, we may encounter dozens, or even hundreds of places, large and small. Daily life helps make us aware of them, even if for only a few seconds: an appealing garden; a well-designed counter in a café; a simple porch with people talking and laughing; a lively street. We look, we quickly make a judgment, maybe not even explicitly aware that we are doing so, and we go on.

These most ordinary things, sometimes remembered and sometimes not, are the ground of our existence in the world, holding it all up. Most of us are in the built world, surrounded by those ordinary things along with some that may be extraordinary, for our entire day. Occasionally elements of that world rise up as something worth paying particular attention to, sometimes belonging to the ordinary world but standing out from it at the same time. This book has described some of those places, famous or not, "architecture" or "building," large or small, beautiful but sometimes not, that have stayed in my memory longer.

ACKNOWLEDGEMENTS AND THANKS

MANY PEOPLE have helped with this complex project, in large and small ways. My thanks, once again, to Fran Ford, who saw the potential of the project and supported me with her comments about my writing; the review board at Routledge who, as it turned out, helped finalize the title; and the external reviewers of the proposal, who had helpful advice for the development of the text.

For being incisive critics of the manuscript, I thank Jenny Young, who read the whole work carefully and provided many important comments that helped me eliminate the not-so-useful and give the book more clarity; Tom Kerr, whose early reading of the manuscript helped me give each entry the emphasis it needed; Judith Kenny, who helped me understand how the book should be seen by its readers; Nick Seemann, who read a couple of reflections every day with his morning coffee in Sydney and encouraged me to give each reflection more information. Don Corner provided useful insights about the title and purpose of the book, and suggestions at critical times about the text. Thanks to Alvin Comiter for many conversations about the book, Paris, and the French photographer Eugène Atget. Thanks also to Tom Hubka for setting the example of what it means to write a good book, David Week for his basic questions of the purpose of the book, and Luke Janzen for helpful conversations at the beginning of writing. Thanks also for help and useful talks, large and small, to August Stolba, Hajo Neis, Dorit Fromm, Caleb Bean, Maksym Rokmaniko, Jim Givens, Ilona Givens and Philip Shelley.

For helping me navigate particular places, I am grateful to Artemis Anninou in Greece, Gernot Mittersteiner and Michi Bier in Vienna, Achyuthan Ramaswamy in south India, Nalini Thakur in Delhi, Azhar Tyabji in Ahmedabad and Delhi, Nick Seemann in Nepal, Ashley Dhanani, Matt Brown, Francesca Froy, Frances Holliss and Adam Hart in London, Myron Stachiw in Ukraine, Virginia Cartwright for connecting me with architects in Finland, Tom Kerr in India and Thailand, Esther Hagenlocher in Germany, Jean Castex in Paris, Ron Lovinger in Japan, Malcolm Fraser and Helen Lucas in Edinburgh, and Andrea Torreblanca, Carmen Cuenca, Michael Krichman and Felipe Orensanz in Mexicali. Particular thanks go to Siân Thérèse and Neil Weightman with whom I visited Liverpool, and for wonderful days looking at villages and ruins in Shropshire, Derbyshire, West Sussex, Kent and the counties near Abbotsley—not to mention London. Thanks to my brother, Bob Davis, for arranging for the digitization of home movies of Brooklyn from decades ago, Aya Brackett for her photographs of the house her father built in California, Oregon architecture students, now alumni, Ryan Arreola and Yash Akhouri for their photographs in Lugano, Rigel Wakil for his photograph of Kyoto, Christian Wallenborg for locating photographs (and the photographer) of the Lewerentz church in Stockholm, Manas Murthy and Vanicka Arora for their research on brickwork in Nepal.

For the illustrations, I had excellent and committed help from Ian Nielsen-Fox, who skillfully and effectively did most of the drawings, Erik Larson, who developed several of the complex three-dimensional drawings, and other students who helped with the illustrations, including Jonah Nees, Cole Persons, Erin Davis, and Gita Akkihal. Sheri Pyron and Zachary Leonard brought artists' sensibilities to the paintings. Many thanks to Alvin Comiter who helped with photo editing and color management. And thanks also to Oregon colleagues Erik Steiner, Peter Keyes, Judith Sheine, and Abe Kelso.

Finally, big thanks to copyeditor Patricia Teasdale, whose deliberately soft touch was greatly appreciated, and to Alex Lazarou, who carried the book design through with understanding, skill and a strong aesthetic sensibility. What the book looks and feels like is the result of Alex's good work.

WORKS CONSULTED

Ahlin, Janne, *Sigurd Lewerentz, Architect: 1885–1975*. Stockholm: Byggforlaget, 1987.

Alexander, Christopher, *A Pattern Language*. New York: Oxford University Press, 1977.

Alexander, Christopher et al., "Perception and Modular Coordination." *Journal of the Royal Institute of British Architects* (1959) 66 (12): 425–429.

Alexander, Christopher, *The Nature of Order, vol. 1, The Phenomenon of Life*. Berkeley: Center for Environmental Structure, 2001.

Alexander, Christopher, *The Timeless Way of Building*. New York: Oxford University Press, 1979.

Alexander, Christopher, Howard Davis, Don Corner, and Julio Martinez, *The Production of Houses*. New York: Oxford University Press, 1985.

Arora, Vanicka and Manas Murthy, "Inventing Tradition in Bhaktapur, Nepal: The Trajectories of Lime in Heritage Reconstruction." *Change Over Time* (2023) 12 (1): 34–51.

Ballon, Hilary. *The Greatest Grid: The Master Plan of Manhattan 1811–2011*. New York: Columbia University Press, 2012.

Bendiner-Viani, Gabrielle, *The Cities We Need: Essential Stories of Everyday Places*. Cambridge, MA: MIT Press, 2024.

Benjamin, Walter, *The Arcades Project*. Cambridge and London: The Belknap Press of Harvard University Press, 1999.

Bergdoll, Barry, *Karl Friedrich Schinkel: An Architecture for Prussia*. New York: Rizzoli, 1994.

Blau, Eve, *Red Vienna*. Cambridge, MA: MIT Press, 1999.

Calvino, Italo, *Invisible Cities*. New York: Harcourt Brace Jovanovich, 1978.

Cardwell, Kenneth, *Bernard Maybeck: Artisan, Architect, Artist*. Santa Barbara: Peregrine Smith, 1977.

Caviness, Madeline H. and Jeffrey Hamburger, "Reply to Filler." *The New York Review of Books*, daily, Dec. 17, 2014.

Chatwin, Bruce, *In Patagonia*. New York: Penguin, 1988.

Clarke, Linda, *Building Capitalism: Historical Change and the Labour Process in the Production of the Built Environment*. London: Routledge, 1992.

Clausen, Meredith, "Belluschi and the Equitable Building in History." *Journal of the Society of Architectural Historians* (1991) 50 (2): 109–129.

Coffin, Christie Johnson and Jenny Young, *Making Places for People: 12 Questions Every Designer Should Ask*. New York: Routledge, 2017, second edition 2024.

Critchfield, Richard, *Villages*. New York: Garden City, 1983.

Davis, Howard (Ed.), *Early and Unpublished Writings of Christopher Alexander*. London: Routledge, 2022.

Davis, Howard. "Learning from Vellore." *Arcade: The Northwest Journal for Architecture and Design*, March/April 1993.

Davis, Howard, *Living Over the Store: Architecture and Local Urban Life*. London: Routledge, 2012.

Davis, Howard, *The Culture of Building*. New York: Oxford University Press, 1999, reprinted in paperback 2006.

Davis, Howard, *Working Cities: Architecture, Place and Production*. London: Routledge, 2020.

Davis, Howard and Adam Hart, "From the Bottom Up: Gillett Square in London." In Adnan Morshed, ed., *Spatial (In)justice: How Does It Manifest in the Built Environment?* Hoboken: Wiley, 2026.

Davis, Howard and Ashley Dhanani. "The Winkley Estate." *U + D Urban Form and Design*, special issue on "Retail Environment" (2019) 11/12 (VI).

Davis, Howard and David Week. "The Village Meets the City." *Architecture + Design (New Delhi)*, March–April 1993.

De Soto, Hernando, *The Mystery of Capital*. New York: Basic Books, 2003.

Dickens, Charles. *The Uncommercial Traveller*. Oxford: Oxford University Press, 2022.

Didion, Joan, "Why I Write." *The New York Times*, Dec. 5, 1976.

Fermor, Patrick Leigh, *Mani: Travels in the Southern Peloponnese*. New York: New York Review Books, 2006.

Fermor, Patrick Leigh, *Roumeli: Travels in Northern Greece*. New York: New York Review Books, 2006.

Fermor, Patrick Leigh, *The Broken Road: From the Iron Gates to Mount Athos*. New York: New York Review Books, 2013.

Filler, Martin, "A Scandalous Makeover at Chartres." *The New York Review of Books*, daily, Dec. 14, 2014.

Ford, Edward R., *The Details of Modern Architecture, vol. 1*. Cambridge: MIT Press, 2003.

Goethe, Johann Wolfgang von, *Italian Journey*. San Francisco: North Point Press, 1982.

Goodyear, Dana, "From the Ground Up." *The New Yorker*, Oct. 12, 2020, pp. 54–55.

Grabow, Stephen, *Christopher Alexander: The Search for a New Paradigm in Architecture*. London: Routledge, Kegan + Paul, 1983.

Habraken, N. J., *The Structure of the Ordinary: Form and Control in the Built Environment*. Cambridge, MA: MIT Press, 1998.

Hansen, Maria Fabricius, *The Eloquence of Appropriation: Prolegomena to an Understanding of Spolia in Early Christian Rome*. Rome: "L'Erma" di Bretschneider, 2004.

Herzfeld, Michael, *Evicted from Eternity: The Restructuring of Modern Rome*. Chicago: University of Chicago Press, 2009.

Holliss, Frances, *Beyond Live/Work: The Architecture of Home-Based Work*. London: Routledge, 2015.

Holzer, Harold, *Lincoln at Cooper Union: The Speech That Made Abraham Lincoln President*. New York: Simon & Schuster, 2006.

Hurwit, Jeffrey M., *The Acropolis in the Age of Pericles*. Cambridge: Cambridge University Press, 2004.

Jacobs, Allan, Elizabeth MacDonald, and Yodan Rofe, *The Boulevard Book: History, Evolution, Design of Multiway Boulevards*. Cambridge: MA: MIT Press, 2002.

Jacobs, Jane, "Diamonds in the Tough." In Jane Jacobs, *Vital Little Plans: The Short Works of Jane Jacobs*, edited by Samuel Zipp and Nathan Storring. New York: Random House, 2016.

Jain, Kulbhushan and Minakshi Jain, *Architecture of the Indian Desert*. Ahmedabad, India: AADI Centre, 2000.

Jain, Shikha, *Havelis: A Living Tradition of Rajasthan*. Gurgaon, India: Shubhi Publications, 2004.

James, John, *The Masons who Built Chartres*. London: Routledge & Kegan Paul, 1985.

Katchor, Ben. *Cheap Novelties: The Pleasure of Urban Decay*. London: Penguin, 1991.

Katchor, Ben. *Julius Knipl, Real Estate Photographer*. New York: Pantheon, 2000.

Kazin, Alfred, *A Walker in the City*. New York: Harcourt, Brace and Company, 1951.

Keeler, Charles, *The Simple Home*. Santa Barbara and Salt Lake City: Peregrine Smith, 1979. Reprint of original 1904 edition published by P. Elder, San Francisco.

Landmarks Preservation Commission, Designation List 282, LP-1963, June 17, 1997 (Brooklyn Public Library).

Le Corbusier, *Oeuvre Complet, 1952–57*. Zurich: W. Boesiger, 1958.

Le Corbusier, *The Journey to the East*. Translated by Ivan Zaknic. Cambridge, MA: MIT Press, 1987.

Lima, Renata Priori, *Avenida Paulista Como Centro Urban Lineal: Espacios Colectivos, Plug-ins and Interfaces*. Madrid: Fundacion Arquia, 2020.

Livingston, Morna, *Steps to Water: The Ancient Stepwells of India*. New York: Princeton Architectural Press, 2002.

London Borough of Tower Hamlets, "Old Bethnal Green Road Conservation Area (Winkley Estate and Surrounding Area): Character Appraisal and Management Guidelines." 2009.

Mamidipudi, Annapurna, *Towards a Theory of Innovation in Handloom Weaving in India*. Doctoral Thesis, Maastricht University, 2016. Maastricht University. https://doi.org/10.26481/dis.20160414am

Marcus, Sharon, *Apartment Stories: City and Home in Nineteenth-Century Paris and London*. Berkeley: University of California Press, 1999.

Mari, Francesca, "Imagine a Renter's Utopia. It Might Look Like Vienna." *The New York Times Magazine*, May 23, 2023.

McCoy, Esther, *Five California Architects*. New York: Reinhold, 1960.

Millhauser, Steven, *Martin Dressler: The Tale of an American Dreamer*. New York: Crown, 1996.

Minton, Anna, "Newcastle's noble failure of an estate." *The Guardian,* May 21, 2015. https://www.theguardian.com/cities/2015/may/21/byker-wall-newcastles-noble-failure-of-an-estate-a-history-of-cities-in-50-buildings-day-41

Minton, Anna, *Big Capital: Who is London For?* London: Penguin, 2017.

Moholy-Nagy, Sibyl, *Native Genius in Anonymous Architecture*. New York: Horizon, 1957.

Morshed, Adnan, ed., *How Does Spatial Justice Manifest in the Built Environment?* Hoboken: Wiley. Projected publication Spring 2026.

Mumford, Lewis, *The Brown Decades: A Study of the Arts in America*. New York: Dover Publications, 1955.

Naegele, Daniel, "Seeing What Is Not There Yet: Le Corbusier and the Architectural Space of the Photograph." Presented at the international symposium "INTER—Photography and Architecture: at the University of Navarra, Spain, November 2–4, 2016. *Architecture Conference Proceedings and Presentations*, p. 90, 2016. https://lib.dr.iastate.edu/arch_conf/90. Accessed 10 August 2021.

Orum-Nielsen, Jorn, in collaboration with Mike Pease, *Dwelling: At Home, In Community, On Earth: The Significance of Tradition in Contemporary Housing*. Copenhagen: The Danish Architectural Press, 1996.

Pajares-Ayuela, Paloma, *Cosmatesque Ornament: Flat Polychrome Geometric Patterns in Architecture*. New York: W.W. Norton & Co., 2001.

Palaasma, Juhani. "Rationality and Domesticity." In *Alvar Aalto Architect, The Aalto House 1935–36*. Helsinki: Alvar Aalto Foundation, 2014, p. 80.

Peponis, John, *Architecture and Spatial Culture*. New York: Routledge, 2024.

Perec, Georges, *An Attempt at Exhausting a Place in Paris*. Cambridge, MA: Wakefield Press, 2010.

Perec, Georges, *Species of Spaces and Other Pieces*. London: Penguin Classics, 2008.

Pevsner, Nikolaus, *An Outline of European Architecture*. Harmondsworth: Penguin, 1963.

Polano, Sergio, *Hendrik Petrus Berlage: Complete Works*. New York: Rizzoli, 1988.

Priore Lima, Renata, *The Avenida Paulista as a Linear Urban Centre: Collective Spaces, Plug-Ins and Urban Interfaces*. Madrid: Fundacion Arquia, 2020.

Ramm, Benjamin, "A Controversial Restoration that Wipes Away the Past." *The New York Times*, Sept. 1, 2017. https://www.nytimes.com/2017/09/01/arts/design/chartres-cathedral-restoration-controversial.html

Rhodes, Robin Francis, *Architecture and Meaning on the Athenian Acropolis*. Cambridge: Cambridge University Press, 1995.

Romero, Simon, "Medellín's Nonconformist Mayor Turns Blight to Beauty." *The New York Times*, July 15, 2007. https://www.nytimes.com/2007/07/15/world/americas/15medellin.html

Rudofsky, Bernard, *Architecture Without Architects*. New York: Doubleday & Co., 1964.

Ruskin, John, *The Stones of Venice*. New York: J. Wiley & Sons, 1881.

Saalman, Howard, *Filippo Brunelleschi: The Buildings*. London: Zwemmer, 1993.

Scalbert, Irénée, *A Real Living Contact with the Things Themselves: Essays on Architecture*. Zurich: Park Books, 2018.

Scientific American, vol. 104 no. 21 (May 1911).

Scully, Vincent, *The Earth, The Temple and the Gods: Greek Sacred Architecture*. New York: Praeger, 1969.

Seemann, Nicholas, "Mapping the Mandala: an Approach to Community-Based Architecture in Kathmandu, Nepal." MS thesis, Department of Architecture, University of Oregon, 2000.

Sergel, Ruth, *See You in the Streets: Art, Action and Remembering the Triangle Shirtwaist Fire*. Iowa City: University of Iowa Press, 2016.

Shellenbarger, Michael, *Harmony in Diversity: The Architecture and Teaching of Ellis F. Lawrence*. Eugene, OR: University of Oregon Press, 1989.

Sheppard, F.H.W., General Editor, *Survey of London, Volume XXIX, The Parish of St. James Westminster, Part One, South of Piccadilly*. London: The Athlone Press, University Of London, 1960.

Shield, René Rose, *Diamond Stories: Enduring Change on 47th Street*. Ithaca and` London: Cornell University Press, 2002.

Smithson, Alison and Peter Smithson. *Ordinariness and Light: Urban theories 1952–1960 and their application in a building project 1963–1970.* Cambridge, MA: MIT Press, 1970.

Steffens, Martin, *K. F. Schinkel 1781–1841: An Architect in the Service of Beauty.* Cologne: Taschen, 2003.

Steichen, Edward, ed., *The Family of Man.* New York: The Museum of Modern Art, 1955.

Stern, Robert A. M., Gregory Gilmartin, and John Montague Massengale, *New York 1900: Metropolitan Architecture and Urbanism 1890–1915.* New York: Rizzoli, 1983.

Stewart, Andrew F. "History, Myth and Allegory in the Program of the Temple of Athena Nike, Athens." *Studies in the History of Art* 16 (1985). *Symposium Papers IV: Pictorial Narrative in Antiquity and the Middle Ages* (1985), pp. 53–73. Published by the National Gallery of Art.

Stilgoe, John, *Outside Lies Magic: Regaining History and Awareness in Everyday Places.* London and Somerville, MA: Walker Books, 1998.

Stone-Ferrier, Linda, *The Little Street: The Neighborhood in Dutch Art and Culture.* New Haven and London: Yale University Press, 2022.

Sutton, Peter C., *Pieter De Hooch.* Ithaca, NY: Cornell University Press, 1980.

Sweeney, Robert and Judith Sheine, *Schindler, Kings Road and Southern California Modernism.* Berkeley: University of California Press, 2012.

Swenarton, Mark. *Cook's Camden: The Making of Modern Housing.* London: Lund Humphries, 2017.

Szarkowski, John, *Looking at Photographs: 100 Pictures from The Collection of the Museum of Modern Art.* New York: The Museum of Modern Art, 1973.

Szarkowski, John, *The Work of Atget*, volume 3, *The Art of Old Paris.* New York: The Museum of Modern Art, 1982.

Tandberg, Jorgen, "Revisit: Hedmark Museum in Hamar, Norway by Sverre Fehn." *The Architectural Review*, 9 August 2021. https://www.architectural-review.com/essays/revisit/revisit-hedmark-museum-in-hamar-norway-by-sverre-fehn

Tange, Kenzo and Noboru Kawazoe, with photographs by Yoshio Watanabe, *Ise: Prototype of Japanese Architecture.* Cambridge, MA: MIT Press, 1965.

Taut, Bruno, *Houses and People of Japan.* London: John Gifford Ltd., 1938.

Ubbelohde, M. Susan, "The Dance of a Summer Day: Le Corbusier's Sarabhai House in Ahmedabad, India." *Traditional Dwellings and Settlements Review*, Vol., 14 no. 2, Spring 2003, pp. 65–80.

Uldall, Kai, *Frilandsmuseet: English Guide.* Copenhagen: The National Museum, 1980.

Upton, Dell, "Architecture in Everyday LIfe." *New Literary History* (2002) 33: 707–723.

Vogtherr, Christoph Martin, "Views and Approaches: Schinkel and Landscape Gardening." In John Zukowsky, ed., *Karl Friedrich Schinkel 1781–1841, The Drama of Architecture.* Tubingen/Berlin: Ernst Wasmuth Verlag, 1994.

Wagner, Otto, *Modern Architecture.* Santa Monica, CA: Getty, 1998.

West, Rebecca, *Black Lamb and Grey Falcon: A Journey Through Yugoslavia.* London: Penguin, 2007.

White, Stephen, *Building in the Garden: The Architecture of Joseph Allen Stein in India and California.* Delhi: Oxford University Press, 1993.

Wilson, Colin St. John, "Leiviska at Myyrmaki." *Architectural Review*, (1987) 181 (1084): 63–67.

Wittkower, Rudolf, *Architectural Principles in the Age of Humanism.* New York: W. W. Norton, 1971.

Woolf, Virginia, *Mrs. Dalloway.* London: The Hogarth Press, 1925.

Wray, Nicola, Bob Hawkins, and Colum Giles, *'One Great Workshop': The Buildings of the Sheffield Metal Trades.* London: English Heritage, 2001.

Youngson, A. J., *The Making of Classical Edinburgh.* Edinburgh: Edinburgh University Press, 1966.

Zipp, Samuel and Nathan Storring, eds., *Vital Little Plans: The Short Works of Jane Jacobs.* New York: Penguin Random House, 2016.

Zukowsky, John, ed., *Karl Friedrich Schinkel 1781–1841, The Drama of Architecture.* Tübingen/Berlin: Ernst Wasmuth Verlag, 1994.

Zumthor, Peter. *Thinking Architecture.* Basel: Birkhauser, 2006.

INDEX

TYPES

NAMES AND PLACES